To B.J.
    Hope you have
fun Quilting and making
  thing's.
                Love you
                 Aunt Betty Jo

O9-CFT-434

Scrap Basket Crafts

Scrap Basket Crafts

Over 50 Quick-and-Easy Projects to Make from Fabric Scraps

◆

Nancy Reames

CONTRIBUTING WRITERS: STACEY L. KLAMAN
AND DONNA BABYLON

EDITED BY JANE TOWNSWICK

Rodale Press, Emmaus, Pennsylvania

OUR MISSION

We publish books that empower people's lives.

RODALE BOOKS

Copyright © 1994 by Rodale Press, Inc.

Photographs copyright © 1994 by Rodale Press, Inc.

The authors and editor who compiled this book have tried to make all of the contents as accurate and as correct as possible. Plans, illustrations, photographs, and text have all been carefully checked and cross-checked. However, due to the variability of local conditions, construction materials, personal skill, and so on, the authors and editor do not assume any responsibility for any injuries suffered or for damages or other losses incurred that result from the material presented herein. All instructions and plans should be carefully studied and clearly understood before beginning construction.

All rights reserved. No part of this publication may be reproduced or transmitted in any form or by any means, electronic or mechanical, including photocopy, recording, or any other information storage and retrieval system, without the written permission of the publisher.

Printed in the United States of America on acid-free ∞, recycled ♻ paper, containing 10 percent post-consumer waste

Executive Editor: **Margaret Lydic Balitas**
Editor: **Jane Townswick**
Senior Associate Editors: **Stacey L. Klaman** and **Nancy Reames**
Copy Editor: **Carolyn R. Mandarano**
Production Coordinator: **Jodi Schaffer**
Copy Manager: **Dolores Plikaitis**
Office Manager: **Karen Earl-Braymer**
Administrative Assistant: **Susan Nickol**
Art Director: **Michael Mandarano**
Book Designers: **Patricia Field** and **Darlene Schneck**
Cover Designer: **Patricia Field**
Cover Photographer: **Mitch Mandel**
Interior Photographer: **John P. Hamel**
Photo Stylist: **Marianne G. Laubach**
Illustrators: **Charles M. Metz** and **Frank Rohrbach**

If you have any questions or comments concerning this book, please write to:

Rodale Press, Inc.
Book Readers' Service
33 East Minor Street
Emmaus, PA 18098

Library of Congress Cataloging-in-Publication Data

Reames, Nancy.
    Scrap basket crafts : over 50 quick-and-easy projects to make from fabric scraps / Nancy Reames ; contributing writers: Stacey L. Klaman and Donna Babylon.
        p.   cm.
    ISBN 0–87596–620–9   hardcover
    1. Patchwork—Patterns. 2. Patchwork quilts. 3. Soft sculpture.
4. Pillows. I. Klaman, Stacey, L. II. Babylon, Donna. III. Title.
TT835.R38 1994
746.46—cd20   94–9112
                                                                        CIP

Distributed in the book trade by St. Martin's Press

2 4 6 8 10 9 7 5 3 1 hardcover

Contents

SCRAP QUILTS

COUNTRY BAZAAR

GIFTS GALORE

SANTA CLAUS
IS COMING TO TOWN

HOLIDAYS AND SPECIAL
OCCASIONS

Acknowledgments

The Projects

Our sincere thanks to the following people for reaching into their own scrap baskets and coming up with the wonderful designs that appear in this book.

Doreen Burbank Christmas Tree Quilt

Phyllis Dunstan Agnes the Angel; Blooms, Bands, and Barrettes; Fabulously Fun Button Covers; Fang the Fanny Pack

Connie J. Nordstrom Midnight Flowers Quilt

Quilter's Newsletter Magazine Christmas Card Baskets; Pretty Petunias Quilt; Snowball and Arrowroot Pillow Quilt

Nancy Reames Babushka Doll Trio; Easter Basket Pillow; Elmo the Elf; Floral Cardigan Sweatshirt; Folk Art Flag Wallhanging; Happy the Scraposaurus; Hungry Chicks Place Mats; Paper Doll Sweatshirt

Gale Rose Christmas Stockings

Shery Hendricks Sebald Patches the Bear

Margaret Sindelar Crazy Patchwork Photograph Album Cover; Fabric-Covered Picture Frames; Lace Patchwork Ring Bearer's Pillow; Patchwork Purse; Plaid Pieced Place Mats; Spring Flowers Pillow; Yo-Yo and Button Vest

Suzie Treinen Divine Denim Jacket; Holiday Kitchen Magnets; Partridge Tableau

Linda Trexler Halloween Trick-or-Treat Bag

Nancy Young Braided Denim Basket; Jeans Rug

The Photographs

The following people and stores very generously donated the use of the decorative items that appear along with the projects in the photographs.

Pumpkin Masters
P.O. Box 61456
Denver, CO 80206
Haunted house pumpkin

Patches
Country Gifts, Pottery, Dolls,
    Collectibles
173 Main St.
Emmaus, PA 18049
Child's cupboard

Ellen Halloran
P.O. Box 825
Village Station
New York, NY 10014
18K yellow gold wedding bands

Introduction

At one time or another, every sewer encounters the same question: What do you do with the bits and pieces of fabric that are left over after finishing a project? The answer is almost universal—toss them into a scrap basket! Whether you stash a cache of cottons in a drawer or display a rainbow of bright fabrics on open shelves, one thing is certain. If you sew, you save scraps.

A scrap basket is a personal portrait in fabric, evoking as many memories as a beloved photo album. What sorts of treasures have found their way into your own scrap collection? Have you saved snippets of silk from your first prom dress? Precious pieces of satin and lace from a wedding trousseau? Or remnants of a flannel nightgown you loved as a child? Perhaps you've been lucky enough to inherit fabric from your mother's or grandmother's sewing basket. Whatever the contents, a scrap basket is often a real lifesaver for any sewer, yielding soft bandages for emergency teddy bear repair, colorful patches for a pair of jeans, or a glamorous evening gown for a Barbie doll.

Your scrap basket is sure to contain an array of exciting projects just waiting to happen. And whether you're an enthusiastic beginner or a dyed-in-the-wool sewing veteran, *Scrap Basket Crafts* will help make those projects reality. From quick-and-easy projects like Elmo the Elf (shown on the back cover) and the Paper Doll Sweatshirt (on page 66) to more detailed projects like the Midnight Flowers Quilt (on page 2) or the Folk Art Flag Wallhanging (on page 220), *Scrap Basket Crafts* will keep you delving into your scrap basket with delight for many years to come.

How to Use This Book

Whether you're making your first project or your fiftieth, the step-by-step instructions, detailed illustrations, and colorful photographs in *Scrap Basket Crafts* will enable you to reproduce all of the projects just as the designers made them. If you're new to crafting, sewing, and quilting, start by reading through the basic techniques in the "General Instructions," beginning on page 256. If your skills are more advanced, you may enjoy referring to this section to brush up on techniques you've used in the past or to sample a few new methods. The following features in each project will make your sewing time more enjoyable and help you achieve professional-looking results for every project.

Full-size pattern pieces are given wherever possible. For patterns too large to show on one page, the pieces are shown in sections. Each section is numbered and labeled with placement lines to make it easy to trace a complete pattern piece.

Numbered step-by-step instructions guide you through making each project. When special sewing or quilting techniques, such as embroidering or making covered piping, are required, you'll find a helpful cross-reference directing you to additional information in the "General Instructions," beginning on page 256.

Detailed illustrations accompany the step-by-step instructions, making it easy to know at a glance that you're following the correct sewing process. A crosshatch pattern indicates the wrong side of the fabric, making it easy to position fabrics together correctly.

Color photographs of each project show all of the important details clearly, providing a handy visual reference guide as you sew.

Complete fabrics and supplies lists specify how much fabric is needed for each project and where each fabric is used, making it easy to reproduce the exact look of the original project. And if you want to change any or all of the fabric colors, the color wheel on page 258 will help you experiment with pleasing color combinations. The supplies lists detail every item you'll need to make each project, from tools and thread to the correct number of buttons or beads.

Size listings at the top of each project provide the finished dimensions of each project.

"Bits 'n' Pieces" boxes included with most projects offer shortcuts, innovative ways to save time or money, and creative ideas for varying designs to create an entirely new look for the project.

Scrap Quilts

- ❖ **Midnight Flowers Quilt**
- ❖ **Pretty Petunias Quilt**

Midnight Flowers Quilt

Spring flowers bloom in bright colors in this quick and simple-to-piece quilt. Make one entirely in deep jewel-toned Amish solids, or create a country look by using pastel prints and plaids.

❖ *Size: The quilt is 39 inches square.*

Fabric Requirements

- 1⅛ yards of charcoal solid for the sashing strips, inner and outer borders, and binding
- 1 yard of black solid for the patchwork blocks and the corner squares in the outer border
- ⅜ yard of medium green solid for the leaves in the patchwork blocks
- ⅛ yard of medium pink solid for the middle border
- Nine 1½ × 20-inch strips of assorted solids for the flower petals
- Nine 1½ × 5-inch strips of assorted solids for the flower centers
- 1¼ yards of fabric for the backing

Other Supplies

- 43-inch square of batting
- Rotary cutter
- Cutting mat
- Wide plexiglass ruler
- Black sewing and quilting threads
- Size 10 or 12 betweens

Instructions

Note: Prewash and press all fabrics. All measurements include ¼-inch seam allowances.

Cutting

1. From the charcoal solid, cut four 4 × 32½-inch strips for the outer borders.

2. From the same charcoal solid, cut four 1½ × 29½-inch strips for the inner borders.

3. From the same charcoal solid, cut one 1½ × 44-inch strip. From this strip cut twenty 1½-inch squares for the corner squares between sashing strips and the inner border corners.

4. From the same charcoal solid, cut four 1½ × 44-inch binding strips.

5. From the same charcoal solid, cut forty 1½ × 5½-inch sashing strips.

6. From the black solid, cut four 2½ × 40-inch strips for the patchwork blocks. Also cut twenty-seven 1½ × 10-inch strips for the patchwork blocks.

7. From the same black solid, cut four 4-inch corner squares for the outer border.

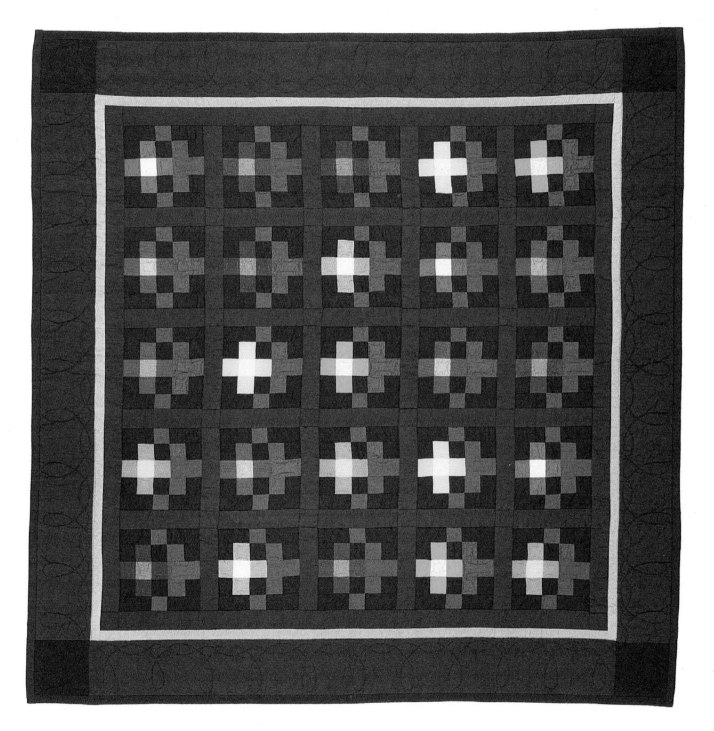

8. From the green solid, cut two 1½ × 40-inch strips, nine 1½ × 10-inch strips, and nine 2½ × 5-inch strips for the patchwork blocks.

9. From the pink solid, cut two 1 × 32½-inch strips and two 1 × 31½-inch strips for the middle border.

10. From the 20-inch assorted solid strips, cut nine 1½ × 10-inch strips for the flower petals. Also cut two 1½ × 5-inch strips of each fabric for the flower petals.

Piecing the Flower Blocks

Note: For color placement of the flower petals and centers, refer to the **Fabric Key.** Use black thread to piece the entire quilt. Press each seam toward the darker fabric unless specified otherwise.

| Black | Green | Petals | Center |

Fabric Key

1. To make one A unit, stitch one 1½ × 40-inch green strip and two 2½ × 40-inch black strips together, as shown in **Diagram 1.** Repeat to make a second A unit.

2. From each A unit, cut twenty-five 1½-inch rows, as shown in **Diagram 2.**

3. To make one B unit, sew three 1½ × 10-inch black strips, one 1½ × 10-inch green strip, and one

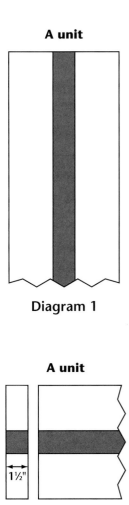

A unit

Diagram 1

A unit

1½"

Cut 50 rows total

Diagram 2

1½ × 10-inch assorted solid petal strip together, as shown in **Diagram 3** on the opposite page. Make a total of nine B units with a different color for the petals in each unit.

4. From each B unit, cut six rows, each 1½ inches wide, as shown in **Diagram 4** on the opposite page.

B unit

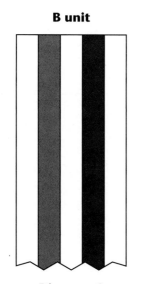

Diagram 3

C unit

Diagram 5

6. Cut each C unit into three rows, each 1½ inches wide, as shown in **Diagram 6.**

C unit

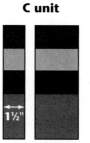

Cut 27 rows total

Diagram 6

B unit

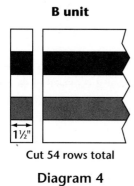

1½"

Cut 54 rows total

Diagram 4

5. To make one C unit, sew three 1½ × 5-inch strips for the petals and flower center and one 2½ × 5-inch green strip together, as shown in **Diagram 5.** Make nine C units with a different flower center strip in each unit.

7. To piece one flower block, lay out two A unit rows, two B unit rows, and one C unit row, as shown in **Diagram 7** on page 6. Sew them together and press the seams.

8. Make three flower blocks in each of seven different color combinations and two flower blocks in each of two other color combinations for a total of 25 blocks, each 5½ inches square.

A B C B A

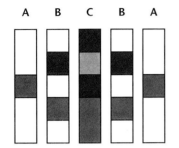

Flower Block

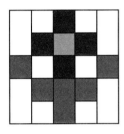

Diagram 7

Assembling the Quilt

1. Referring to **Diagram 8** and the photograph on page 3 for color placement, sew together a row of five flower blocks with sashing strips between them. Press the seams. Make five rows, beginning and ending each with a flower block.

Flower block   Sashing strip

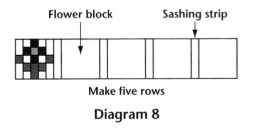

Make five rows

Diagram 8

2. Sew a row of five sashing strips with corner squares between them, as shown in **Diagram 9**. Repeat to

make a total of four rows of sashing strips and corner squares.

Sashing strip   Corner square

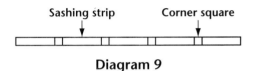

Diagram 9

3. Sew a 1½ × 29½-inch charcoal inner border to the bottom of one row of flower blocks, as shown in **Diagram 10**. Press the seams toward the border.

Flower block   Sashing strip

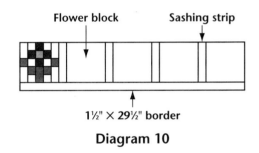

1½" × 29½" border

Diagram 10

4. Referring to **Diagram 11**, sew the remaining rows of flower blocks together, with rows of sashing strips and corner blocks between them.

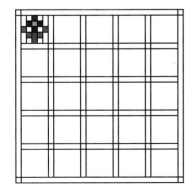

Diagram 11

5. Sew the 1½ × 29½-inch charcoal inner border at the top of the final row of flower blocks and press the seam.

6. Referring to **Diagram 11**, sew a charcoal corner square to each end of a 1½ × 29½-inch charcoal inner border strip. Sew this strip to one side of the quilt. Repeat to make the final inner border strip for the opposite side of the quilt.

Adding the Remaining Borders

1. Sew a 1 × 31½-inch pink middle border to the sides of the quilt. Press the seams toward the borders. Sew a 1 × 32½-inch middle border to the top and bottom of the quilt and press the seams toward the borders.

2. Sew a 4 × 32½-inch charcoal outer border to the top and bottom of the quilt. Press the seams toward the borders.

3. Sew a 4-inch black corner square to each end of a 4 × 32½-inch black outer border and press the seams toward the corner squares. Repeat to make a second outer border. Sew an outer border to each side of the quilt, pressing the seams toward the borders.

Layering and Quilting

Note: For information on layering and quilting, refer to the "General Instructions" on page 268.

1. Referring to the photograph on page 3, quilt curves inside each flower petal, leaf, and center. Begin stitching at the corner of each square, curving gently to

Bits 'n' Pieces

Try This Variation: Quilting in the ditch between seams over the entire surface of a patchwork quilt can be a daunting prospect. As an easier alternative to fighting with seam allowances, why not try quilting diagonal crossed lines in the flower blocks? And when it comes to the borders, using ¾-inch masking tape as a guide will let you quilt diagonal lines easily. Place a piece of tape at the proper angle on the quilt top and quilt next to the edge. Then move the tape, align it with the previously quilted line, and quilt next to the edge of it again. That produces evenly spaced, parallel lines of quilting without the need to mark them with a pencil or chalk marker first.

¼ inch inside the seam line, then curving gently back to the adjacent corner of the square.

2. Referring to **Diagram 12**, quilt in the ditch around each flower block and border.

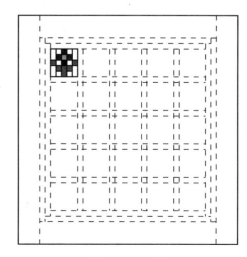

Diagram 12

3. In the outer borders, use the quilting design at the top of the opposite page or a design of your choice.

4. In the corner squares of the outer borders, use the quilting design at the bottom of the opposite page or another design of your choice.

Binding the Quilt

1. Press the four binding strips in half lengthwise with wrong sides together.

2. Layer the backing, batting, and quilt top, then trim the batting and backing to within ½ inch of the quilt top.

3. With right sides together, place a binding strip along the bottom of the quilt, matching raw edges. Using a ¼-inch seam, stitch through all layers, backstitching at each end of the seam. Trim the quilt top, batting, and backing even with the seam allowance, and then trim the ends of the binding even with the sides of the quilt. Repeat for the top edge of the quilt.

4. Fold these binding strips around to the back side of the quilt and hand stitch them, as shown in **Diagram 13.**

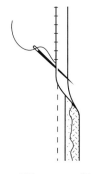

Diagram 13

5. Lay a binding strip along one side of the quilt so that it extends slightly beyond the previously sewn bindings. Stitch through all layers of the quilt, backstitching at each end of the seam. Trim the quilt top, batting, and backing even with the seam allowance. Repeat for the opposite side of the quilt.

6. Fold these binding strips around to the back side of quilt, tucking the edges in to create smooth, square corners, and hand stitch them in place.

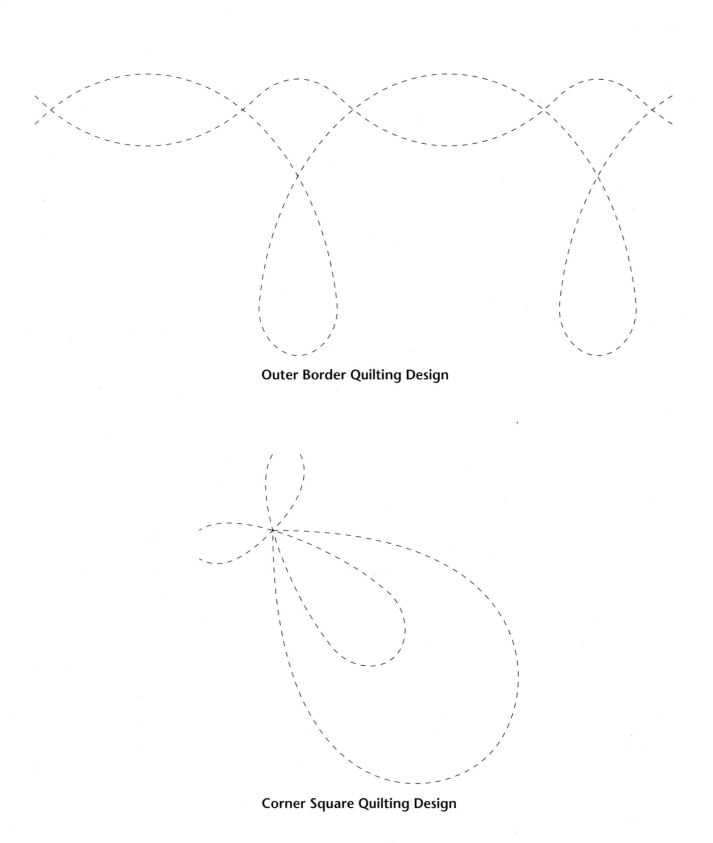

Outer Border Quilting Design

Corner Square Quilting Design

Pretty Petunias Quilt

The petunias in this patchwork garden will bloom brightly year-round. Dig through your scrap basket and piece six flowers in summery shades of pink, orange, and purple. Surround the blossoms with leafy green prints, add a sprinkling of tiny yellow French knots, and fence them in with a path of prairie points.

❖ *Size: The quilt is approximately 47 × 65 inches, including prairie points.*

Fabric Requirements

- ❖ 1½ yards total of three dark green prints for the sashing strips and leaves
- ❖ 1 yard total of assorted medium brown prints for the basket and basket handles
- ❖ ½ yard of dark brown print for the basket
- ❖ 2 yards of pale yellow solid for the background pieces and borders
- ❖ Scraps of assorted light brown prints for the basket
- ❖ Scraps of assorted light, medium, and dark prints in six color combinations for the flowers
- ❖ Scraps of three medium and dark pink prints for the setting pieces
- ❖ Scraps of assorted light, medium, and dark prints for the prairie points
- ❖ 3 yards of a coordinating solid for the backing

Other Supplies

- ❖ 51 × 72-inch piece of batting
- ❖ Template plastic
- ❖ Fine-point black permanent marker
- ❖ One skein of dark green embroidery floss
- ❖ One skein of yellow embroidery floss
- ❖ One skein of bright pink pearl cotton size 3 for tying the quilt
- ❖ Embroidery needle

Instructions

Note: Each pattern piece includes ¼-inch seam allowances. Press each seam toward the darker fabric immediately after sewing it, unless specified otherwise.

Cutting

1. Trace the pattern pieces on pages 20–25 onto template plastic, transferring all markings, and cut out the templates.

2. From the dark green prints, cut 24 E sashing strips. Also cut one M, one M reverse, one N, one N reverse, and two K triangles for each of the six petunia blocks.

3. From the medium brown print, cut 6 A, 6 B, 6 B reverse, and 12 C shapes. Also cut 24 Q triangles.

4. From the dark brown print, cut six S and six S reverse shapes.

5. From the pale yellow solid, cut two 4½ × 48-inch borders and two 4½ × 68-inch borders. These measurements are longer than necessary. The excess fabric will be trimmed after the border corners are mitered. From the remaining yellow fabric, cut 24 D, 12 H, 36 I, 12 J, 12 K, and 12 L shapes.

6. From the light brown print, cut 12 R triangles.

7. From each of the six fabric combinations for the flowers, cut the following pieces. From a dark print, cut two K and four H shapes. From a medium print, cut four O shapes. From a light (or another medium) print, cut four O reverse, two P, and two P reverse shapes.

8. From the medium and dark pink prints, cut 24 F, 24 F reverse, and 24 G shapes.

9. From the assorted light, medium, and dark prints, cut 144 prairie points, each 3 inches square.

10. Cut the backing fabric in half, from selvage edge to selvage edge.

Piecing the Petunia Blocks

Note: The following instructions apply to piecing one petunia block. Follow the same steps to piece the remaining five blocks, for a total of six.

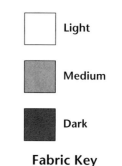

Fabric Key

1. Sew a medium print O reverse piece to a light print O reverse piece, as shown in **Diagram 1.** Repeat three more times to make a total of four O/O reverse units.

Diagram 1

2. Referring to **Diagram 1,** sew a dark print or solid H triangle and a yellow I triangle to each corner of an O/O reverse unit. Repeat, sewing triangles to the remaining three O/O reverse units. This forms a flower unit.

3. Sew the four flower units together, as shown in **Diagram 2.**

Diagram 2

4. Sew a medium print P and P reverse to a dark print K triangle, as shown in **Diagram 3.** Repeat to make a second P/K/P reverse unit (refer to **Diagram 5**).

Diagram 3

5. Sew a dark green K triangle and a dark print H triangle to a P/K/P reverse unit, as shown in **Diagram 4.** Repeat for the other P/K/P reverse unit.

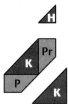

Diagram 4

6. Sew the three units together, as shown in **Diagram 5.**

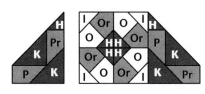

Diagram 5

7. Sew a yellow I triangle and a yellow J triangle to a dark green M shape, as shown in **Diagram 6.** Referring to **Diagram 6,** repeat for an M reverse shape.

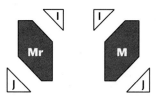

Diagram 6

8. Sew a yellow L triangle and a yellow K triangle to a dark green N shape, as shown in **Diagram 7.** Repeat for a dark green N reverse shape.

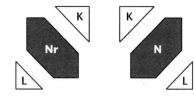

Diagram 7

9. Sew the K/N reverse/L, the I/M reverse/J, the I/M/J, and the K/N/L units together, as shown in **Diagram 8.** This forms a leaf unit.

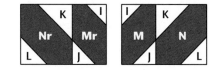

Diagram 8

10. Sew the pieced leaf and flower units together, as shown in **Diagram 9** on page 14.

11. Sew a medium brown print B reverse shape to the left side of the pieced leaf/flower unit. Sew a medium brown A shape to the top of the

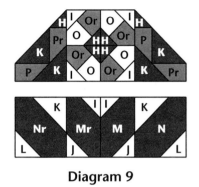

Diagram 9

unit and a medium brown B shape to the right side, as shown in **Diagram 10.**

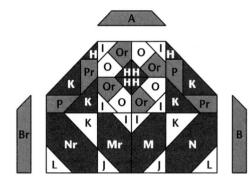

Diagram 10

12. Sew four medium brown print Q triangles together, as shown in **Diagram 11.**

Diagram 11

13. Sew a light brown R triangle to each side of the Q triangle unit, as shown in **Diagram 12.**

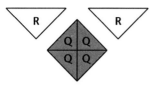

Diagram 12

14. Sew a yellow D triangle to one side of a dark brown print S, as shown in **Diagram 13.** Repeat for an S reverse shape.

Diagram 13

15. Sew the S reverse/D and S/D units to each side of the R/Q triangle unit, as shown in **Diagram 14.**

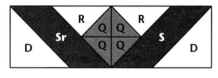

Diagram 14

16. Sew the unit just completed to the unit completed in Step 11, as shown in **Diagram 15** on the opposite page.

17. Sew a medium brown print C shape to a yellow D triangle, as shown in **Diagram 16** on the opposite page. Repeat to make another D/C unit.

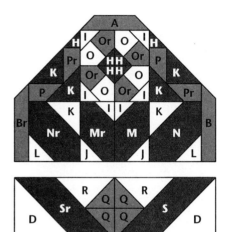

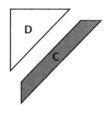

18. Sew the two D/C units to the previously pieced unit, as shown in **Diagram 17.**

19. Sew a pink F and F reverse shape to each side of a dark green E shape, as shown in **Diagram 18.** Repeat to make four F/E/F reverse units.

Diagram 18

20. Sew an F/E/F reverse unit to each side of the petunia block, as shown in **Diagram 19.** Start and stop ¼ inch in from the beginning and end of each seam, backstitching to reinforce the seam.

Diagram 15

Diagram 16

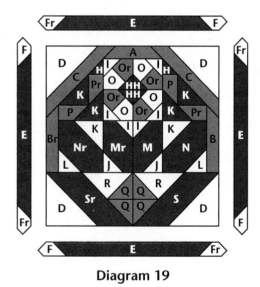

Diagram 19

21. Miter each corner seam of the petunia block, beginning at the corner point of the block where the F and F reverse shapes meet and sewing to the outer edge of fabric.

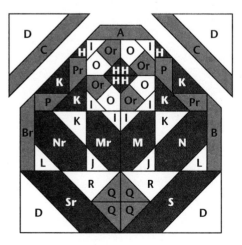

Diagram 17

22. Sew a pink G triangle to each of the four corners, as shown in **Diagram 20.** This completes the petunia block.

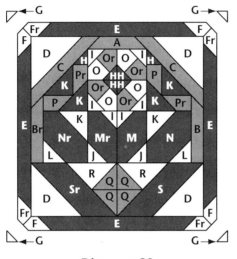

Diagram 20

23. Repeat Steps 1 through 22 to make a total of six blocks.

Embroidering the Petunia Blocks

1. Using three strands of yellow floss, embroider French knots, as indicated on each H and K pattern piece, in each petunia block. For more information on embroidery stitches, see pages 273–275 in the "General Instructions."

2. Using three strands of green floss, outline stitch the veins in each petunia block, as indicated on the M, M reverse, N, and N reverse pattern pieces.

Assembling the Quilt Top

1. Sew the six petunia blocks together, as shown in the **Assembly Diagram** on the opposite page.

2. Fold one of the $4\frac{1}{2} \times 68$-inch border strips in half crosswise and press it lightly to mark the midpoint. Align the midpoint of the border with the midpoint on one side of the quilt. With right sides together, pin the border to the side of the quilt.

3. Sew the border to the quilt, beginning and ending the seam $\frac{1}{4}$ inch in from each corner. Repeat for the border on the opposite side of the quilt.

4. In the same manner, sew the $4\frac{1}{2} \times 48$-inch borders to the top and bottom of the quilt, mitering the corners. For information on mitering border corners, see page 266 in the "General Instructions."

Making Prairie Points

1. Fold each 3-inch assorted print square in half diagonally, wrong sides together, as shown in **Diagram 21.**

Diagram 21

2. Fold each square in half again, as shown in **Diagram 22.**

Diagram 22

Assembly Diagram

3. Place the prairie points along each edge of the right side of the quilt top, overlapping them approximately ½ inch, as shown in **Diagram 23.** Baste the triangles in place.

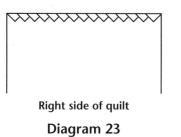

Right side of quilt

Diagram 23

Finishing

1. Remove the selvage edges from the two pieces of backing fabric, then sew the pieces together so that the seam runs horizontally across the width, as shown in **Diagram 24** on page 18. Press the seam open.

2. Cut the backing and the batting the same size as the completed quilt top.

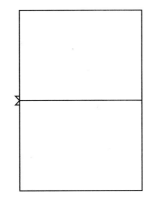

Diagram 24

3. On a large, flat work surface, layer the quilt in the following order: first the batting, then the quilt top right side up, and, finally, the backing right side down. Make sure that all edges are even, then pin the three layers of the quilt sandwich together.

Bits 'n' Pieces

Try This Variation: For a traditional-style binding with a scrap look, why not create a pieced binding strip from many different fabrics? Start by cutting squares and rectangles from scraps of the prints and solids used in the quilt. Cut each square 1½ inches square. Cut each rectangle 1½ inches wide by whatever length you like. Sew enough of these squares and rectangles together to make a binding strip that is 1½ inches wide and 7 yards long. Press all of the seams open and bind the quilt as you would for a solid-binding strip. For more information on binding a quilt, see page 269 in the "General Instructions."

4. Sew around all four sides of the quilt, catching the prairie points in the seam and leaving a 12-inch opening along one side for turning.

5. Trim the corners diagonally and turn the quilt right side out through the 12-inch opening. Blindstitch the opening closed.

Quilting

1. To prepare the quilt for quilting and tying, baste the layers together with thread or pins. For more information on basting, see page 264 in the "General Instructions."

2. Machine quilt in the ditch of the vertical seams on the sides and in the center. In the same manner, quilt in the ditch of each horizontal seam, as shown in **Diagram 25** on the opposite page. Also quilt in the ditch of the seams in each petunia block, as shown.

Tying

1. Thread an embroidery needle with approximately 1 yard of pearl cotton and pull it so that the ends are even. Do not tie a knot in the thread.

2. At each corner of the petunia blocks, insert the needle from the right side of the quilt through all of the layers. Bring it back up ¼ inch away and pull the threads through until there is an approximately 3-inch tail. Tie a square knot and trim the thread even with the 3-inch tail.

Diagram 25

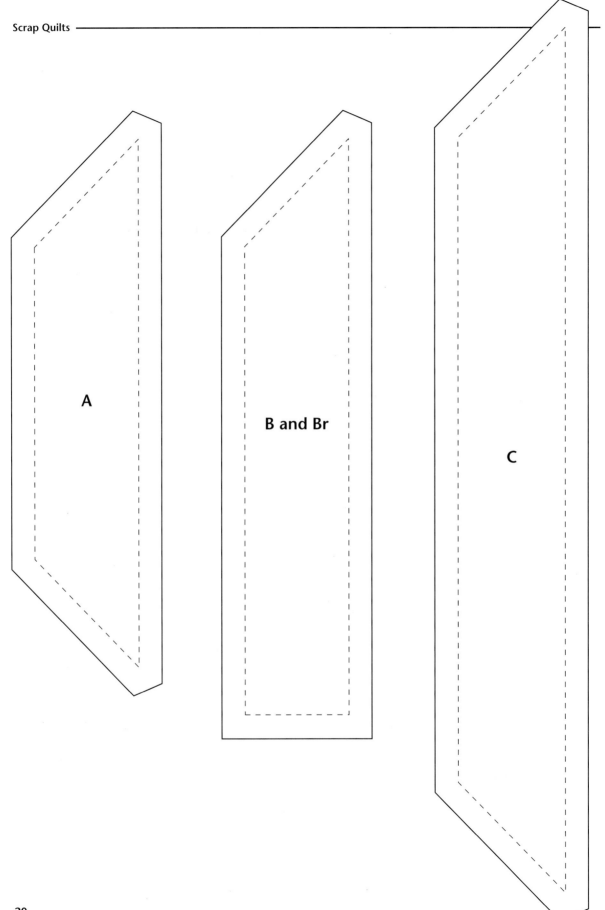

A

B and Br

C

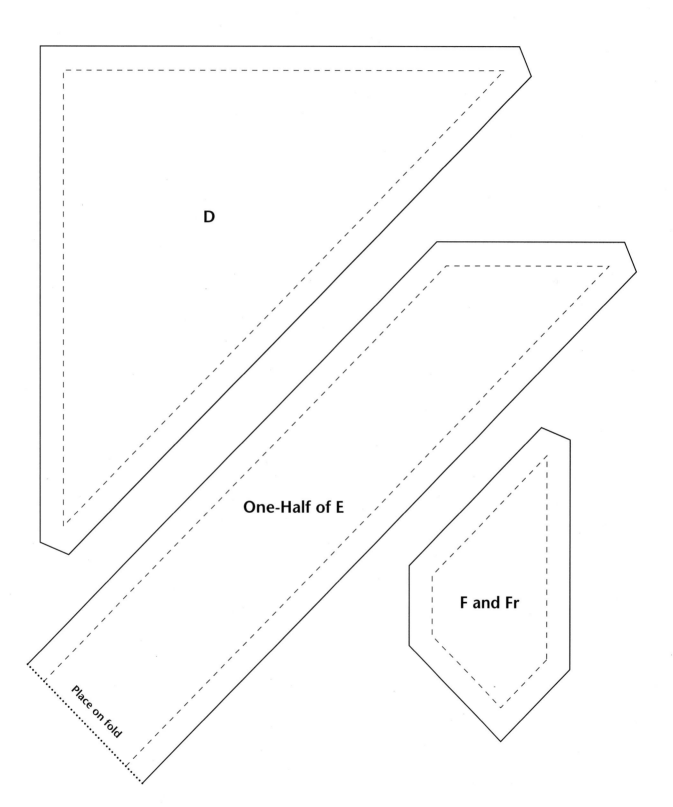

D

One-Half of E

F and Fr

Place on fold

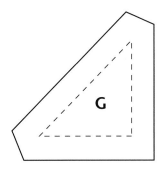

G

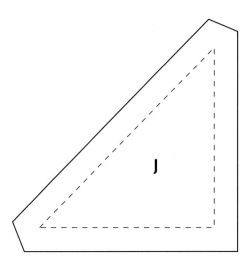

J

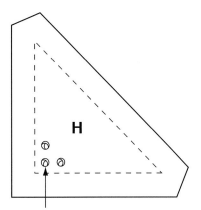

H

French knot embroidery for petunia

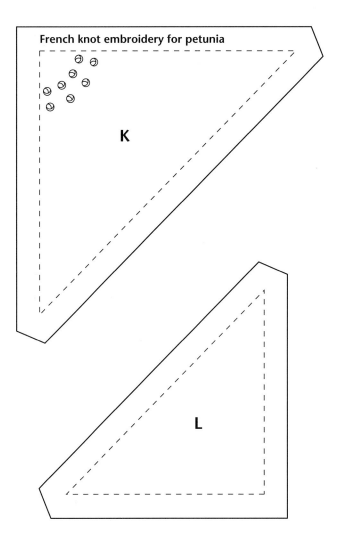

French knot embroidery for petunia

K

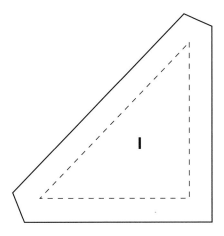

I

L

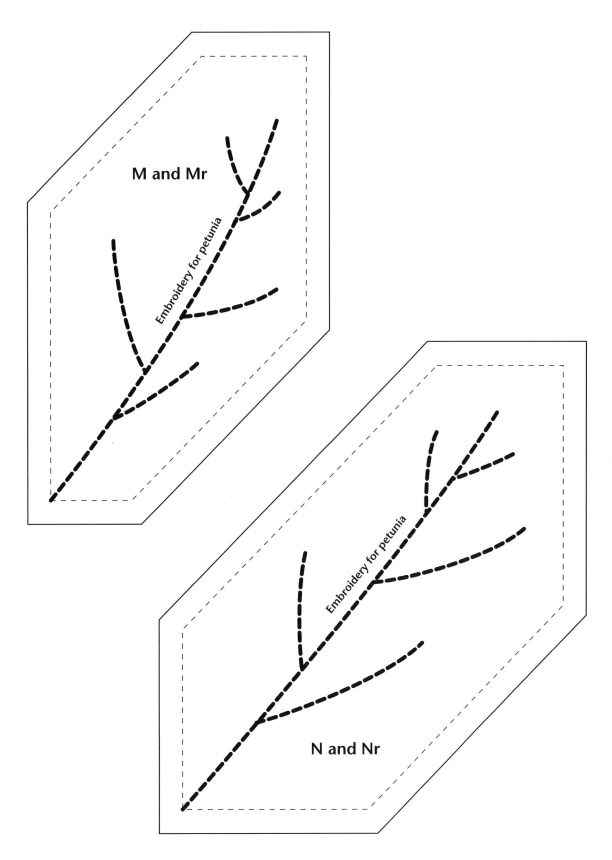

M and Mr

Embroidery for petunia

Embroidery for petunia

N and Nr

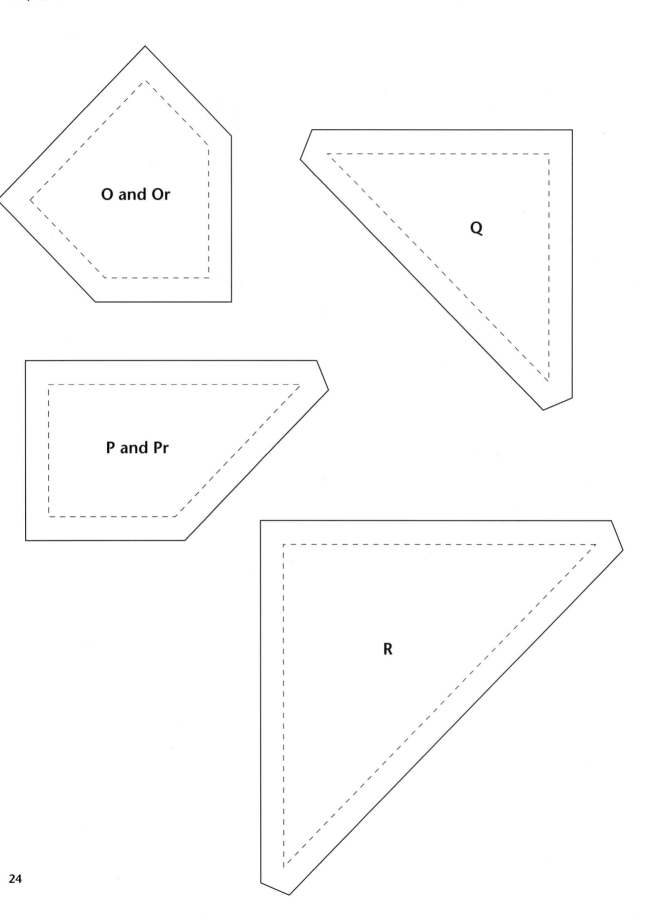

O and Or

Q

P and Pr

R

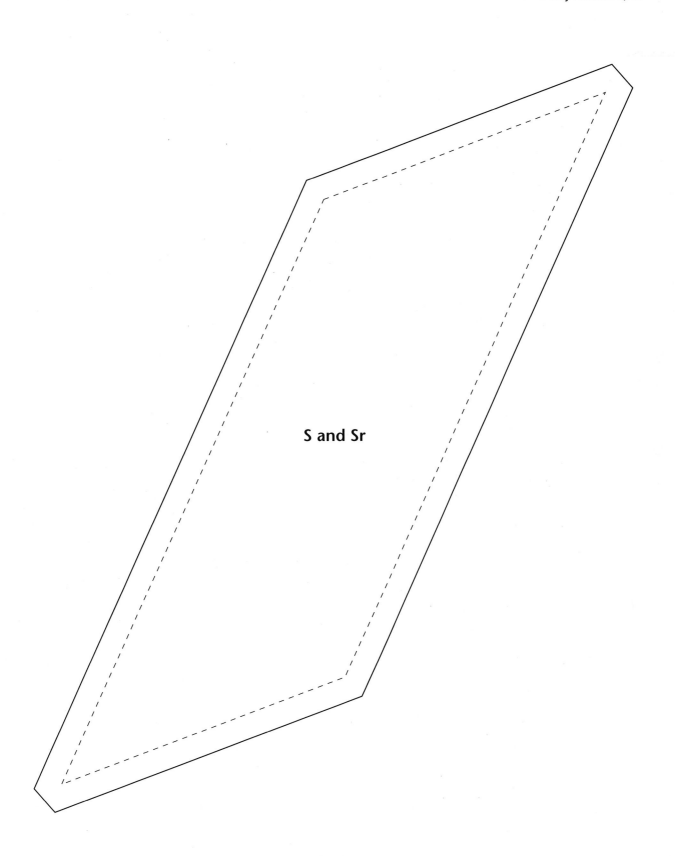

S and Sr

Country *Bazaar*

- ♥ **Blooms, Bands, and Barrettes**
- ♥ **Hungry Chicks Place Mats**
- ♥ **Babushka Doll Trio**
- ♥ **Patches the Bear**
- ♥ **Fabulously Fun Button Covers**
- ♥ **Paper Doll Sweatshirt**
- ♥ **Plaid Pieced Place Mats**
- ♥ **Jeans Rug**
- ♥ **Patchwork Purse**
- ♥ **Braided Denim Basket**

Blooms, Bands, and Barrettes

Sprinkle bright three-dimensional flowers over a purchased headband, or accent a purchased barrette with subtly shaded triangles to create fabulous spring or summer hair decorations. And if you like the no-sew approach, tie a row of fabric strips onto a barrette and top them off with a row of fabric buttons.

Scrappy Rag Barrette

Fabrics and Supplies

- ♥ 4-inch purchased metal clip barrette
- ♥ Scraps of assorted blue and yellow fabrics for the rag strips
- ♥ Scrap of red solid for the buttons
- ♥ Spray fabric sizing
- ♥ Fray-Check
- ♥ Sewing thread
- ♥ Polyester fiberfill
- ♥ Tracing paper or template plastic
- ♥ Fine-point black permanent marker
- ♥ Fabric glue

Instructions

COVERING THE BARRETTE

1. Tear several ½-inch strips from the assorted blue and yellow print scraps of fabric. Cut the strips into 6-inch lengths.

2. Tie enough strips over the top of the barrette to completely cover it. Alternate prints to create a scrappy look.

3. Trim the ends of each strip diagonally to approximately 1½ inches on either side of the barrette. Cut

off any loose threads. Coat the strips with spray fabric sizing and press the edges. If you wish, coat the edges of each strip with Fray-Check after testing it on a scrap of fabric.

MAKING THE BUTTONS

1. Trace the button pattern on page 32 onto tracing paper or template plastic and cut it out.

2. Draw around the button pattern on the wrong side of the red solid fabric and cut out six buttons.

3. Sew a gathering thread around one fabric button ⅛ inch from the edge.

4. Place a small piece of polyester fiberfill in the center of the wrong side of the button fabric. Pull the gathering thread around the polyester fiberfill, creating a soft button. Take a few stitches to close the fabric. Repeat to make five more buttons.

5. Use fabric glue to attach the buttons to the center of the barrette, covering the knots in the fabric strips. Allow the glue to dry.

Folded Fabric Barrette

Fabrics and Supplies

- ♥ 1½ × 4-inch purchased metal barrette set (or refer to "Bits 'n' Pieces" on page 31 to make your own)
- ♥ Scraps of light pink, rose, light aqua, and medium aqua solids
- ♥ Fusible interfacing
- ♥ 1 pink 12 mm faceted square plastic jewel
- ♥ Fabric glue
- ♥ Tracing paper or template plastic
- ♥ Fine-point black permanent marker
- ♥ Pencil or removable fabric marker

Instructions

COVERING THE BARRETTE

Remove the top section of the barrette from the bottom section and use it as a fabric cutting guide. Cut a rectangle of light pink fabric large enough to cover the top section of the barrette and tuck under the edges. Center the top section on the wrong side of the fabric rectangle. Remove the top section and apply fabric glue to it. Then reposition the top section on the fabric and bring the edges of the fabric to the inside. Replace the top section over the bottom section, pressing firmly until the two pieces click together.

Bits 'n' Pieces

Try This Variation: To make a barrette with a more elegant look, cover it with satin ribbons instead of fabric scraps. Top off the ribbons with a row of clear plastic "gemstones" set in glitzy fabric paint, or glue some shiny brass buttons down the center of the barrette.

One way to attach the gemstones is to use fabric paint that matches their color. Squeeze a large dot of paint onto the ribbons. The dot of paint should be a little smaller than the gemstone you use. Press the gemstone into the paint, gently squeezing the paint up over the edge of the gemstone. When the paint dries, the gemstone will be secure.

For a no-sew way to attach buttons to the barrette, dab a bit of white craft glue onto the back of each button. Press the buttons onto the ribbon on the top of the barrette.

MAKING THE TRIANGLES

1. Iron fusible interfacing onto the wrong side of the remaining three scraps of fabric.

2. Trace the A rectangle on page 33 onto tracing paper or template plastic, transferring all markings, and cut it out.

3. Draw two A rectangles on the wrong side of each of the rose, light aqua, and medium aqua solid fabrics and cut them out.

4. To form triangles from the two rose and two medium aqua A rectangles, first fold each rectangle lengthwise with right sides together. Then fold each top corner down to meet in the middle, as shown in **Diagram 1.** Stitch across the bottom edge of each triangle, turn each triangle right side out through the center back opening, and press.

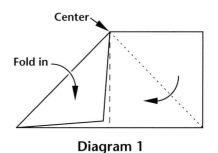

Diagram 1

5. To form the base triangles, fold the two light aqua A rectangles with wrong sides together, following the method in Step 4. Stitch across the bottom raw edges and press, but don't turn the triangles right side out.

6. Following **Diagram 2,** center the light aqua base triangles ½ inch apart on the top section of the barrette. Glue them in place. Glue the longest edge of the medium aqua tri-

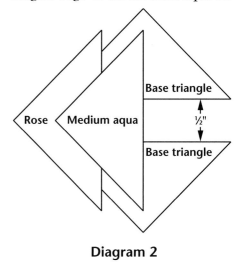

Diagram 2

angles in place over the base triangles. Glue the rose triangles over the sides of the base triangles, slipping the long edges underneath the medium aqua triangles. Allow the glue to dry completely.

7. Glue the pink plastic square jewel over the medium aqua triangles at the center of the barrette. Allow the glue to dry.

Flowering Headband

Fabrics and Supplies

- ♥ Purchased fabric-covered headband
- ♥ 5-inch square of white solid for the flowers
- ♥ 3-inch square of green felt for the leaves
- ♥ 1 package of narrow yellow rickrack
- ♥ 1 package of narrow green rickrack
- ♥ 1 package of ½-inch multicolored bias tape
- ♥ Red sewing thread
- ♥ Red acrylic fabric paint for the flowers
- ♥ Red fabric paint for outlining the flowers
- ♥ Green fabric paint for outlining the leaves
- ♥ Small paintbrush
- ♥ Fabric glue

Instructions

WRAPPING THE HEADBAND

1. Apply fabric glue to the back side of the bias tape, leaving approximately 1 inch free. Begin at one end of the headband and wrap the bias

tape around it in a spiral fashion, leaving approximately ½ inch between each round of bias tape. Tuck the end of the bias tape under itself on the last round and pin it in place.

2. At one end of the headband, tuck the ends of the yellow and green rickrack under the bias tape and glue them in place. Wrap the yellow and green strips of rickrack around the headband in a crisscross pattern. Finish the other ends by cutting and gluing them down. Glue the bias tape in place at each end of the headband.

Bits 'n' Pieces

Try This Variation: If you can't find a barrette that can be taken apart, you can use a plain barrette and adapt it easily. Just take a quick trip to your local craft or sewing store and look for a plain metal clip barrette and a piece of chipboard. Follow these quick-and-easy steps to make a covered barrette that looks like the one in the photo, or vary the shape of the chipboard to create your own original design.

1. Cut a 1½ × 4-inch rectangle of chipboard.

2. Cut a piece of fabric large enough to cover the top of the chipboard and go over the edges. Iron a piece of fusible webbing onto the wrong side of the fabric and remove the layer of paper.

3. Center the chipboard rectangle on top of the fusible webbing and bring the edges of the fabric around the chipboard. Fuse the fabric to the back of the chipboard.

4. Use a hot-glue gun to attach the back of the fabric-covered chipboard to the top bar of the barrette.

Bits 'n' Pieces

Try This Variation: It's easy to make your own ½-inch bias tape from 45-inch-wide cotton or medium-weight fabric. Here's how:

1. To cut a 2-inch strip of fabric on the true bias grain, bring one corner of the fabric up to the selvage (wrong sides together) to create a 45-degree angle. Press the fold and mark a line 1 inch from the fold. Cut along this line to create a 2-inch bias strip.

2. Fold the 2-inch bias strip in half lengthwise, wrong sides together, and press the fold.

3. Open up the bias strip and fold one of the raw edges in to meet the center fold. Press a crease in this fold.

4. Fold the other side of the bias strip in to meet the center fold and press a crease in this fold.

5. Fold the bias strip in half, creating a ½-inch strip of bias tape.

Note: Commercial bias-tape makers are wonderful tools for making your own bias tape, and they're easy to find in notions departments of most sewing stores. Bias-tape makers create folds on both sides of a fabric strip at the same time, allowing you to simply pull the strip gently through the tool and press both folds in place. The tool is inexpensive, too, so you may want to invest in several sizes for giving your garments and crafts a professional touch.

MAKING THE FLOWERS AND LEAVES

1. Cover the 5-inch square of white fabric with red acrylic fabric paint. When the paint is completely dry, turn the fabric over and paint the other side. Allow the paint to dry.

2. Trace the flower and leaf patterns on the opposite page onto template plastic and cut out each template.

3. Using the flower template as a guide, draw seven flowers on the right side of the 5-inch square of red-painted fabric and cut them out.

4. Using the leaf template as a guide, draw nine leaves on the 3-inch square of green felt and cut them out.

5. Use the red fabric paint to outline the cut edges of one side of each flower. Allow the paint to dry. Turn the flower over and outline the edges on the back of each flower.

6. Use the green fabric paint to outline and draw veins on the top of each leaf.

7. To shape each flower, pinch the center from the back side. Use red sewing thread to tack the pinched center of each flower to the headband. Apply a drop of fabric glue to the center of each flower to reinforce the tacked stitches. Allow the glue to dry.

8. Apply a drop of fabric glue to the back of each leaf and glue one or two leaves under each flower. Allow the glue to dry.

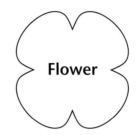

Flower

Leaf

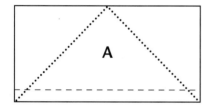

A

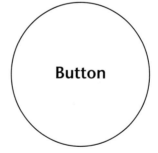

Button

Hungry Chicks Place Mats

Bright-eyed baby chicks dance happily over the surface of this fabric barnyard, pecking for food. Embellished with colorful "seed" beads, tiny prairie points, and easy embroidery stitches, these fanciful place mats are sure to be real kid pleasers.

♥ *Size: Each place mat is 13 × 16 inches.*

Fabric Requirements
(for two place mats)

- ♥ ⅜ yard of gray print for the background of two place mats
- ♥ Scraps of assorted yellow prints for the chicks and wings
- ♥ Scrap of orange solid for the beaks
- ♥ ½ yard of purple print for the borders and backing of one place mat
- ♥ ½ yard of red print for the borders and backing of one place mat

Other Supplies

- ♥ ½ yard of fleece
- ♥ ¼ yard of fusible webbing
- ♥ Yellow and black sewing threads
- ♥ 1 skein of yellow pearl cotton or embroidery floss
- ♥ 1 skein of black embroidery floss
- ♥ Clear nylon thread or thread that matches the background
- ♥ 32 assorted colored seed beads
- ♥ 3⅛ yards of black rayon corded piping
- ♥ Six 3-inch squares of freezer paper
- ♥ Pencil or removable fabric marker
- ♥ Template plastic
- ♥ Fine-point black permanent marker

Instructions

Note: All patterns include ¼-inch seam allowances, except for the appliqué patches, which are finished size.

Cutting

1. From the gray print, cut two 10½ × 13½-inch backgrounds.

2. Following the chick and wing patterns on page 37, trace five chicks and five wings on the paper side of the fusible webbing. To trace the sixth chick and wing, reverse the direction of the pattern pieces. Iron the fusible webbing onto the wrong side of the assorted yellow scraps and cut out the six chicks and six wings.

3. Trace the beak pattern on page 37 onto template plastic and cut out the pattern piece. On a scrap of orange fabric, draw around the beak and cut it out.

4. From the purple print, cut a 13½ × 16½-inch backing piece. Cut two 2 × 15-inch border strips and

two 2 × 18-inch border strips. Repeat to cut the border strips and backing for the second place mat from red print.

5. Cut two 13 × 16½-inch pieces of fleece.

Assembling the Place Mats

1. Referring to **Diagram 1,** fold the beak. Make a total of six beaks.

2. Referring to **Diagram 2** on page 36, place each chick on the background fabric. Make a loop for the top knot at each chick's head by wrapping one strand of yellow pearl cotton or embroidery floss four times loosely around a pencil. Cut the thread and pin the yellow loops so they will lie under the edge of the chick's head on the

Step 1. Fold in half

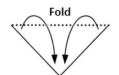

Step 2. Fold two corners down to the center point

Step 3. Insert beak under chick's head to dashed line

Diagram 1

background fabric. Place an orange beak under the chick's head and fuse the chick in place on the background fabric. Repeat for the remaining chicks.

3. Cut a scrap of fleece small enough to fit under the center of each wing. Fuse a wing onto each chick, centering the fleece under the wing.

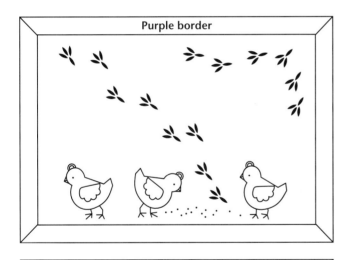

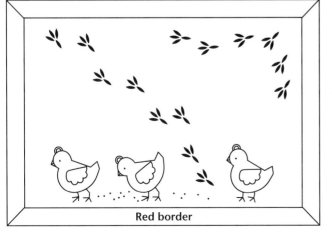

Diagram 2

4. Iron the shiny side of a square of freezer paper onto the wrong side of the background fabric opposite where the chicks are placed. Using yellow thread and a narrow zigzag stitch, machine appliqué around each wing and chick. Allow the point of each beak to remain free. Remove the freezer paper after you have finished stitching.

5. Using a pencil or other removable fabric marker, draw legs and feet beneath the body of each chick. Using black thread and a narrow zigzag stitch, machine appliqué the legs and feet.

6. Using the pencil or removable fabric marker, draw footprints randomly over the background. Draw an eye on each chick. With six strands of black embroidery floss, embroider a French knot for each eye and make the footprints with a lazy daisy stitch. For more information on embroidery stitches, see pages 273–275 in the "General Instructions."

7. Using clear nylon thread or thread that matches the background, sew seed beads randomly near the feet of the chicks bending over on each place mat. The beads should be placed close to the bottom of the background fabric in order to avoid scratching dishes or plates when they're placed on top of the mat.

8. With right sides together, sew the short red border strips to the short sides of the background fabric,

Bits 'n' Pieces

Try This Variation: With your scrap bag handy, try piecing the border with odds and ends of fabric—prints, plaids, and solids. Scrappy borders will create place mats with a country feel. And if you like the look of planned color schemes, use the color wheel on page 258 to play with various colors. Try combining a dusty tan background print with ocher chicks, and piece the borders from brown, terracotta, and red plaids or stripes. The possibilities are endless.

beginning and ending the seams ¼ inch in from each edge of the background fabric. In the same manner, stitch the long red border strips to the long sides of the background fabric. Miter each of the corner seams. For more information on mitering corners, see page 270 in the "General Instructions." Repeat for the place mat bordered in purple.

9. Place the corded piping and the top of the place mat bordered in red print right sides together. Align the raw edges and overlap the ends of the piping. Using a zipper foot, sew the piping to the place mat, stitching next to the cording. For more information on making and attaching piping, see page 272 in the "General Instructions." Repeat for the place mat bordered in purple print.

10. Place the top of the place mat bordered in red print and its backing fabric right sides together. Place the fleece on top of the backing. Use a zipper foot to stitch around the edges of the place mat, leaving a 4-inch opening on one side for turn-

ing. Stitch as close as possible to the piping. Turn the place mat right side out and blindstitch the opening closed. Repeat for the place mat bordered in purple print.

11. Beginning with the place mat bordered in red print, machine quilt in the ditch of the seam between the border and the center of the place mat. Repeat for the place mat bordered in purple print.

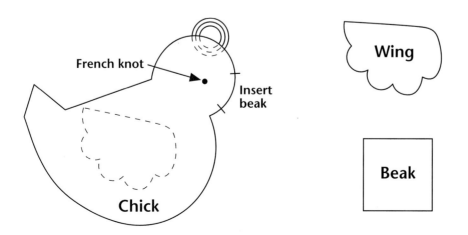

French knot

Insert beak

Chick

Wing

Beak

Babushka Doll Trio

Modeled after wooden Russian nesting dolls called matryoshkas, *these babushka-clad maidens are decorative as well as functional. Collect colorful fabric scraps, bits of floss, some ribbon roses, and seed beads, and create a sweet trio of dolls to welcome guests at your front door. Their friendly faces will add a touch of hospitality and warmth to your home.*

♥ *Size: The small doll is 7¼ inches tall, the medium doll is 8¾ inches tall, and the large doll is 10 inches tall.*

Small Doll

Fabric Requirements

- ♥ 12 × 14-inch piece of muslin for the front and back bases, body bottom, arms, hands, and head/bodice
- ♥ 6 × 10-inch piece of lavender solid for the scarf
- ♥ 6 × 14-inch piece of pink-and-blue stripe for the dress back and dress front bottom
- ♥ 6 × 6-inch square of blue pindot for the apron
- ♥ 1½ × 4½-inch piece of pink solid for the tie

Other Supplies

- ♥ 3 yards of fusible webbing
- ♥ Thread in accent colors for machine appliqué
- ♥ 3 yards of freezer paper
- ♥ 1 skein each of gold, black, dark green, dark blue, and coral embroidery floss
- ♥ 9 to 12 pink, blue, and off-white ribbon roses
- ♥ ¾ yard of ⅛-inch pink satin ribbon
- ♥ Pink powder blusher
- ♥ 14 pearl white seed beads for the buttons
- ♥ 16-ounce bag of polyester fiberfill

- ♥ 32-ounce bag of plastic pellets
- ♥ Template plastic or tracing paper
- ♥ Fine-point black permanent marker
- ♥ Lead pencil or removable fabric marker

Medium Doll

Fabric Requirements

- ♥ 12 × 18-inch piece of muslin for the front and back bases, body bottom, arms, hands, and head/bodice
- ♥ 7 × 10-inch piece of blue solid for the scarf
- ♥ 7 × 14-inch piece of navy print for the dress back and dress front bottom
- ♥ 7-inch square of rose print for the apron
- ♥ 1¾ × 5¼-inch piece of dark blue solid for the tie

Other Supplies

- ♥ 3 yards of fusible webbing
- ♥ Thread in accent colors for machine appliqué
- ♥ 3 yards of freezer paper
- ♥ 1 skein each of gold, black, dark green, dark blue, and coral embroidery floss

- ♥ 9 to 12 pink, blue, and off-white ribbon roses
- ♥ ¾ yard of ⅛-inch dark rose satin ribbon
- ♥ Pink powder blusher
- ♥ 14 pearl white seed beads for the buttons
- ♥ 16-ounce bag of polyester fiberfill
- ♥ 32-ounce bag of plastic pellets
- ♥ Template plastic or tracing paper
- ♥ Fine-point black permanent marker
- ♥ Lead pencil or removable fabric marker

Large Doll

Fabric Requirements

- ♥ 12 × 22-inch piece of muslin for the front and back bases, body bottom, arms, hands, and head/bodice
- ♥ 8 × 11-inch piece of rose solid for the scarf

- ♥ 8 × 16-inch piece of teal-and-purple print for the dress back and dress front bottom
- ♥ 8-inch square of blue print for the apron
- ♥ 2 × 6-inch piece of dark purple solid for the tie

Other Supplies

- ♥ 3 yards of fusible webbing
- ♥ Thread in accent colors for machine appliqué
- ♥ 3 yards of freezer paper
- ♥ 1 skein each of gold, black, dark green, dark blue, and coral embroidery floss
- ♥ 9 to 12 pink, blue, and off-white ribbon roses
- ♥ ¾ yard of ⅛-inch lavender satin ribbon
- ♥ Pink powder blusher
- ♥ 14 pearl white seed beads for the buttons
- ♥ 16-ounce bag of polyester fiberfill

♥ 32-ounce bag of plastic pellets
♥ Template plastic or tracing paper
♥ Fine-point black permanent marker
♥ Lead pencil or removable fabric marker

Instructions

Note: Patterns include ¼-inch seam allowances unless specified otherwise. These directions are for making the medium doll. To make the small and large dolls, follow the instructions on page 42 for reducing or enlarging the patterns.

Medium Doll

CUTTING

1. Trace the patterns on pages 43–49 onto tracing paper or template plastic, transferring all information, and cut them out.

2. Iron fusible webbing onto the wrong side of the fabrics for the scarf, dress, and apron. Cut a 3 × 6-inch piece of muslin for the head/bodice and iron fusible webbing onto the wrong side.

3. Use a pencil or fabric marker to draw around the front and back base patterns on muslin, leaving 2 inches between them. Trace the outlines of the hands, arms, scarf, bodice, apron, and face to the front base and transfer all marks for the scarf, dress, and apron to the back base. Draw around the body bottom pattern on the muslin. Do not cut out the front base, back base, or body bottom at this time.

4. Place the head/bodice pattern on the paper side of the 3-inch piece of muslin. Draw around the pattern with a pencil. Do the same for the hands pattern on the remaining piece of muslin. Cut out these appliqué pieces.

5. Place the scarf front and scarf back patterns on the paper side of the scarf fabric and draw around them with a pencil. Cut out these appliqué pieces.

6. Place the apron front and apron back patterns on the paper side of the apron fabric and draw around them with a pencil. Cut out these appliqué pieces.

7. Place the dress front bottom, dress back, body bottom, and arm patterns on the paper side of the dress fabric. Draw around the patterns with a pencil, reversing the arm pattern for the second arm. Cut out these appliqué pieces.

8. Fold the tie fabric in half lengthwise, right sides together. Place the tie pattern on the fold of the fabric and draw around it with a pencil, transferring all information. Cut out the tie piece. Sew the seam from the fold to the marked opening and turn the tie right side out. Slip stitch the opening closed and make a knot in the center of the tie.

ASSEMBLING THE DOLL

1. Remove the paper from the back of the fusible webbing on the appliqué pieces. Arrange the pieces on the front base and overlap them in the following order. Place the head/bodice piece in position, followed by the dress front bottom, the apron front, the hands, the arms, then the scarf front. As you add each piece, make sure it overlaps the edge of the previous piece. Fuse the appliqué pieces to the front base.

2. Arrange the appliqué pieces for the back base in the following order: the dress back, the apron back, then the scarf back. Fuse the appliqué pieces to the back base.

3. Cut out the muslin body bottom. Fuse the fabric body bottom to the muslin body bottom.

4. Cut out the front and back bases. Iron the shiny side of a piece of freezer paper onto the wrong side of the front and back bases.

5. With a narrow zigzag stitch, machine appliqué over the edges of all pieces, covering the raw edges. Use one color thread for stitching around the edges of the apron and another color for the arms, hands, bodice, scarf, and head. Satin stitch thumb lines inside each hand. Remove the freezer paper from the wrong side of the fabric after you finish stitching.

EMBROIDERING

Note: For step-by-step instructions for working these embroidery stitches, refer to pages 273–275 in the "General Instructions."

1. With two strands of green floss, randomly embroider the

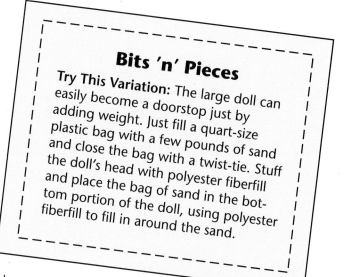

Bits 'n' Pieces

Try This Variation: The large doll can easily become a doorstop just by adding weight. Just fill a quart-size plastic bag with a few pounds of sand and close the bag with a twist-tie. Stuff the doll's head with polyester fiberfill and place the bag of sand in the bottom portion of the doll, using polyester fiberfill to fill in around the sand.

flower stems with long straight stitches, positioning them according to the front base pattern.

2. With two strands of gold floss, embroider the hair with both long and short stitches. Also with two strands of gold floss, embroider each eyebrow with a single straight stitch.

3. With two strands of black floss, embroider the outlines of the eyes with straight stitches. Embroider the nose with two tiny straight stitches. Embroider the lacing on the bodice with long straight stitches, adding 14 seed beads to the bodice as indicated by the large dots on the pattern piece.

4. With two strands of blue floss, embroider the iris of each eye with a French knot.

5. With coral floss, embroider the lips with tiny satin stitches.

6. Put a dab of powder blusher on your fingertip and smooth a bit of color gently over the cheeks.

SEWING, STUFFING, AND FINISHING

1. Place the front and back bases right sides together and sew only the side seams, leaving an opening as indicated on the pattern pieces. Clip or notch the curved seam allowances to make them lie smoothly.

2. With right sides together, baste the body bottom piece to the front and back bases. Sew around the edges and clip the curves. Turn the doll right side out through the side opening.

3. Stuff three-quarters of the doll firmly with fiberfill. Fill the remainder of the doll with plastic pellets and sew the side opening closed.

4. Tack the tie to the scarf under the doll's chin.

5. Sew clusters of three ribbon roses at the tops of the embroidered stems.

6. Tie the ⅛-inch rose satin ribbon into a bow and tack the bow beneath the flowers. Trim the ends of the ribbon.

Large and Small Dolls

To make the large and small dolls, enlarge or reduce the patterns on a photocopy machine.

For the large doll, enlarge each piece to 115 percent of the original size. For the small doll, reduce each pattern piece to 83 percent of the original size. Note that the seam allowances will be inaccurate due to enlarging and reducing. Adjust the seam allowances on your enlarged or reduced patterns to ¼ inch beyond the actual stitching lines. Follow the previous instructions for the medium doll, using a lighter or darker shade of gold floss for the hair and adding French knots or bullion stitches over the long and short stitches to create tiny curls in the hair.

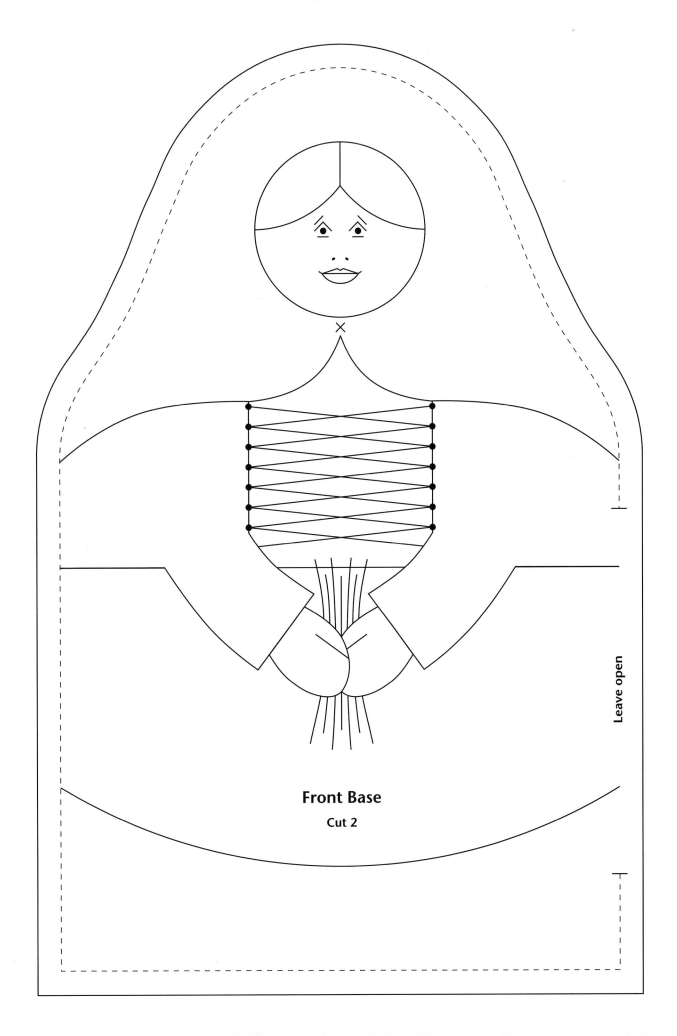

Front Base

Cut 2

Leave open

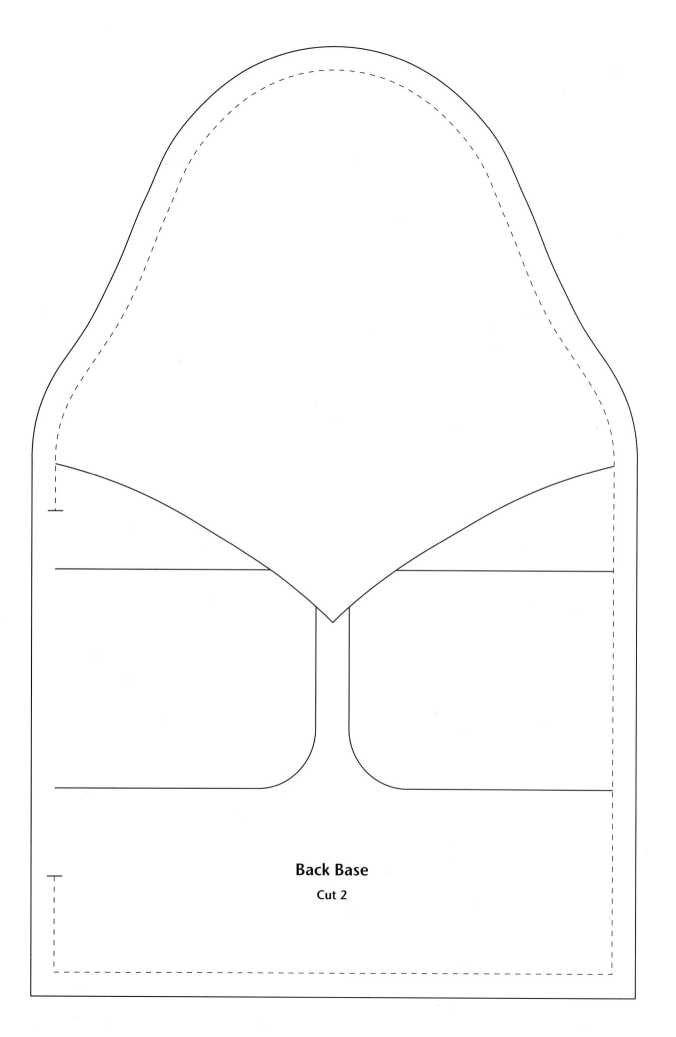

Back Base

Cut 2

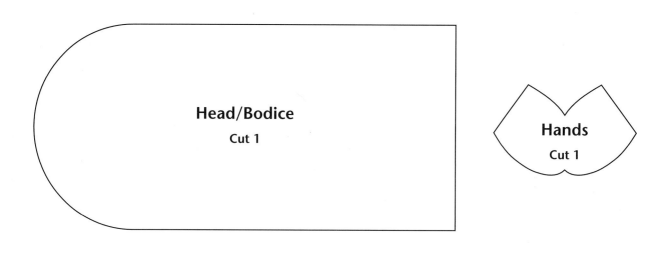

Head/Bodice

Cut 1

Hands

Cut 1

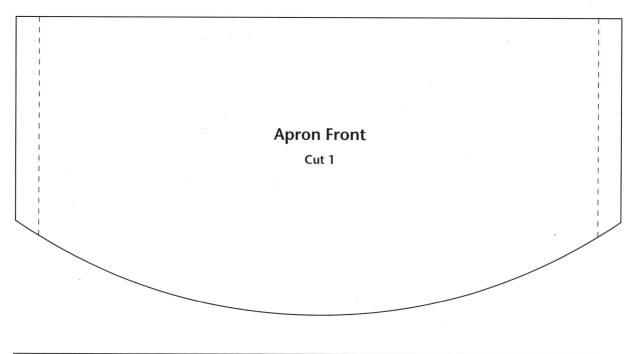

Apron Front

Cut 1

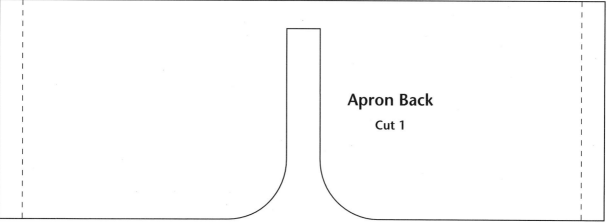

Apron Back

Cut 1

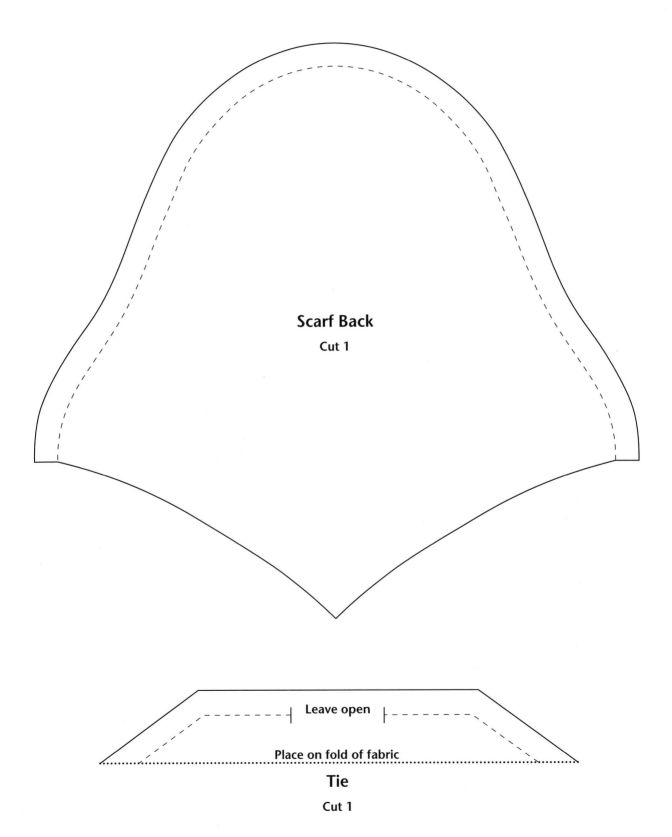

Scarf Back

Cut 1

Leave open

Place on fold of fabric

Tie

Cut 1

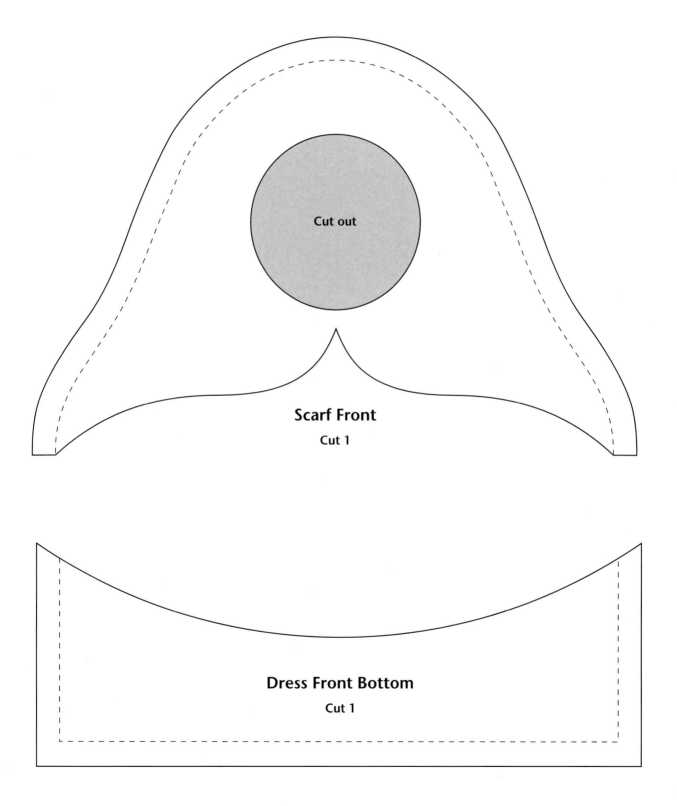

Cut out

Scarf Front

Cut 1

Dress Front Bottom

Cut 1

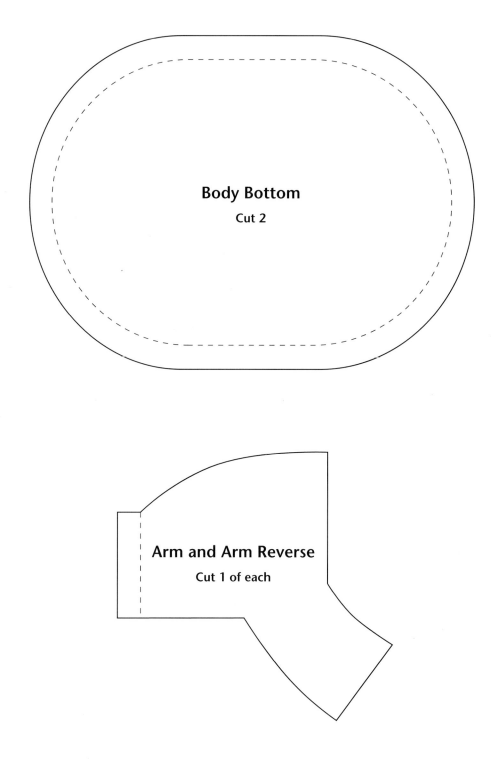

Body Bottom

Cut 2

Arm and Arm Reverse

Cut 1 of each

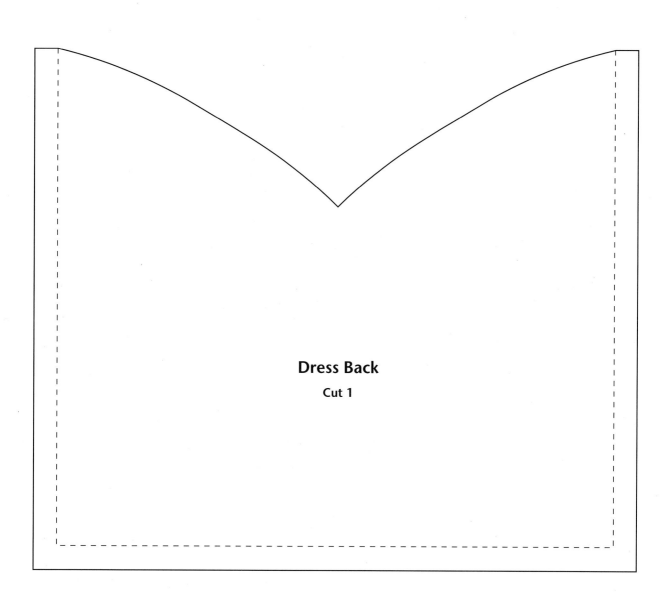

Dress Back

Cut 1

Patches the Bear

It takes just a bit of TLC and a few "bear" necessities to make Patches the Bear. Country plaids and matching muted prints give him a homespun look that will be a welcome addition to any bear collection. Patches even has movable arms and legs, and the best part is that he's "beary" simple to sew!

♥ *Size: The bear is approximately 14 inches high.*

Fabric Requirements

- ♥ ¼ yard of dark blue plaid for the head side and body
- ♥ ¼ yard of brown plaid for the head gusset and body
- ♥ ⅛ yard of medium blue plaid for one arm and one leg
- ♥ ⅛ yard of light blue plaid for one arm and one leg
- ♥ ⅛ yard of black paisley for one arm and one leg
- ♥ ⅛ yard of red print for one arm and one leg
- ♥ ⅛ yard of gold print for the bow
- ♥ 8-inch square of brown print for the ears

Other Supplies

- ♥ 16-ounce bag of polyester fiberfill
- ♥ 4-inch soft-sculpture needle
- ♥ 1 skein of black pearl cotton
- ♥ Two ¼-inch black round buttons for the eyes
- ♥ One ½-inch beige button
- ♥ Sewing thread to match fabrics
- ♥ Hand-sewing needle
- ♥ Template plastic or tracing paper
- ♥ Fine-point black permanent marker
- ♥ Pencil or removable fabric marker for tracing templates on fabric

Instructions

Note: Patterns include ¼-inch seam allowances. Cut all pattern pieces on the right side of the fabric. Trace all markings onto the right side of the fabric.

Cutting

1. Trace the pattern pieces on pages 54–57 onto template plastic or tracing paper, transferring all markings, and cut out the templates. (Transfer the facial markings with the pencil or removable fabric marker.)

2. From the dark blue plaid, cut one head side, one head side reverse, and one body reverse.

3. From the brown plaid, cut one head gusset and one body.

4. From the medium blue plaid, cut one arm and one leg.

5. From the light blue plaid, cut one arm and one leg.

6. From the black paisley, cut one arm reverse and one leg reverse.

7. From the red print, cut one arm reverse and one leg reverse.

8. From the gold print, cut one 2¼ × 26-inch piece for the bow.

9. From the brown print, cut four ears.

Sewing

1. To make one red/light blue arm, pin one arm to one arm reverse with right sides together. Sew the pieces together, leaving a 2-inch opening, as shown in **Diagram 1.** Clip or notch the curved seam allowances to make them lie smoothly and finger press them open. Turn the arm right side out.

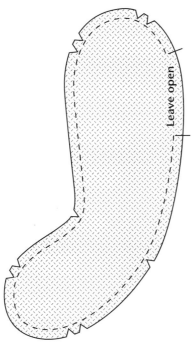

Diagram 1

2. Repeat Step 1 to make the medium blue/black arm, the light blue/black leg, the medium blue/red leg, the dark blue/brown plaid body, and the brown print ears. Notch the curved seams, finger press open, and turn the pieces right side out.

3. To make the head, pin the head side to the head side reverse with right sides together. Beginning at the neck edge and ending at the nose, sew the pieces together, as shown in **Diagram 2.** Clip or notch the curved seam allowances to make them lie smoothly. Finger press this seam open.

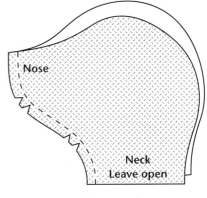

Diagram 2

4. To complete the head, pin each side of the head gusset to each of the head sides, with right sides together and the noses on the patterns aligned. Sew the pieces together, as shown in **Diagram 3** on the opposite page, leaving the neck edge open. Clip or notch the curved seam allowances to make them lie smoothly and finger press them open. Turn the head right side out.

5. Turn under the ¼-inch seam allowance along the bottom edge of the ears. Fold along the pleat lines, as shown in **Diagram 4** on the opposite page. Baste the pleats in place and blindstitch each ear closed.

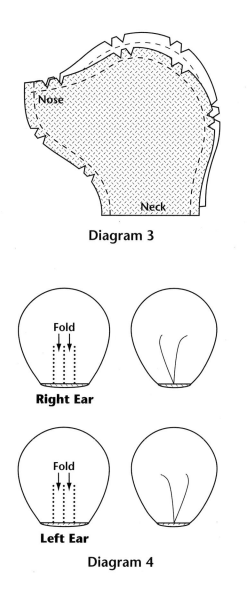

Diagram 3

Right Ear

Left Ear

Diagram 4

Stuffing

1. Stuff the arms, legs, body, and head firmly with polyester fiberfill.

2. Turn under the ¼-inch seam allowance along the opening of each piece and blindstitch it closed.

Assembling

1. With black pearl cotton and a soft-sculpture needle, sew the arms and legs firmly to the body at the

dots indicated on each pattern piece. Attach the head to the body by sewing the seams of each piece together.

2. With matching thread and a hand-sewing needle, sew the ears to the head as indicated on the head.

Finishing

1. With matching thread and a hand-sewing needle, sew the black buttons for the eyes and the beige button at the dots indicated on the patterns.

2. Use black pearl cotton and a soft-sculpture needle to satin stitch the nose, as shown in **Diagram 5.** Embroider the mouth with large straight stitches. Embroider each paw with three straight stitches at the markings indicated on the arms.

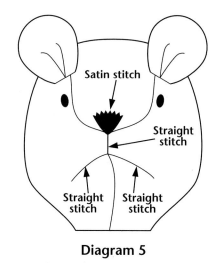

Diagram 5

3. Tie a bow around the neck of the bear with the gold print fabric. Trim the ends of the bow at a 45-degree angle.

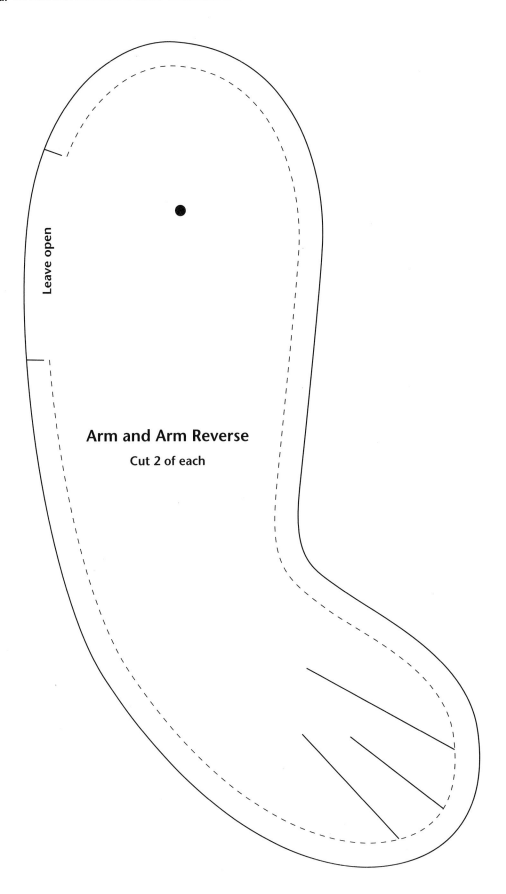

Leave open

Arm and Arm Reverse

Cut 2 of each

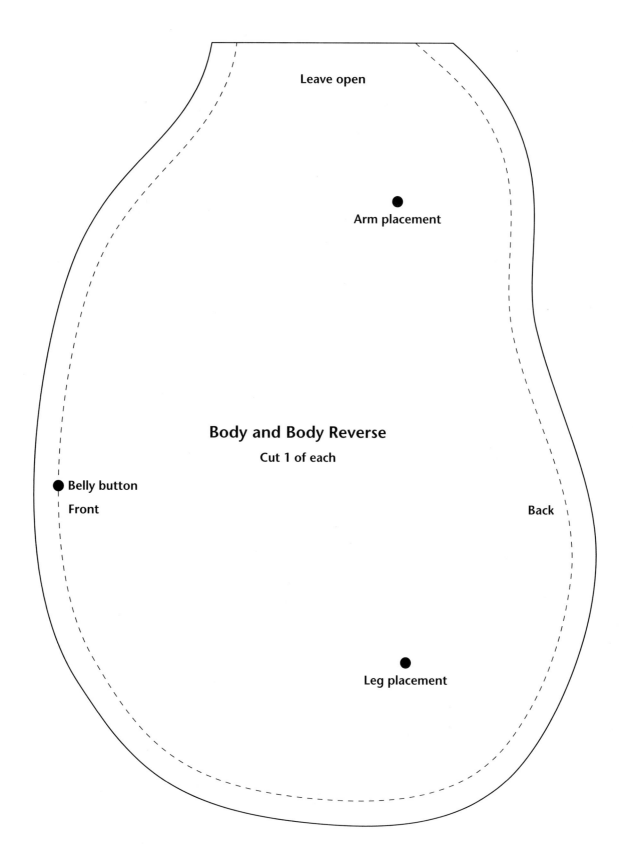

Leave open

Arm placement

Body and Body Reverse

Cut 1 of each

Belly button

Front

Back

Leg placement

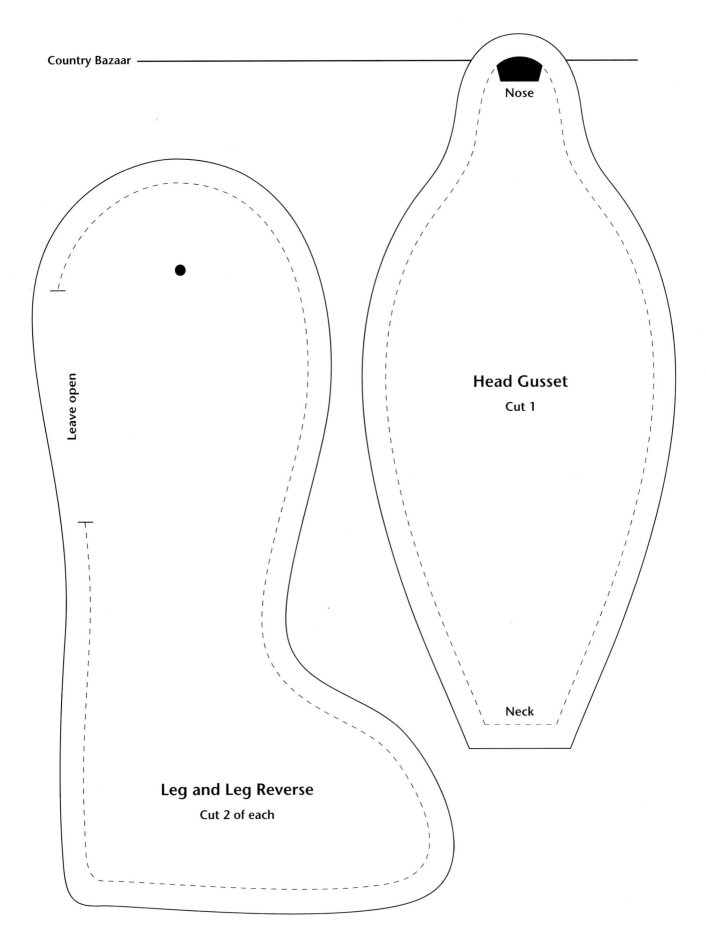

Nose

Head Gusset

Cut 1

Neck

Leave open

Leg and Leg Reverse

Cut 2 of each

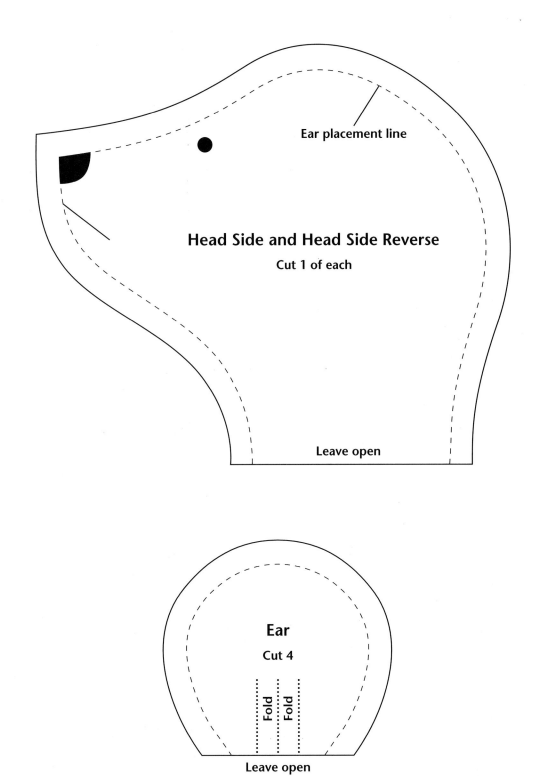

Head Side and Head Side Reverse

Cut 1 of each

Ear placement line

Leave open

Ear

Cut 4

Fold

Fold

Leave open

Fabulously Fun Button Covers

For a quick-and-easy "coverup," snap an honorary medal over the button on a denim shirt pocket, or create a cascade of small ribbon rosettes down the front of a silk blouse. Clip a feathered flapper to a dress collar, or try out the different effects you can achieve with the yo-yo Sunflower, Synthetic Suede, Black Rose, Hook and Snap, and Denim 'n' Lace button covers.

♥ *The button covers listed are the sizes used for the projects in the photo. For your button covers, select a size that will fit the buttons on your garment.*

Honorary Medal Button Cover

Supplies

- ♥ 25 mm button cover blank
- ♥ 7½-inch length of 1½-inch yellow-and-orange striped grosgrain ribbon
- ♥ 7½-inch length of ⅜-inch dark purple satin ribbon
- ♥ 6½-inch length of ⅜-inch orange satin ribbon
- ♥ 5½-inch length of 1-inch medium purple satin ribbon
- ♥ 10-inch length of ⅛-inch black-and-white satin ribbon
- ♥ Two ½-inch decorative coins
- ♥ One 1-inch decorative coin
- ♥ Fray-Check
- ♥ Needle
- ♥ Sewing thread to match striped and dark purple ribbons
- ♥ Extra-thick craft glue
- ♥ Metal glue

Instructions

1. Apply Fray-Check to the cut ends of the grosgrain ribbon. Run a gathering thread ⅜ inch in from the long edge on one side of the ribbon. Pull the gathering thread to draw the ribbon into a circle, and secure the gathers by taking a few stitches with a needle and thread. Overlap the ends of the ribbon and glue them together.

2. Apply Fray-Check to the cut ends of the dark purple ribbon. Run a gathering thread along one long edge of the dark purple ribbon. Pull the thread gently to begin gathering the ribbon into a circle. Place the slightly gathered dark purple ribbon over the center of the striped grosgrain ribbon. Tighten the gathers of the dark purple ribbon around the gathered portion of the grosgrain ribbon and secure the gathers with a needle and thread.

3. Fold the 1-inch medium purple ribbon in half crosswise and glue the top edges of the wrong sides of the ribbon together. Center the raw ends of this ribbon on the front side of the button cover and secure them with metal glue.

4. Fold the ⅜-inch orange ribbon in half crosswise and glue the top edges of the wrong sides of the rib-

bon together. Center the raw ends of this ribbon on the center of the 1-inch purple ribbon on the button cover and secure the top edges in place with craft glue.

5. Cut the ⅛-inch black-and-white ribbon in half. Fold each of the 5-inch pieces in half crosswise and glue the top edges of the wrong sides of each piece together. Glue these ribbons to the sides of the purple ribbon with craft glue.

6. Sew the small gold coins to the ends of the black-and-white ribbons. Sew the large gold coin to the end of the orange ribbon.

7. Using the metal glue, attach the wrong side of the gathered grosgrain ribbon to the button cover, covering the raw ends of the ribbons already glued to the button cover. Let the glue dry completely before wearing the button covers.

Ribbon Rosette Button Cover

Supplies

- ♥ 18 mm button cover blank
- ♥ 7½-inch length of 1-inch purple satin ribbon
- ♥ 7½-inch length of ⅜-inch blue satin ribbon
- ♥ Needle
- ♥ Sewing thread to match ribbons
- ♥ Extra-thick craft glue
- ♥ Metal glue
- ♥ Fray-Check

Instructions

1. Apply Fray-Check to the cut ends of the purple satin ribbon. Run a gathering thread ⅜ inch in from the long edge on one side of the ribbon. Pull the gathering thread to draw the ribbon into a circle, and secure the gathers by taking a few stitches with a needle and thread. Overlap the ends of the ribbon and glue them together.

2. Run a gathering thread along one long side of the blue ribbon. Pull the thread gently to begin gathering the ribbon into a circle. Place the slightly gathered blue ribbon over the center of the purple ribbon. Tighten the gathers of the blue ribbon around the edges of the purple ribbon ,and secure the gathers by taking a few stitches with a needle and thread.

3. Glue the purple-and-blue rosette to the front side of the button cover with the metal glue.

Hook and Snap Button Cover

Supplies

- ♥ 18 mm button cover blank
- ♥ Scrap of lace trim large enough to cover the top of the button cover
- ♥ 8 black hooks from a hook-and-eye set
- ♥ Half of a ¼-inch metal snap
- ♥ Extra-thick craft glue
- ♥ Metal glue

Instructions

1. Using the metal glue, secure the piece of lace trim to the front side of the button cover.

2. Using the craft glue, secure eight hooks in a concentric circle on top of the lace trim. Allow to dry.

3. Center half of the snap on top of the hooks and secure it in place with the craft glue.

Synthetic Suede Knot Button Cover

Supplies

♥ 18 mm button cover blank
♥ 6-inch length of ⅜-inch tan synthetic suede
♥ 6-inch length of ⅜-inch gray synthetic suede
♥ Extra-thick craft glue
♥ Metal glue

Instructions

1. Cut a ⅜-inch-long slit in the center of the tan strip of synthetic suede.

2. Referring to **Diagram 1,** tie the two strips of synthetic suede

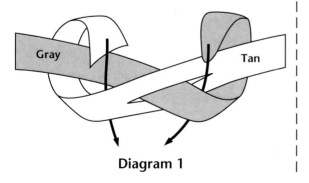
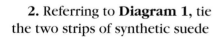

Diagram 1

together by first inserting the end of the gray strip into the slit in the tan strip. Pull the ends of each strip through the loops, as shown.

3. Referring to **Diagram 2,** tighten the strips into a knot. Add a touch of craft glue behind the knot to hold the crossed strips in place, then allow the glue to dry. Trim the ends of each strip diagonally approximately 1 inch below the knot.

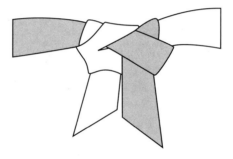

Diagram 2

4. Secure the wrong side of the knot to the front side of the button cover with metal glue.

Flapper Button Cover

Supplies

♥ 25 mm button cover blank
♥ 3-inch scrap of ⅛-inch red-and-gold striped ribbon
♥ 2-inch square of muslin
♥ 2-inch square of quilt batting
♥ Small scrap of brown braided wool roving
♥ One ¼-inch red rhinestone
♥ Small blue, red, tan, and speckled feathers

♥ Tracing paper
♥ Fine-point black permanent marker
♥ Red pencil for the cheeks
♥ 2-inch square of cardboard for the face
♥ Extra-thick craft glue
♥ Metal glue

Instructions

1. Trace the flapper face pattern on page 65 onto tracing paper and cut it out.

2. Draw around the pattern on the cardboard and cut out the circle. Cut a piece of batting the same size and glue it to the cardboard circle.

3. Place the face pattern on the muslin and draw a circle approximately ¼ inch beyond the edge of the pattern. Cut out the muslin circle on the drawn line. Trace the facial features onto the center of the muslin circle with the black fine-point permanent marker. Use red pencil to shade the cheeks.

4. Center the batting circle on the wrong side of the muslin face. Bring the edges of the muslin to the back of the cardboard and glue them in place with craft glue.

5. Untwist a small amount of the braided wool roving to create curly hair. Glue a few small tufts of the wool roving to the top of the face. Wrap the ⅛-inch red-and-gold ribbon around the top of the head for a headband, gluing the ends to the back of the cardboard. Glue a speck-

led feather and a red rhinestone to the headband. Glue a blue, tan, and red feather under the chin.

6. Secure the wrong side of the face to the front side of the button cover with metal glue.

Black Rose Button Cover

Supplies

♥ 25 mm button cover blank
♥ 6-inch length of ¾-inch black fabric
♥ Fabric stiffener
♥ Small plastic bag
♥ Water-base varnish
♥ Paintbrush
♥ Metallic gold paint
♥ Liner brush
♥ Three ⅛-inch rhinestones
♥ Waxed paper
♥ Extra-thick craft glue
♥ Metal glue

Instructions

1. Pour a small amount of fabric stiffener into the small plastic bag. Drop the 6-inch strip of black fabric into the bag and squeeze the fabric stiffener through the fabric. Remove any excess solution by blotting the fabric with another piece of scrap fabric.

2. To form the rose, roll the end of the fabric strip into a small tube. Continue wrapping the strip around the center tube, making each wrap slightly looser than the previous wrap. Twist the strip of fabric occasionally as you wrap to give the rose more dimension. Tuck the end of the strip into the back of the rose and allow it to dry on a piece of waxed paper.

3. Brush the top of the rose with water-base varnish and allow it to dry. Apply a thin line of metallic gold paint along the edges of the ribbon. Allow the paint to dry.

4. Secure the wrong side of the rose to the front side of the button cover with metal glue.

5. Secure three rhinestones to the top of the rose with craft glue, positioning them as desired.

Denim 'n' Lace Button Cover

Supplies

♥ 18 mm button cover blank
♥ 2-inch square of denim
♥ 4-inch length of ½-inch lace trim
♥ Small white ribbon rose
♥ 14 pink seed beads
♥ Tracing paper or template plastic
♥ Fine-point black permanent marker
♥ Extra-thick craft glue
♥ Metal glue

Instructions

1. Trace the denim circle pattern on page 64 onto tracing paper or template plastic; cut out the pattern.

2. Draw around the circle pattern on the wrong side of the denim and cut out the denim circle.

3. Using your fingernail, fray the edges of the denim around the circle. Trim off any long threads.

4. Secure the wrong side of the denim circle to the front side of the button cover with metal glue.

5. Glue the lace trim around the back of the denim circle, overlapping and gluing the ends in place.

6. Glue a circle of 14 seed beads around the denim circle, ⅛ inch in from the edge.

7. Glue a white ribbon rose in the center of the denim circle.

Sunflower Button Cover

Supplies

♥ 18 mm button cover blank
♥ 3-inch square of yellow fabric
♥ 2-inch square of rust fabric
♥ One 2½-inch and one 2-inch square of green fabric
♥ Tracing paper or template plastic
♥ Fine-point black permanent marker
♥ Sewing thread to match fabrics
♥ Black embroidery floss
♥ Small piece of polyester fiberfill
♥ Extra-thick craft glue
♥ Metal glue

Instructions

1. Trace the flower, flower center, and leaf patterns on pages 64–65 onto tracing paper or tem-

Bits 'n' Pieces

Try These Variations: Any of these button covers can be made into earrings or pins by gluing the appropriate hardware to the completed piece. Glue the parts to a small circle of cardboard before gluing on the pin back or the earring clips or posts. For a young girl, decorate a headband or hairclip with several of the sunflowers. Try making daisy flowers using white for the flowers and yellow for the centers. The black rose would make a nice toe clip for a pair of plain pumps. Make the rose larger by using a slightly wider and longer piece of fabric. Experiment with the twists and turns of the fabric as you form the rose.

plate plastic. Cut out the three patterns.

2. Draw around the flower pattern on the wrong side of the yellow fabric. Cut out one sunflower. Draw around the flower center pattern on the wrong side of the rust fabric. Cut out one flower center. Draw around the large and small leaf patterns on the wrong side of the green squares. Cut out one large and one small leaf.

3. Sew a line of gathering stitches ⅛ inch from the raw edge of the rust flower center. Place a small amount of polyester fiberfill in the center of the wrong side of the circle. Pull the gathering stitches to create a small puffed flower center. Secure the thread by running the stitches through the raw ends of the gathered puff, but do not cut the thread.

4. Turn under a ¼-inch hem on the yellow sunflower, sewing a gathering thread ⅛ inch from the fold at the same time. Place the rust flower center in the center of the sunflower on the wrong side of the fabric. Use the thread from the rust flower center to tack the flower center securely in place. Cut the thread.

5. Pull the gathering thread on the sunflower, drawing in the

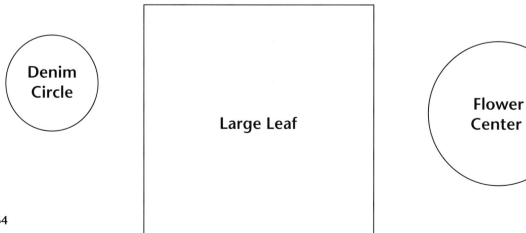

Denim Circle

Large Leaf

Flower Center

edges of the sunflower circle to meet the rust flower center. Take a few backstitches to secure the gathering thread, but do not cut it. With the same thread, tack the gathers of the sunflower around the rust flower center. Secure and cut the thread.

6. Referring to **Diagram 3,** fold the large leaf square of fabric in half, wrong sides together, and finger press a crease at the center. Fold both corners down to meet the raw edges and sew a line of gathering stitches at the lower edge. Pull the thread to gather the base of the leaf. Secure and cut the thread. Repeat for the smaller leaf.

7. Using two strands of black embroidery floss, work a stem stitch down the center of each leaf and make about 25 French knots in the center of the flower.

8. Using the metal glue, attach the wrong sides of the two leaves and the sunflower to the front side of the button cover.

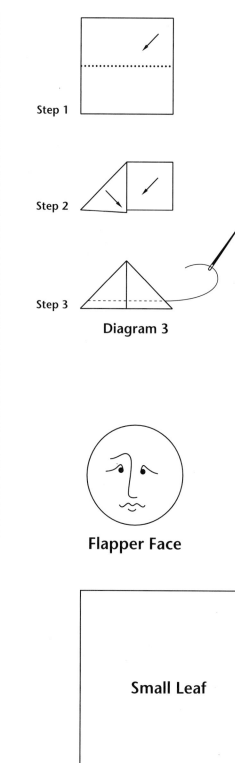

Step 1

Step 2

Step 3

Diagram 3

Flapper Face

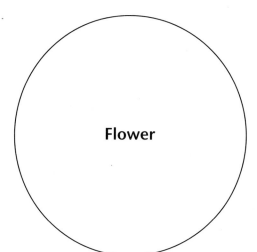

Flower

Small Leaf

Paper Doll Sweatshirt

Do you remember the fun of folding paper and cutting out a row of perfectly matched paper dolls? Why not use the same technique and cut a trio of fabric dolls to decorate a favorite sweatshirt? Dress the dolls in printed gowns with tiny seed beads and add black buttons to create whimsical hairstyles.

♥ *Size: The paper doll motif is 9 × 21 inches.*

Fabrics and Supplies

- ♥ 10 × 24-inch piece of printed muslin for the doll bodies
- ♥ Three 7-inch-square scraps of print fabrics for the dresses
- ♥ 1 large crew neck sweatshirt
- ♥ Sewing thread to match the sweatshirt
- ♥ ¾ yard of fusible webbing
- ♥ 10 × 24-inch piece of fabric stabilizer
- ♥ 57 pearl-color seed beads for the buttons
- ♥ 24 to 30 black buttons of assorted sizes for hair
- ♥ Template plastic
- ♥ Fine-point black permanent marker
- ♥ Pink fabric marker for the cheeks
- ♥ 1 skein of black embroidery floss
- ♥ Sharp pencil

Instructions

Cutting

1. Trace the doll body and doll dress patterns on pages 68–69 onto template plastic and cut out the templates.

2. Cut a 10 × 24-inch piece of fusible webbing. Iron the webbing side onto the wrong side of the printed muslin.

3. Place the doll body template on the left side of the paper side of the webbing and draw around it. Move the template to the right of the first doll, placing it so the hands touch, and draw a second doll body. Move the template to the right again and draw a third doll body, making sure it is joined to the second doll at the hands. Cut out the three dolls, leaving them joined at the hands.

4. Cut three 7-inch squares of fusible webbing. Iron the webbing side onto the wrong side of each print scrap.

5. Place the doll dress template on the paper side of one of the print scraps and draw around it. Repeat for the other two print scraps. Cut out three doll dresses.

Assembling the Sweatshirt

1. Remove the paper backing from the muslin dolls. Center the dolls 3 inches above the ribbing on the front of the sweatshirt. Fuse the dolls to the front of the sweatshirt (see **Diagram 1** on the opposite page).

2. Remove the paper backing from the back of each doll dress.

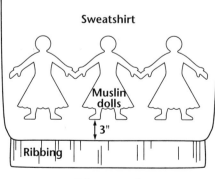

Diagram 1

Place the webbing side of one dress on one doll body; fuse a dress on each doll, as shown in **Diagram 2.**

Diagram 2

3. Pin or fuse the piece of fabric stabilizer to the wrong side of the sweatshirt behind the dolls. Using a narrow zigzag stitch, machine appliqué around the doll bodies, outlining the dresses and the ruffles above the hands and legs. Do not stitch between the hands. Remove the stabilizer.

Bits 'n' Pieces

Try This Variation: To make a sweatshirt that will please any little girl, reduce the doll body and doll dress patterns by 50 percent on a photocopier, which will make the row of dolls measure 4½ × 10½ inches—just right for a petite miss! Instead of using buttons for the hair, tack several strands of embroidery floss at the top of each doll's head. Braid the strands of floss together to make braids that hang down freely, then tie them with colorful bits of ribbon.

Finishing

1. Sew 19 seed beads evenly down the front of each dress, as indicated on the dress pattern.

2. Position and sew several black buttons around the head of each doll. The number of buttons you use will depend on the sizes you select.

3. Use the black marker to draw the mouth and the eyes. Use the pink marker to draw the cheeks.

4. Use six strands of black floss to make French knots for the bangs.

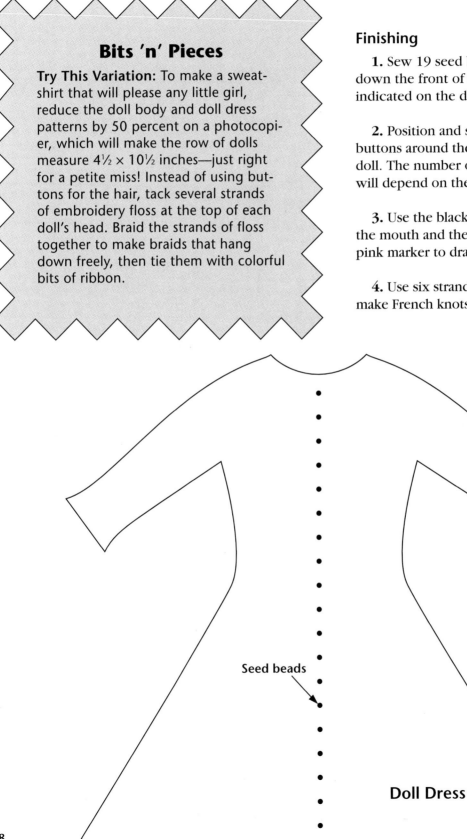

Seed beads

Doll Dress

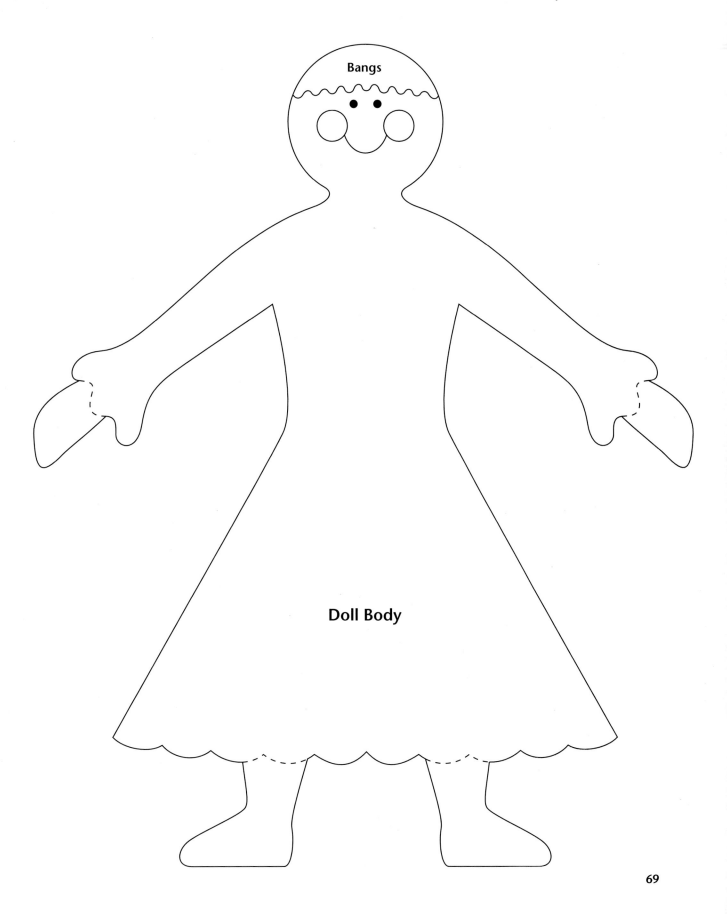

Bangs

Doll Body

Plaid Pieced Place Mats

These quick-and-easy country-style place mats are especially nice when they're pieced from remnants of plaid fabrics. Throw in an occasional solid in a bright accent color for fun. Follow our schematic plan for placement of the pieces or, if you wish, arrange them to suit your own fancy.

♥ *Size: Each place mat is 13 × 18 inches.*

Fabric Requirements
(for four place mats)

- ♥ 7 assorted 18 × 22-inch pieces of light, medium, and dark plaids or stripes
- ♥ 4 different 18 × 20-inch pieces of solid fabric for binding and an occasional square, triangle, or rectangle
- ♥ 1¼ yards of fleece
- ♥ 1 yard of blue or other solid fabric for backing

Other Supplies

- ♥ Template plastic
- ♥ Fine-point black permanent marker
- ♥ Pencil or removable fabric marker
- ♥ White sewing thread or rustproof nickel-plated brass safety pins, size 1 or 2, for basting
- ♥ Off-white or clear nylon thread for machine quilting
- ♥ Sewing threads to match fabrics in each binding strip

Instructions

Note: Cutting and assembly instructions are given for making one place mat. Each place mat consists of a total of 35 pieced and solid squares in 5 horizontal rows of 7 squares each. To determine the total number of pieces you'll need for four place mats, multiply the number of each pattern by 4. All pattern pieces include ¼-inch seam allowances.

Cutting

1. With a permanent marker, trace pattern pieces A, B, C, and D on page 73 onto template plastic.

2. With a pencil or removable fabric marker, draw around the templates on the assorted plaid fabrics. If desired, cut a few of the B, C, and D pieces from solid fabrics, referring to the photo for guidance. Mark around each template on the wrong side of the fabric and cut out the following total number of pieces for one place mat:

- • 8 of square A
- • 40 of triangle B
- • 30 of square C
- • 19 of rectangle D

3. Cut two 1¾ × 20-inch binding strips from different solid fabrics and two 1¾ × 15-inch binding strips from different solid fabrics.

4. Cut one 15 × 20-inch piece of backing fabric.

5. Cut one 15 × 20-inch piece of fleece.

Piecing

Note: The assembly instructions are for piecing one place mat. Wherever possible, press each seam toward the darker fabric.

1. Sew four plaid or striped B triangles together to form a square, as shown in **Diagram 1.** (If desired, use two solid and two plaid or striped B triangles.) Make ten of these pieced squares.

Diagram 1

2. Sew four plaid or striped C squares together (or a combination of plaid or striped and solid C squares) to form a larger square, as shown in **Diagram 2.** Make five of these pieced squares.

Diagram 2

3. Sew two plaid or striped C squares and one plaid or striped D rectangle together to form a square, as shown in **Diagram 3.** Make five of these pieced squares.

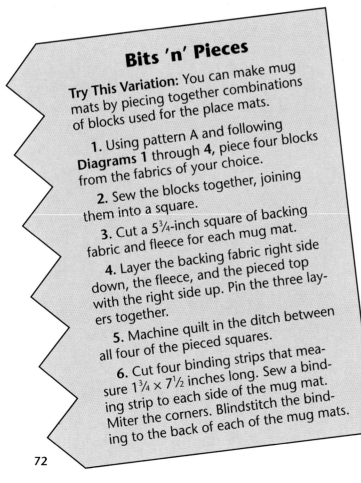

Diagram 3

4. Sew two plaid D rectangles or one plaid and one striped D rectangle together to form a square, as shown in **Diagram 4.** Make seven of these pieced squares.

5. Referring to **Diagram 5** on the opposite page, sew together five

Bits 'n' Pieces

Try This Variation: You can make mug mats by piecing together combinations of blocks used for the place mats.

1. Using pattern A and following Diagrams 1 through 4, piece four blocks from the fabrics of your choice.

2. Sew the blocks together, joining them into a square.

3. Cut a 5¾-inch square of backing fabric and fleece for each mug mat.

4. Layer the backing fabric right side down, the fleece, and the pieced top with the right side up. Pin the three layers together.

5. Machine quilt in the ditch between all four of the pieced squares.

6. Cut four binding strips that measure 1¾ × 7½ inches long. Sew a binding strip to each side of the mug mat. Miter the corners. Blindstitch the binding to the back of each of the mug mats.

Diagram 4

horizontal rows of seven squares each. Combine plaid or striped A squares with pieced squares.

6. Sew the five horizontal rows of squares together to assemble the place mat, as shown in **Diagram 6** on the opposite page.

7. Place the backing fabric right side down on a table and center the fleece on top of it. Place the pieced place mat right side up on top of the fleece and baste the three layers together, using white sewing thread or rustproof, nickel-plated brass safety pins.

8. Machine quilt horizontally and vertically across the place mat, stitching in the ditch around each 2½-inch square.

9. Trim the backing and fleece even with the edges of the place mat.

10. Sew the two longer binding strips to the long sides of the place mat. Sew the shorter binding strips to the short sides of the place mat. Miter the corner seams as described on page 270 in the "General Instructions." Blindstitch the binding to the back of the place mat by hand, matching the thread to the color of each binding strip.

11. Repeat the cutting and piecing instructions to make the remaining three place mats.

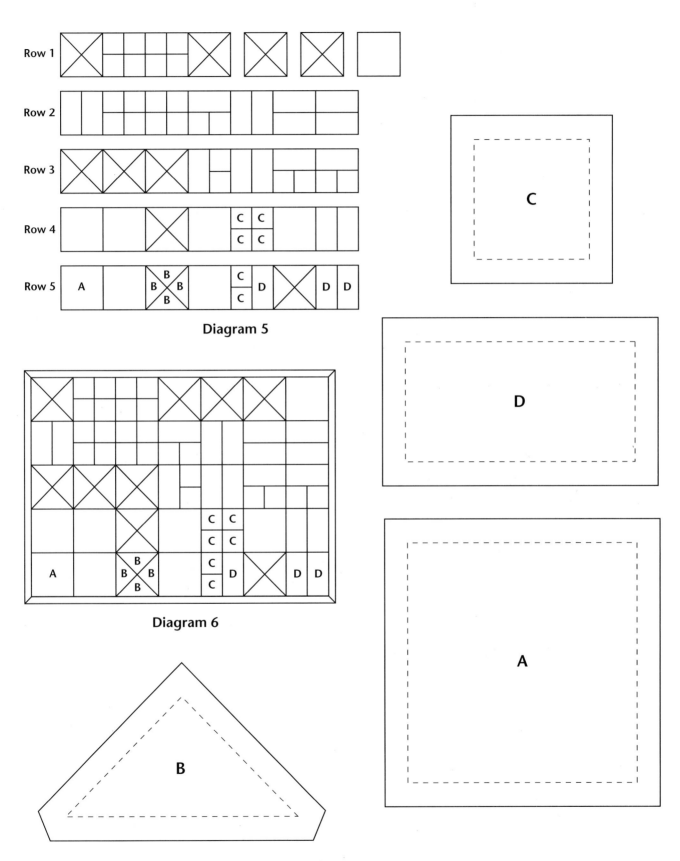

Row 1

Row 2

Row 3

Row 4

Row 5

Diagram 5

Diagram 6

A

B

C

D

Jeans Rug

Braid new life into old, worn jeans and create a reversible, durable rug for any area of your home at the same time. This truly American craft goes back to the early 1800s, when it was popular for making rugs to protect and complement tables, chests, beds, and other household furniture. As you plait narrow strips of denim together, you can take pride in giving this time-honored American tradition a modern-day twist.

♥ *Size: The oval rug is approximately 19 × 29 inches.*

Fabrics and Supplies

- ♥ 4 pairs of adult-size blue jeans
- ♥ Sewing thread to match fabric
- ♥ Quilting thread to match fabric
- ♥ Curved lacing needle
- ♥ Sewing needle
- ♥ Sharp scissors
- ♥ Safety pins or straight pins
- ♥ Removable fabric marker
- ♥ Hole punch

Instructions

Cutting

1. Beginning at the bottom of one pant leg and ending at the other, cut open a pair of blue jeans along the inner seam.

2. Carefully cut out the zipper, preserving as much of the jeans fabric as possible.

3. Cut along the center back seam to separate the legs of the jeans. Remove and discard the pockets. If there is a leather tag attached to the waist, remove it and set it aside for finishing the rug.

4. Cut off the waistband.

5. Referring to **Diagram 1,** cut as many 2-inch strips from each pant leg as possible, discarding any strip that is less than 5 inches long. Cut the strips to incorporate decorative topstitching, rivets, or patches.

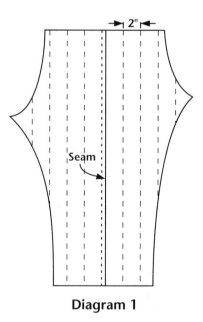

Diagram 1

6. Repeat Steps 1 through 5 for each of the remaining pairs of blue jeans. Divide all the strips into three equal groups.

Joining the Strips

1. Place two strips right sides together to form a right angle, as shown in **Diagram 2** on page 76, and sew a diagonal seam. Trim the seam allowance to ¼ inch and press it open. Continue sewing together the strips from one group in the same manner, using diagonal seams and trimming and pressing each of the seams open. This will form Strip A. Roll Strip A into a ball, folding the fabric in half lengthwise, wrong sides together, as you work.

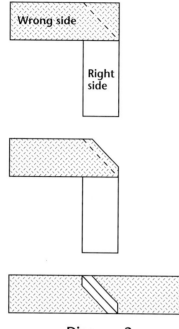

Diagram 2

2. Sew all of the strips from both remaining groups into one long strip that is twice as long as Strip A. This will form Strip B-C, as shown in **Diagram 3.** Mark the midpoint of Strip B-C with a dot. Roll both ends of this strip toward the midpoint, folding the fabric in half lengthwise, wrong sides together, as you work.

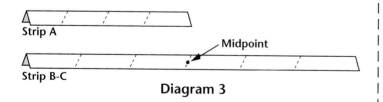

Diagram 3

Forming the T

Referring to **Diagram 4,** form a T by inserting Strip A between the folded layers of Strip B-C at the midpoint. Secure the T by machine sewing or hand stitching 4 inches across Strip A.

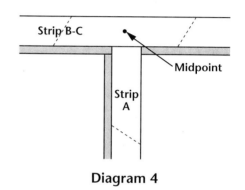

Diagram 4

Braiding the Rug

1. Hold the T so that the open side of Strip C is on the right, as shown in **Diagram 4.** Hold the T securely between the left thumb and forefinger. Then fold Strip B over your thumbnail to form a loop, as shown in **Diagram 5** on the opposite page. (You will use this loop later to lace the rug together.) Fold Strip C over Strip B and then fold Strip A over Strip C. This establishes the braiding sequence. Remove your thumb from the braid and slightly adjust the size of the first loop to make it match the others.

2. Continue braiding the strips until the braid measures 11 inches. Create a turn in the braid, which

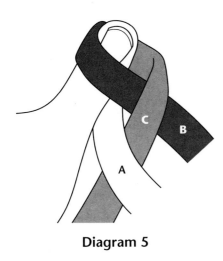

Diagram 5

Bits 'n' Pieces

Try This Variation: Try your hand at designing your own rag rug with a color scheme and fabric selection that will accent any room in your home. A secondhand shop is often a treasure chest offering an unlimited variety of fabric. Soft wool or flannel plaids will add cozy comfort to a bedroom. Or mix and match cotton fabrics in pretty pastels, gingham checks, stripes, or calico patterns for a down-home country look. For an exotic safari look, try a specialty fabric shop for leopard-spotted designs, imitation leather, and imitation snakeskin.

will form the center of the rug, by using a double twist, as shown in **Diagram 6.** Start by placing the right strip over the center strip. Repeat, so that there are two loops on the right. Then place the left strip over the center strip, and repeat this entire sequence. The twist on the right will make the braid turn to the left. When you've finished, fasten the ends of the strips together with a safety pin. After you have created this center portion of the rug, continue braiding straight for the entire length of

the strips. The rug will take shape when you lace the braid around the center portion of the rug.

Lacing the Rug

1. Lace on a flat surface. Referring to **Diagram 7,** form the first seam to be laced by laying the section before and after the double twist next to each other. The double twist will create the first curve in the rug.

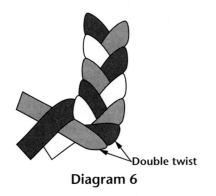

Diagram 6

Double twist

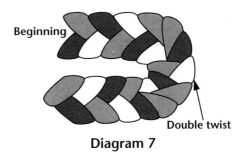

Beginning

Double twist

Diagram 7

2. Thread the lacing needle with quilting thread that matches the denim fabric. Referring to **Diagram 8** and working from right to left, bring the lacing needle up through the bottom of loop 1 and down through the top of loop 2. Fasten the thread in a secure knot to prevent it from unraveling.

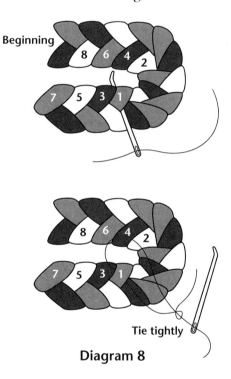

Diagram 8

3. Referring to **Diagram 9,** continue lacing the center seam by bringing the needle up through loop 3, down through loop 4, and up through loop 3. This forms the E-lacing. Continue lacing by bringing the needle up through loop 5, down through loop 6, and up through loop 5. Then bring the needle up through loop 7, down through loop 8, and up through loop 7. Complete the center seam by lacing it to the thumb loop.

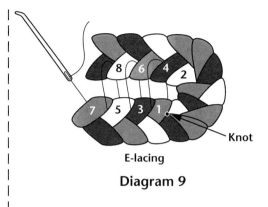

E-lacing

Diagram 9

4. Use a straight lacing stitch to ease the braid around the thumb loop by bringing the needle up through the bottom of the thumb loop and down through it, as shown in **Diagram 10.**

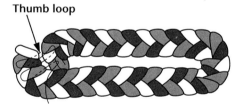

Diagram 10

5. Continue lacing the braid to the center of the rug in a clockwise direction until the next curve. Do not skip any loops on the straight side.

6. To ensure that the rug will lie flat around the next and subsequent curves, work about six extra loops around the curve. To do this, wrap the braid around the curve and fasten it to the rug with a large safety pin where the braid comes out of the curve, as shown in **Diagram 11** on the opposite page.

7. As shown in **Diagram 11**, fasten the braid to the center of the rug with six straight pins, spaced evenly around the curve.

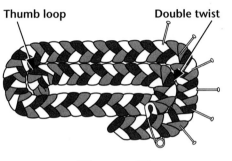

Thumb loop   Double twist

Diagram 11

8. To lace the curve, skip a loop on the braid you are working on and lace the next loop on the braid to the center of the rug. Repeat this procedure until there are six loops that have not been laced to the center of the rug in between six loops that have been laced to the center of the rug.

Finishing the Rug

1. To taper the braid as the rug is near completion, unbraid about 6 inches from the end of the braid. Cut each of the strips, creating a gradual taper by modifying the points, as shown in **Diagram 12.**

2. Slip stitch the end of each strip closed. Rebraid these strips, then interweave each end into successive loops on the rug, pulling each end through a loop and weaving it back in a zigzag pattern to secure, as shown in **Diagram 13.**

3. If you saved a leather tag from the jeans, use a hole punch or sharp

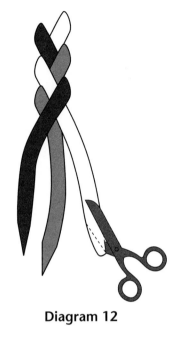

Diagram 12

sewing needle to pierce a hole in it. Insert a strand of quilting thread through the hole in the tag and through one loop on the rug. Tie the ends of the thread in a secure knot.

Diagram 13

Patchwork Purse

A great way to complement any casual outfit is to carry a matching purse. Make a colorful tote bag and highlight it with these easy-to-quilt Flying Geese. Outline their flight with a hint of red piping, or be adventurous and vary the pieced design to suit yourself. All it takes is an assortment of red and blue scraps, a bit of fleece, and your own imagination.

♥ *Size: The purse is 12 inches high, and the oval base measures 6 × 9 inches.*

Fabric Requirements

- ♥ ¾ yard of blue print for the background
- ♥ ¼ yard of muslin or muslin print for the Flying Geese triangles
- ♥ ¼ yard of red print for the Flying Geese triangles, piping, and end caps of the drawstrings
- ♥ ¼ yard of navy print for the Flying Geese triangles and drawstrings
- ♥ ¼ yard of red-and-blue print for the casing and binding

Other Supplies

- ♥ 1½ yards of ⅛-inch cording for piping around the Flying Geese triangles
- ♥ 2 yards of ¼-inch cording for piping for the drawstrings
- ♥ 1 yard of ½-inch cording for piping for the base of the purse
- ♥ ½ yard of extra-loft fleece
- ♥ 8 × 12-inch piece of medium-weight cardboard
- ♥ 8 × 12-inch piece of fusible webbing
- ♥ Off-white quilting thread
- ♥ Template plastic
- ♥ Fine-point black permanent marker

Instructions

Note: Pattern pieces include ¼-inch seam allowances, unless specified otherwise. Press seam allowances toward the darker fabric, unless stated otherwise.

Cutting

1. Trace the A and B triangles, the C circle, and the base pattern on pages 84–85 onto template plastic and cut them out.

2. From the muslin, cut 32 B triangles.

3. From the red print, cut four A triangles and two C end caps. Cut the remaining red fabric into 2-inch bias strips.

4. From the navy print, cut four A triangles. Cut the remaining navy fabric into two strips, each 2 × 37 inches, for the drawstrings.

5. From the red-and-blue print, cut eight A triangles. Cut the remaining red-and-blue print into 2 × 12½-inch casing strips and one 3 × 26-inch strip to cover the ⅛-inch cording.

6. From the blue print background fabric, cut one 3 × 24½-inch strip, one 19½ × 24½-inch rectangle, and two base pieces.

7. From the fleece, cut one 14 × 24½-inch rectangle and one base piece.

8. From the cardboard, cut one base piece.

9. From the fusible webbing, cut one base piece.

Assembling the Purse Top

1. Referring to **Diagram 1,** make one Flying Geese unit by stitching two B triangles to one A triangle.

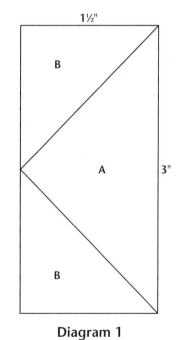

Diagram 1

Bits 'n' Pieces

Try This Variation: To make a purse with a completely different look, try changing the colors and/or the design of the pieced and quilted strip. Why not experiment with diamonds, squares, and rectangles? For inspiration and ideas, look at pieced borders on several patchwork quilts, or if appliqué appeals to you, use a floral motif rather than a patchwork design.

It's easy to draft most patchwork designs on a piece of graph paper. Treat each square of the graph paper as 1 inch and simply draw in the shapes of the design. If the design you choose has different dimensions from those given for the Patchwork Purse, you can use the measurements from your graphed design to alter the size of the purse you make. Refer to **Diagram 3** on the opposite page to determine the cutting sizes for the casings, background fabric, and fleece. Draft the remaining parts of the purse on the graph paper, remembering that each square of the paper stands for 1 inch of fabric. When you cut out the actual pattern pieces, add ¼-inch seam allowances on each side.

Repeat to make a total of 16 Flying Geese units.

2. Stitch the 16 Flying Geese units together to form a strip measuring 3½ × 24½ inches. Referring to the photograph on page 81, alternate the colors of the A triangles.

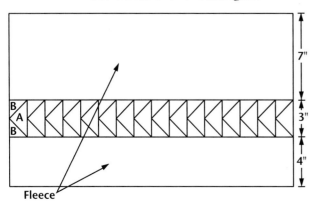

Diagram 2

3. Referring to **Diagram 2**, pin the Flying Geese strip to the fleece, with the lower edge 4 inches above the bottom edge of the fleece.

4. Sew the short ends of the red bias strips together to make a bias strip long enough to cover 1½ yards of ⅛-inch cording.

5. Cover the ⅛-inch cording with the red bias strip. Using a zipper foot, stitch a seam as close as possible to the cording. Trim the seam allowance to ¼ inch and cut the piping in half.

6. Align the raw edge of one piece of piping with the raw edge of the Flying Geese strip. Sew the piping to the strip through all layers, using a zipper foot to stitch as close as possible to the cording. Attach the second piece of piping to the other edge of the Flying Geese strip in the same manner.

7. Hand quilt ⅛ inch inside the A triangles and ⅛ inch from the diagonal seams in the B triangles.

8. Place the 3 × 24½-inch background strip and the Flying Geese strip right sides together, aligning raw edges. Sew the background strip to the Flying Geese strip through all layers and press the seam allowance toward the fleece.

9. Place the 19½ × 24½-inch background rectangle and the other side of the Flying Geese strip right sides together, aligning raw edges. Stitch through all layers and press the seam allowance toward the fleece.

10. Fold the top half of the blue background fabric over the top of the fleece, covering the fleece on the back to create the lining. Baste the raw edges of the lining, fleece, and purse top together at the bottom edge.

Making the Casings for the Handles

1. Turn under ¼ inch on each edge of the casing strips and press. Stitch across each of the short ends to hem them.

2. Referring to **Diagram 3,** place the wrong sides of the two casing pieces on the right side of the purse, 1 inch below the top and ¼ inch in from each side. Topstitch ¹⁄₁₆ inch from the edges at the top and bottom of the casings, stitching though all thicknesses.

Sewing the Purse Sides and Bottom

1. Trim the background fabric below the Flying Geese strip so that it measures 2¼ inches (see **Diagram 3**).

2. Cut a 24½-inch-long strip of ½-inch cording. Turn under a ¼-inch hem on one short end of the 3-inch red-and-blue print strip. Fold the red-and-blue print strip lengthwise, wrong sides together, inserting the cording between the two layers. Using a zipper foot and a basting stitch, sew as close to the cording as possible. Trim the seam allowance of the piping to ¼ inch. With right sides together and raw edges aligned, stitch the piping to the bottom of the purse front.

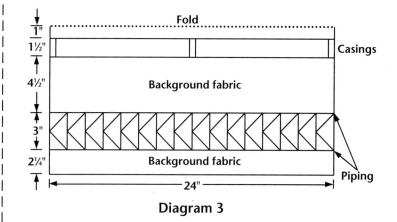

Diagram 3

3. With right sides of the purse front together, sew the side seam of the purse, stopping just short of the piping. Insert the raw end of the piping into the end of the piping that has been turned under, butting the cording ends up against each other. Slip stitch the two ends together where they meet, as shown in **Diagram 4.**

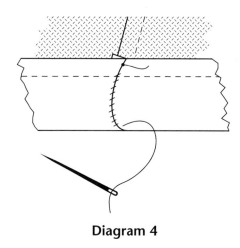

Diagram 4

4. Baste the fleece base to the wrong side of one background fabric base piece. With right sides together, baste and stitch the purse top to the base, matching one side of the purse to the triangle at one end of the oval base. Clip the curves along the base so the seams lie flat and turn the purse right side out.

5. Iron the webbing base onto the wrong side of the other background fabric base piece. Remove the paper from the webbing and center the fabric base on one side of the cardboard base. Fuse the fabric and cardboard bases together. Make clips in the fabric every ½ inch around the cardboard to make it easier to fold the fabric over the edges of the cardboard. Fuse the fabric to the wrong side of the cardboard. Place this inner base, fabric side up, in the bottom of the purse.

6. To make the drawstrings, fold a 2-inch navy strip in half lengthwise, right sides together, and stitch ¼ inch from the raw edges. Repeat for the second drawstring. Turn both fabric tubes right side out. Cut the length of the ¼-inch cording in half and thread one piece through each fabric tube.

7. Thread one of the drawstrings through both casings, then thread the other drawstring through the casings in the opposite direction. Tie the ends of each drawstring into a knot and trim the ends close to the knots.

8. To make end caps to cover the knot at the end of each drawstring, turn under ¼ inch around each red circle. Sew a line of gathering stitches ⅛ inch from the folded edge. Gather and tighten the circle over each knot. Secure the end caps to the drawstrings by taking a few stitches through the cording.

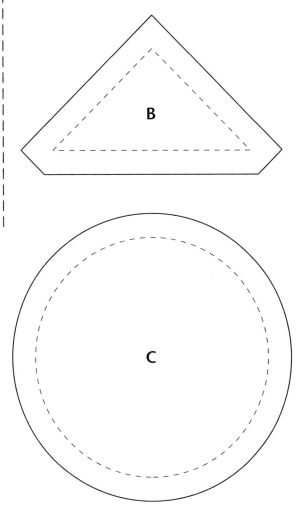

B

A

C

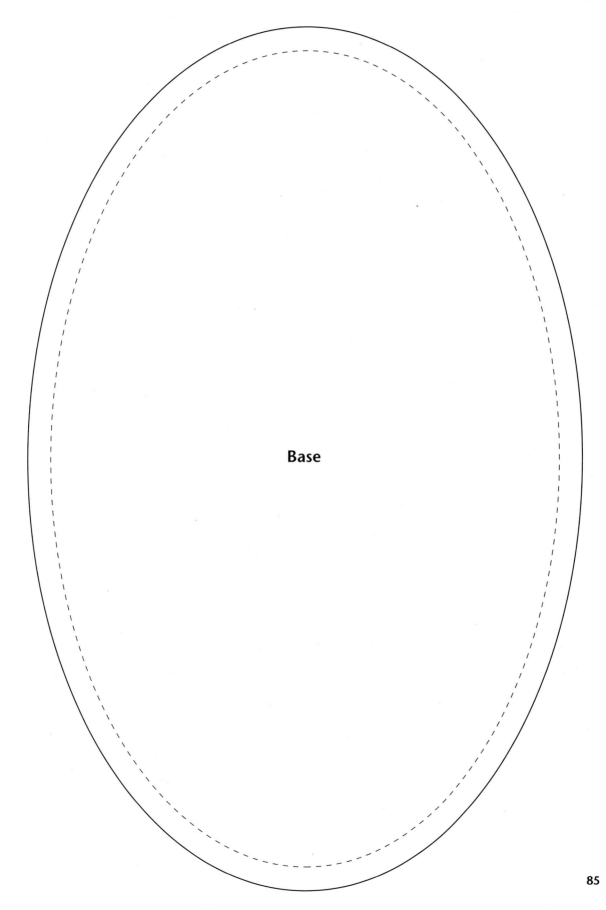

Base

Braided Denim Basket

Making a denim rag basket is a surefire way to get your teenagers to part with their old jeans. This handy container will hold their hair accessories, make-up, or sewing supplies—and the best part is that you can braid one in no time at all.

♥ *Size: The braided denim basket is 6 inches in diameter and 3 inches high.*

Fabrics and Supplies

- ♥ 1 pair of adult-size blue jeans
- ♥ Sewing thread to match fabric
- ♥ Quilting thread to match fabric
- ♥ Curved lacing needle
- ♥ Sharp scissors
- ♥ Safety pins or straight pins
- ♥ Removable fabric marker

Instructions

Cutting

1. Beginning at the bottom of one pant leg and ending at the other, cut open the pair of blue jeans along the inner seam.

2. Carefully cut out the zipper, preserving as much fabric as possible.

3. Cut along the center back seam to separate the legs of the jeans. Remove and discard the pockets and the leather tag, if there is one.

4. Cut off the waistband.

5. Referring to **Diagram 1,** cut as many 2-inch strips from each pant leg as possible. Discard any strip that is less than 5 inches long. Cut the strips to incorporate interesting

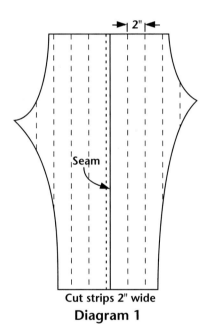

Cut strips 2" wide
Diagram 1

stitching, rivets, or patches. Divide the strips into three equal groups.

Joining the Strips

1. Place two strips right sides together, forming a right angle, as shown in **Diagram 2** on the opposite page. Sew a diagonal seam. Trim the seam allowance to ¼ inch and press the seam open. Continue joining the strips from one group in the same manner, forming one long strip. This will be Strip A. Roll Strip A into a ball, folding the fabric in half lengthwise, wrong sides together, as you work.

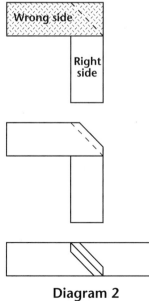

Diagram 2

2. Sew the strips from both remaining groups into one long strip that is

twice as long as Strip A. This will form Strip B-C, as shown in **Diagram 3** on page 88. Mark the midpoint of Strip B-C with a dot. Roll both ends of this strip toward the midpoint, folding the fabric in half lengthwise, wrong sides together, as you work.

Forming the T

Referring to **Diagram** 4 on page 88, form a T by inserting Strip A between the folded layers of Strip B-C at the midpoint. To secure the T, machine sew or stitch by hand 4 inches across Strip A.

Braiding the Basket

1. Hold the T securely between the left thumb and forefinger with the open side of Strip C on the right.

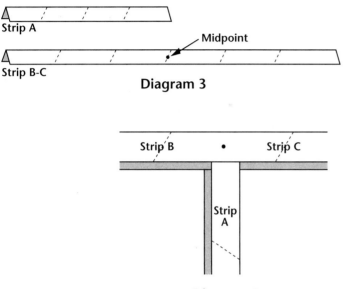

Diagram 3

Diagram 4

2. The basket begins with five double twists on the right to establish a natural coil. Make the double twists by folding Strip B directly over the left thumbnail to form a loop, as shown in **Diagram 5.** (You will use this loop later when you lace the basket together.)

Diagram 5

3. Referring to **Diagram 6,** fold Strip C over Strip B. Then fold Strip B back over Strip C. Fold Strip A

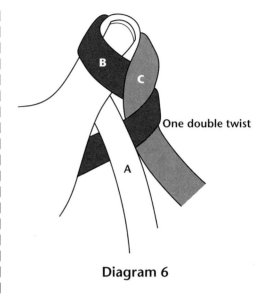

Diagram 6

over Strip C. Repeat this sequence four more times.

4. To continue making a straight braid for the remainder of the basket, alternately fold the right strip over the center strip, and the left strip over the center strip. When you're finished, fasten the ends together with a safety pin.

Lacing the Basket

1. Always lace on a flat surface. Thread the needle with quilting thread. Referring to **Diagram 7** on the opposite page, insert the needle into the thumb loop and run the needle back through five more loops.

2. Bring the needle out and tie the tail of this thread to the thread coming out of the thumb loop. This will draw the braid in, forming a small circle, as shown in **Diagram 8** on the opposite page. This small circle will become the base.

3. Referring to **Diagram 9** on the opposite page, begin lacing, skip-

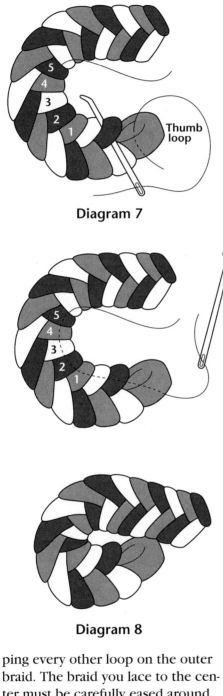

Diagram 7

Diagram 8

ping every other loop on the outer braid. The braid you lace to the center must be carefully eased around the base of the basket in order for the base to lie flat.

4. Continue lacing until there are two complete rows around the center circle. Beginning with the third row, gradually turn and place the

Diagram 9

braid perpendicular to the basket as you stitch, forming the basket sides.

Finishing the Basket

To taper the braid and complete the basket, undo 6 inches from the end of the braid. Cut the end of each strip in graduated lengths to a modified point. Slip stitch the ends closed. Rebraid these strips, interweaving each into successive loops on the basket, as shown in **Diagram 10.** Stitch the ends of the tail together.

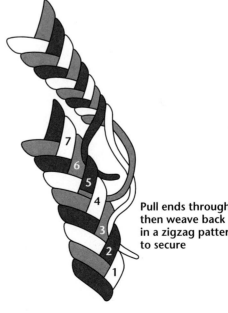

Pull ends through, then weave back in a zigzag pattern to secure

Diagram 10

Gifts Galore

Happy the Scraposaurus

Happy the Scraposaurus has a rainbow of prairie point scales marching playfully down his back, and he's happy to know he's not extinct. If you love "dino-mite" dinosaurs, there are plenty more where he came from. Check to see whether he doesn't have a second cousin lurking somewhere inside your scrap basket.

✦ *Size: Happy measures approximately 17 inches long and 8½ inches high.*

Fabric Requirements
✦ ¼ yard of turquoise solid for the body and legs
✦ Scraps of assorted fabrics for the prairie points

Other Supplies
✦ Sewing threads to match fabrics
✦ Polyester fiberfill
✦ 3-inch dollmaker's needle
✦ Red pearl cotton size 5 for sewing on the legs
✦ Black pearl cotton size 5 for embroidering the face
✦ Tracing paper
✦ Fine-point permanent marker

Instructions

Cutting

Note: All pattern pieces include ¼-inch seam allowances.

1. Trace the patterns on pages 95–97 onto tracing paper, transferring all markings, and cut them out.

2. Join the body pattern pieces together on the placement lines to make one complete pattern.

3. Draw two body patterns on the turquoise solid and cut them out.

4. Draw four each of the leg and leg reverse pattern on the turquoise solid and cut out the eight legs.

5. Draw around the prairie point square pattern on the assorted scraps. Cut out 20 squares.

Sewing

1. Refer to **Diagram 1** on the opposite page to make each prairie point. Fold the square in half, then fold the corners down to meet in the center along the raw edges.

2. With right sides together and raw edges aligned, baste the prairie points to one body piece. Begin placing them at the arrow on the head, overlapping them slightly and decreasing them in height as they reach the arrow on the tail. Referring to **Diagram 2** on the opposite page, trim the raw edges of the prairie points in the tail area so they are even with the raw edges of the body.

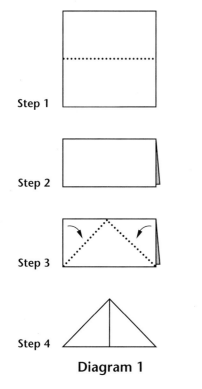

Step 1

Step 2

Step 3

Step 4

Diagram 1

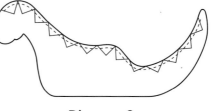

Diagram 2

3. Place the right sides of the two body pieces together with the prairie points sandwiched between them. Sew the two pieces together, leaving the bottom open for turning and stuffing, as indicated on the pattern. Turn the body right side out.

4. Place the right sides of one pair of legs together and sew around the foot, leaving an opening for turning. Repeat for the other three legs.

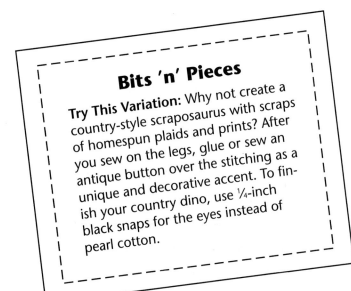

Bits 'n' Pieces

Try This Variation: Why not create a country-style scraposaurus with scraps of homespun plaids and prints? After you sew on the legs, glue or sew an antique button over the stitching as a unique and decorative accent. To finish your country dino, use ¼-inch black snaps for the eyes instead of pearl cotton.

5. Turn all four of the legs right side out through the opening in the back seams.

Assembling the Dinosaur

1. Stuff the legs firmly with polyester fiberfill. Slip stitch the openings closed. Using the dollmaker's needle and the red pearl cotton, sew through one leg and into one side of the unstuffed body at the X mark indicated on the leg. Bring the needle out of the other side of the body at the X and into a second leg. Sew back and forth through the body and two legs several times to secure them. As you work, do not pull the threads too tightly inside the body so that you can stuff it with polyester fiberfill. Knot the pearl cotton next to the body on the underside of one of the legs. Repeat for the other two legs.

2. Stuff the body firmly with polyester fiberfill and blindstitch the opening closed.

3. Using the black pearl cotton, sew through the head at the large dot for the eye. Make a large French knot for the eye by wrapping the thread around the needle four times. Bring the needle through the head and out at the large dot on the other side of the head. Make another large French knot for the second eye.

Insert the needle back into the head and bring it out at the small dot for the nostril. Make a French knot by wrapping the thread around the needle twice. Insert the needle into the head and bring it out the other side at the small dot. Make another French knot for the second nostril.

Insert the needle back into the head and bring it out on one side at the mouth. Make a long straight stitch around the outside of the mouth, inserting the needle back into the head at the the other side of the mouth. Bring the needle out just to the left of the mouth and slip it under the long straight stitch. Insert the needle back into the head just to the right of the long straight stitch. Bring the needle out on the other side of the head and finish the mouth in the same manner. Knot the pearl cotton and pop it through the head, lodging the knot in the fiberfill. Trim the end of the thread.

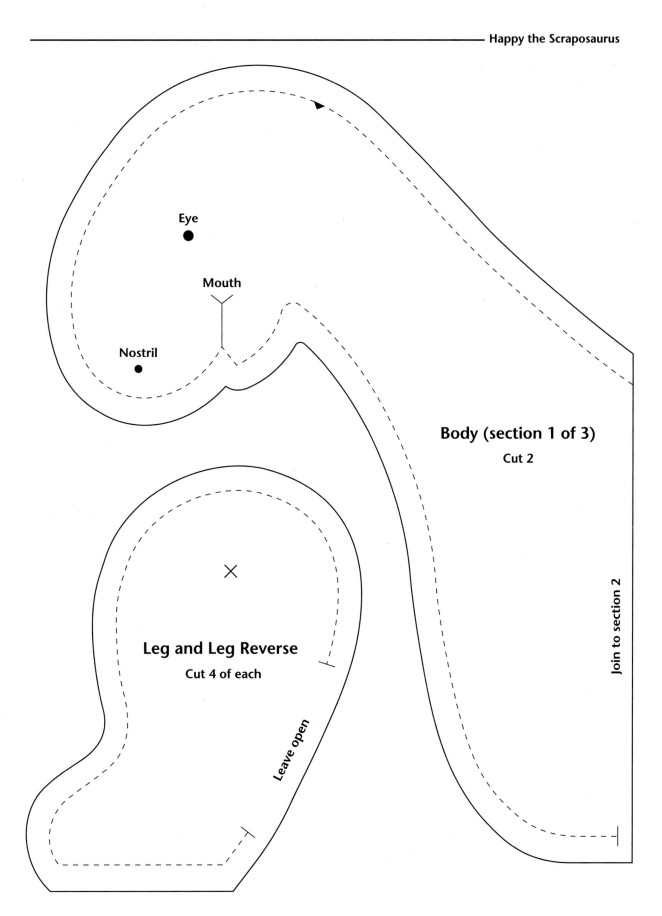

Eye

Mouth

Nostril

Body (section 1 of 3)
Cut 2

Join to section 2

Leg and Leg Reverse
Cut 4 of each

Leave open

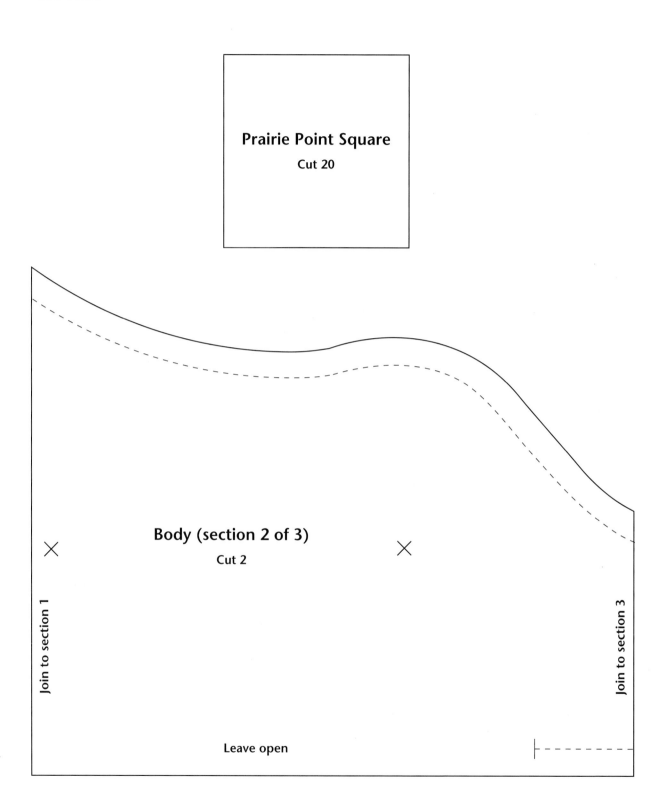

Prairie Point Square

Cut 20

Body (section 2 of 3)

Cut 2

Join to section 1

Join to section 3

Leave open

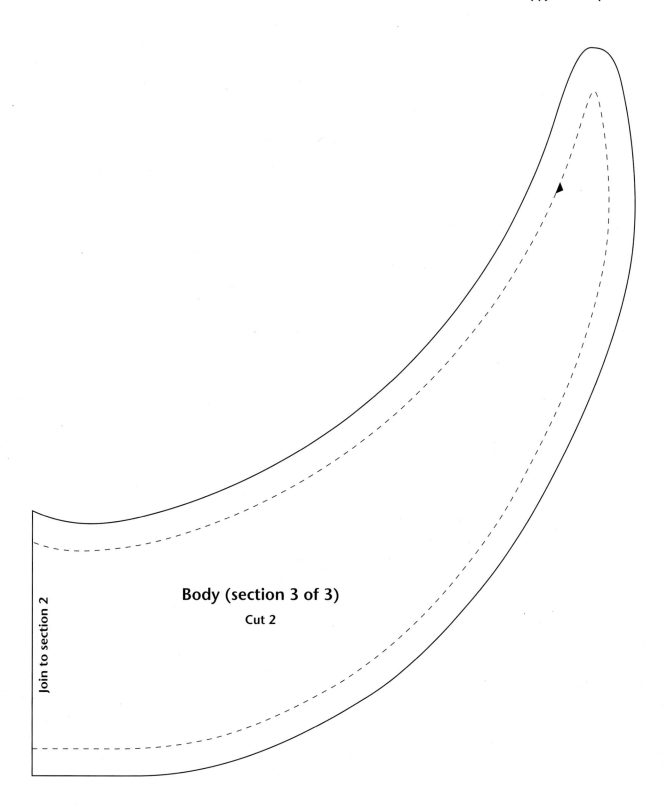

Body (section 3 of 3)

Cut 2

Join to section 2

Fang the Fanny Pack

Bright bits of felt and a scrap of rainbow-striped cotton fabric make Fang a ferociously funny friend for any young dinosaur fan. And he's so quick and easy to make, you could become the hit of your child's birthday party by making several fanny packs as gifts for the guests.

✦ *Size: Fang measures 8 × 10 inches.*

Fabric Requirements

- ✦ 12-inch square of heavyweight black solid for the back
- ✦ 9-inch square of heavyweight rainbow-striped fabric for the body
- ✦ Scraps of red, purple, yellow, aqua, and white felt

Other Supplies

- ✦ 7-inch black metal zipper
- ✦ 6-inch length of 1-inch black nylon belt webbing
- ✦ Black sewing thread
- ✦ 2 black beads for the eyes
- ✦ Small amount of polyester fiberfill for the legs and head
- ✦ Fabric glue or hot-glue gun
- ✦ Tracing paper
- ✦ Pencil
- ✦ Fine-point black permanent marker
- ✦ Pencil or removable marker for marking fabric

Instructions

Cutting

Note: All pattern pieces include ¼-inch seam allowances unless specified otherwise.

1. Trace the patterns on pages 101–105 onto tracing paper, transferring all markings. Cut out the patterns.

2. With a pencil or removable fabric marker, draw around the back body and the gusset on the wrong side of the black solid; cut out each piece. Cut the belt webbing into three 2-inch pieces.

3. Draw around the front body (top) and the front body (bottom) on the wrong side of the striped fabric and cut out each piece.

4. Draw two eyes on white felt, the head on purple felt, and two nostrils on yellow felt. Cut out each piece. Referring to the photo on the opposite page, draw two small circles freehand on purple felt and three circles on yellow felt for the leg accents; cut them out.

5. Draw around the spine on a double thickness of red felt. Topstitch with black thread along the dashed line on the spiked side of the spine. Cut out the spine, trimming close to the topstitching. Cut ¼ inch beyond the solid line at the bottom of the spine for the seam allowance.

6. Draw around the leg on a double thickness of purple felt and top-

stitch along the dashed line. Cut out the leg, trimming close to the top-stitching and ¼ inch beyond the top of the leg. Repeat to make the second leg from yellow felt.

7. Draw around the teeth on a double thickness of aqua felt and topstitch along the dashed line. Cut out the teeth, trimming close to the topstitching.

Assembling the Fanny Pack

1. Space the three pieces of black nylon belt webbing evenly across the back body and pin them in place according to the pattern. Machine zigzag across the top and bottom of each piece. Align the straight raw edges of the red spine with the raw edge of the top of the back body, right sides together. Baste the spine to the back body.

2. Lightly stuff each leg with fiberfill. Place the top edge of each leg between the lines marked at the bottom edge of the back body. Baste the legs in place.

3. Fold under and press a ⅜-inch hem along the marked edge of the front body (top) and front body (bottom). Place the folded edge of the front body (top) over the right side of the zipper and baste it to the zipper. Place the folded edge of the front body (bottom) over the other side of the zipper and pin it in place. When you have finished basting, check to see that the back body is the same size as the front body. If the two halves of the fanny pack do not match, adjust the fold of the front body (bottom) before basting it to the right side of the zipper.

Bits 'n' Pieces

Try This Variation: A Claws the Kitty fanny pack would be "purrfect" for feline fanciers. Simply round the shape of Fang's head slightly to resemble the head of a cat and omit the spine. Cut two little pink felt triangles for ears and six tiny V-shaped pieces of black felt for the claws. Cut a small curved pink felt tongue. Glue the claws on the toes, ears on the head, and the tongue on the teeth placement line. On a piece of black felt, draw a curvy tail and sew it into the seam at the back of the fanny pack. Referring to the diagram, tack the tip of the tail to the front of the fanny pack to hold it in place.

4. Using a zipper foot, topstitch $1/16$ inch from the fold of the fabric along both sides of the zipper. Stitch across both ends of the zipper. Trim any portion of the zipper that extends beyond the edges of the front body. Remove the basting stitches.

5. Position the two eyes on the head. With black thread, topstitch the eyes to the head, stitching $1/16$ inch from the edges.

6. With right sides together, align the neck of the head to the neck of the front body. Place the head and the front body right sides together and stitch across the neck edge.

7. Open the zipper, then place the front and back bodies right sides together, with the spine sandwiched between them. Stitch the front and back bodies together, beginning and ending at the marks indicated and leaving the bottom open. The seam allowance around the head is only $1/8$ inch wide. As you sew around the body, narrow the width of the seam allowance from $1/4$ to $1/8$ inch between the marked dots. Do not turn the fanny pack right side out yet.

8. With right sides together, pin the gusset to the back body, aligning the dots on the gusset with the lines marked on the back body. Beginning and ending at the lines, stitch the gusset to the back body, catching the legs in the seam.

9. Pin the front body (bottom) to the gusset, matching the lines marked on the front body to the dots on the gusset. Beginning and ending at the lines, stitch the gusset to the front body. Clip the curves and corners on the front and back body pieces and turn Fang right side out through the open zipper.

10. Lightly stuff the head with polyester fiberfill and stitch across the neck through all layers.

Finishing

1. Glue the teeth and nostrils to the face. Glue the felt accent circles for the toes on the legs.

2. Sew a black bead to each eye.

3. Slip a child's belt through the three loops on Fang's back.

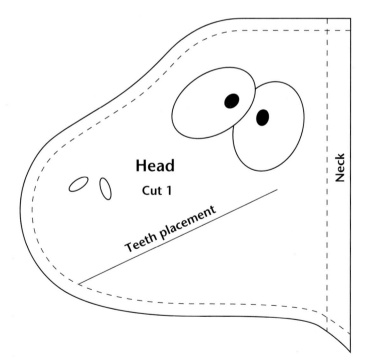

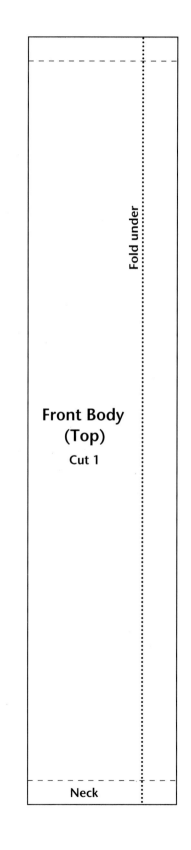

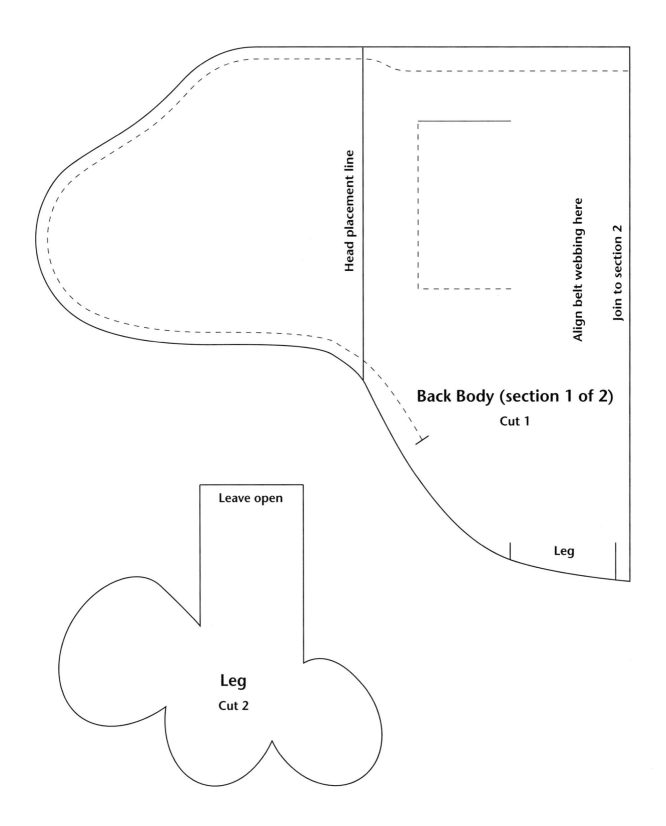

Head placement line

Align belt webbing here

Join to section 2

Back Body (section 1 of 2)

Cut 1

Leg

Leave open

Leg

Cut 2

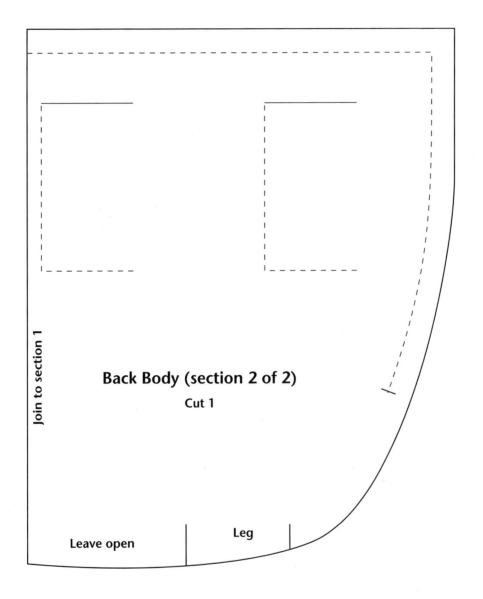

Join to section 1

Back Body (section 2 of 2)

Cut 1

Leave open

Leg

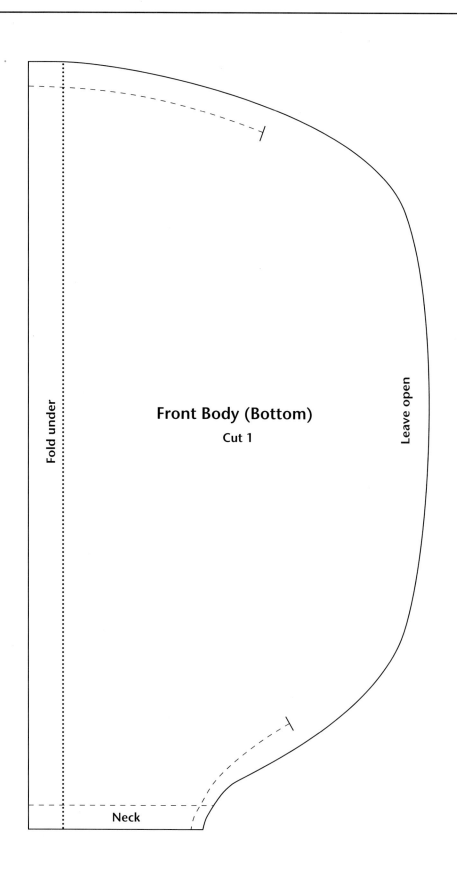

Fold under

Front Body (Bottom)

Cut 1

Leave open

Neck

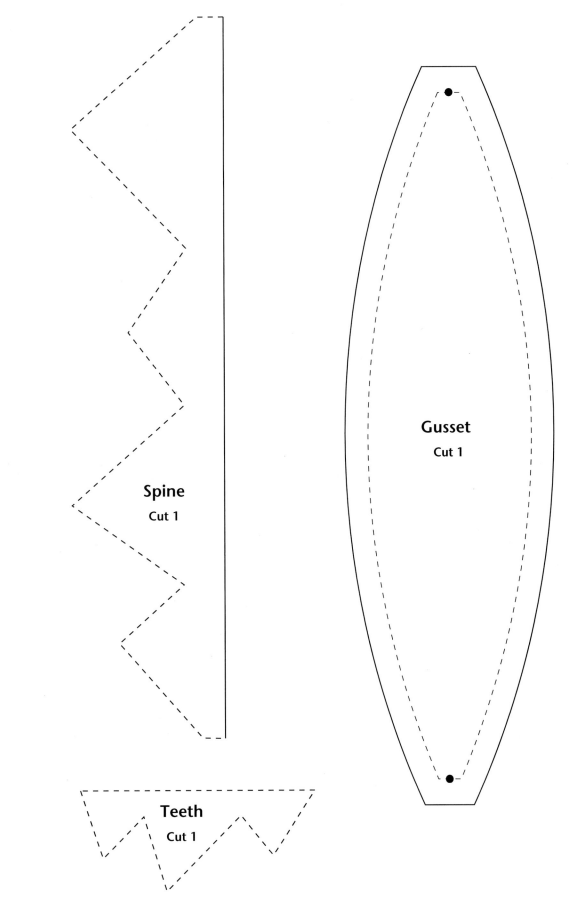

Spine

Cut 1

Teeth

Cut 1

Gusset

Cut 1

Spring Flowers Pillow

A beautiful bouquet of flowers brightens any room. Select an array of floral prints and vibrant solids and appliqué a spray of ruched flowers, pleated rosebuds, and gathered bluebells on a square pillow. And when you're in the mood to dream up your own design, look for inspirational ideas in the blocks of an antique Baltimore album quilt.

✦ *Size: The pillow is 18 inches square, including the shirred piping.*

Fabric Requirements

- ✦ 20-inch square of white solid or muslin for the pillow front
- ✦ 1 yard of purple print for the bow, shirred piping, and pillow back
- ✦ ¼ yard of green print for the stems and calyx
- ✦ ⅛ yard of yellow print for the rosebuds and narrow piping
- ✦ Scraps of assorted green prints and solids for the small, medium, and large leaves
- ✦ Scraps of blue print for the bluebells
- ✦ 12-inch square of rose print for the ruched rose
- ✦ ⅝ yard of muslin for the pillow form

Other Supplies

- ✦ 16-inch square of fusible interfacing
- ✦ 16-inch square of fleece
- ✦ Sewing threads to match fabrics
- ✦ 2 yards of ⅛-inch cording for the pillow piping
- ✦ 2¼ yards of ½-inch cording for the shirred piping
- ✦ Polyester fiberfill
- ✦ ⅜-inch bias presser bar
- ✦ Template plastic
- ✦ Fine-point black permanent marker
- ✦ Pencil or removable fabric marker
- ✦ Protractor

Instructions

Cutting

Note: Trace around the appliqué templates on the right side of the fabric and add a ³⁄₁₆-inch seam allowance to each piece as you cut it out. Use ½-inch seam allowances for all other seams unless directed otherwise.

1. Trace the patterns on pages 113–115 onto template plastic, transferring all markings. Cut out the templates.

2. From the rose print, cut one ruched rose.

3. From the yellow print, cut two rosebuds.

4. From the blue print, cut two bluebells.

5. From the assorted green print and solid scraps, cut two A leaves, two B leaves, two C leaves, and four D leaves.

6. From the ¼ yard of green print, cut six bias strips, each 1 inch wide. From the same green print, cut two calyxes.

7. From the purple print, cut one bow loop and one bow tail. Reverse both templates and cut one more of each piece. Cut one bow knot.

8. From the same purple print, cut three strips, each 5 × 44 inches, for the shirred piping. From the remaining fabric, cut a 16-inch square for the pillow back.

9. From the remaining piece of yellow print fabric, cut 2-inch-wide bias strips for the narrow piping.

10. From the muslin, cut two 18-inch squares for the pillow form.

Appliquéing the Design

Note: Use **Diagram 1** on page 108 as a guide when placing the appliqué pieces on the background fabric. Enlarge the design several times and use a pencil or removable fabric marker to mark the placement of the design on the 20-inch muslin square.

Diagram 1

Making the Stems, Leaves, and Calyxes

1. To make a bias stem, fold a green print bias strip in half lengthwise, wrong sides together, and stitch a ¼-inch seam. Repeat for each of the green bias strips.

2. Slip the bias bar inside one tube and press it, centering the seam on one side. Remove the presser bar and trim the seam allowance to ⅛ inch. Repeat for each of the stems.

3. Cut one of the stems in half for the two stem pieces below the bow. Turn under ¼ inch on each end and press.

4. Referring to **Diagram 1,** appliqué the stems in place, layering the center stem over the two side stems. For more information on hand appliqué, see page 263 in the "General Instructions."

5. Referring to **Diagram 1,** appliqué the leaves in place.

6. Referring to **Diagram 1,** appliqué the curved edge of each calyx to the top of the stem on each side of the center stem, leaving the top edges open.

Making the Rosebuds

1. Hand sew a line of gathering stitches ⅛ inch in from the raw edge of one yellow rosebud, as shown in **Diagram 2.**

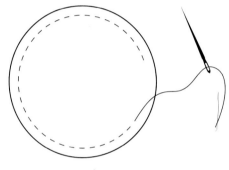

Diagram 2

2. Referring to **Diagram 3,** gather the circle to resemble a yo-yo. Knot the thread to secure the gathers and clip the thread close to the knot.

Diagram 3

3. Referring to **Diagram 4** on the opposite page, turn the gathered circle so the opening is to the wrong side. Fold a ¼-inch pleat in the circle and tack the pleat in place.

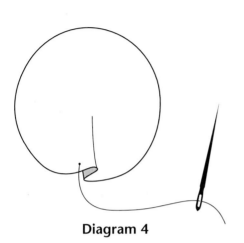

Diagram 4

4. Referring to **Diagram 5**, slip the completed bud under the top edge of the calyx. Appliqué the bud and the top of the calyx in place.

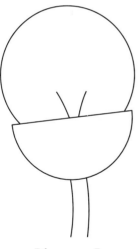

Diagram 5

5. Repeat Steps 1 through 4 to complete the second rosebud.

Making the Bluebells

1. Referring to **Diagram 6**, fold one bluebell in half lengthwise, right sides together. Hand sew a ¼-inch seam along the open side.

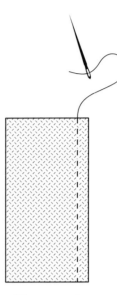

Diagram 6

2. Referring to **Diagram 7**, sew a line of gathering stitches ¼ inch from one short end. Pull the thread to gather and secure it with a knot.

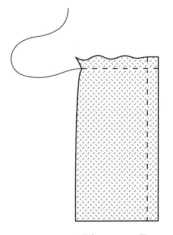

Diagram 7

3. Turn the bluebell right side out. Turn under ¼ inch twice on the other end of the bluebell. This end is a finished edge and will remain open. Sew a line of gathering stitches ⅛ inch from the fold of

the hem. Place your thumb inside the bluebell and gather the stitches around it, as shown in **Diagram 8,** so that the end of the flower will remain open. Knot the thread.

Diagram 8

4. Arrange the bluebell so that it is flat on the back side and the front of the flower is pleated. Appliqué the bluebell in place over the end of one lower side stem.

5. Repeat Steps 1 through 4 for the second bluebell.

Making the Ruched Rose

1. Turn under ¼ inch around the edge of the ruched rose circle. Finger press the fold and baste it in place.

2. Referring to **Diagram 9,** fold the circle in half with right sides together and steam press the fold. Repeat this process until there are eight pie-shaped wedges around the circle. Open the circle and remove the basting thread.

3. Using a protractor, mark placement dots ⅜ inch in from the edge

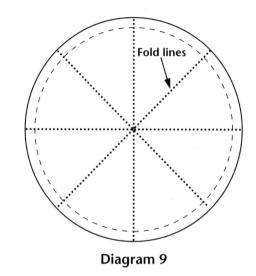

Diagram 9

of the circle. Space the dots 15 degrees apart to indicate the outer curves of the scallops, as shown in **Diagram 10.**

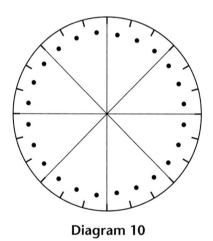

Diagram 10

4. At the outer edge of the circle, mark placement lines 15 degrees apart to indicate the inner points of the scallops. Center these lines to fall midway between each of the previous dots, as shown in **Diagram 10.**

5. Referring to **Diagram 11** on the opposite page, fold the circle

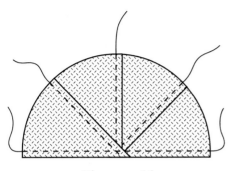

Diagram 11

right sides together along one of the four folds. Hand sew a running stitch across the circle, sewing close to the fold through both layers of the fabric. Repeat for each of the other three folds. Begin and end each stitching line without a knot and leave at least 5 inches of thread free on each side of the circle. These threads are for gathering the rose and appliquéing it to the pillow front.

6. Referring to **Diagram 12,** bring a new thread up at one of the

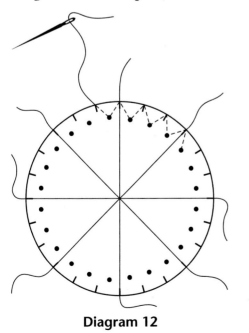

Diagram 12

inside placement dots on the right side of the circle. Begin sewing a line of tiny running stitches in a zigzag pattern from this placement mark to the next placement mark at the outside edge and then to the following inside placement mark.

7. Referring to **Diagram 13,** continue sewing running stitches between inside and outside placement marks. Pull the thread gently to form a scalloped edge, then loop the thread around the edge of the circle to secure each scallop. Take care to leave the 5-inch threads free.

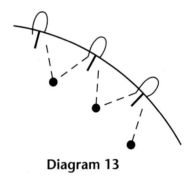

Diagram 13

8. Pin the ruched rose over the top of the center stem. Gently pull on each of the 5-inch threads to gather the center of the rose. Thread your needle with these threads and appliqué the scalloped edges of the rose to the pillow front.

Making the Bow

1. Appliqué the bow loops and the bow tails over the center stem and the two short bottom stems, taking care to cover the raw edges on each stem.

Bits 'n' Pieces

Try This Variation: If people in the nineteenth century could design beautiful floral quilts with nothing more than paper, pencil, and the inspiration of nature's beauty, you can, too!

Start by browsing through books to find a photo of a floral block that pleases you. Then decide how large a block you want to design. Draw a square that size on a piece of graph paper. With a pencil, sketch in rough oval shapes or rectangles to block out the spaces where you want to place flowers, stems, vines, vases, leaves, or other design elements. Then cut out pieces of freezer paper in approximately the same dimensions as your ovals or rectangles. On each piece of freezer paper, sketch a flower, leaf, or any other shape. Fold the paper in half and cut the shape out symmetrically. Do the same for all other shapes in the design. Open up the pieces of freezer paper and arrange your cut appliqué shapes on the graph paper square.

If you like the way they look, it's easy to trace around them to create a finished floral design. If the shapes you've cut are not exactly what you want, you can easily enlarge, reduce, or refine them. Just fold another piece of paper, trace a cut shape again, and then alter any line, curve, width, or length of the piece. Cut out the new shape and see what the revised piece looks like on the graph paper square. Continue to experiment with cut paper shapes until you're pleased with your results. Give yourself permission to play, as well as to make mistakes as you work. The key to success in designing is simply to continue experimenting until you create something you really like.

2. Appliqué the bow knot at the center of the bow, covering the raw edges of the bow loops and bow tails.

Making the Pillow

1. Trim the pillow front so that the design is centered in a 16-inch square. Stitch the fleece to the wrong side of the pillow front along all four edges.

2. Sew the short ends of the yellow bias strips together to make one strip measuring 68 inches long.

3. Fold the yellow strip lengthwise, wrong sides together, inserting the ⅛-inch cording between the two layers. Using a zipper foot and a basting stitch, sew as close to the cording as possible. Trim the seam allowance on the piping to ½ inch. Refer to page 272 in the "General Instructions" for more information on making piping.

4. With right sides together, align the raw edges of the pillow front and the piping and pin them together, overlapping the ends of the piping. Use a zipper foot to sew the piping to the pillow front, stitching as close to the cording as possible.

5. Sew the short ends of the purple print strips right sides together to make one long strip. Turn under and press a ¼-inch hem at each end of the long purple strip.

6. Fold the long purple strip in half lengthwise, wrong sides together, and insert the ½-inch cording between the two layers. Anchor one end of the cording just inside the short end of the strip with a few hand stitches. Maintaining a ½-inch seam allowance, baste along the length of the strip, stopping every few feet to pull on the cording to gather the piping. Continue to baste and gather the strip until you reach the end. Make a few hand stitches in the other end of the cording to secure it just inside the end of the shirred piping. Check to make sure that there is enough shirred piping to go around the pillow front. Sew along the basting seam to secure the gathers. Refer to page 272 in the "General Instructions" for more information on making shirred piping.

7. Align the raw edges of the shirred piping and the yellow piping on the pillow front. Stitch the shirred piping to the pillow front.

Slip stitch the ends of the shirred piping together.

8. Fuse the interfacing to the wrong side of the pillow back.

9. Place the pillow front and the pillow back right sides together and align the raw edges. Stitch them together, leaving a 12-inch opening in the middle of one side. Turn the pillow right side out.

10. To make the inner pillow form, stitch two muslin squares together, leaving a 4-inch opening on one side. Turn the pillow form right side out and stuff it firmly with polyester fiberfill. Slip stitch the opening closed.

11. Insert the pillow form inside the pillow and slip stitch the opening closed.

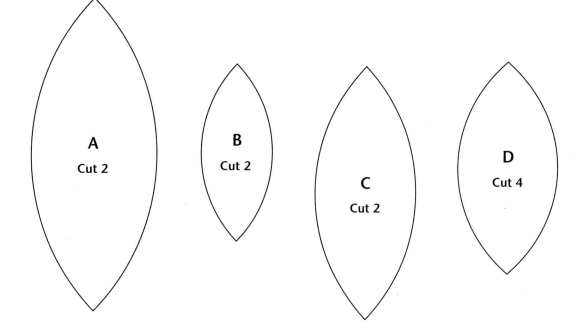

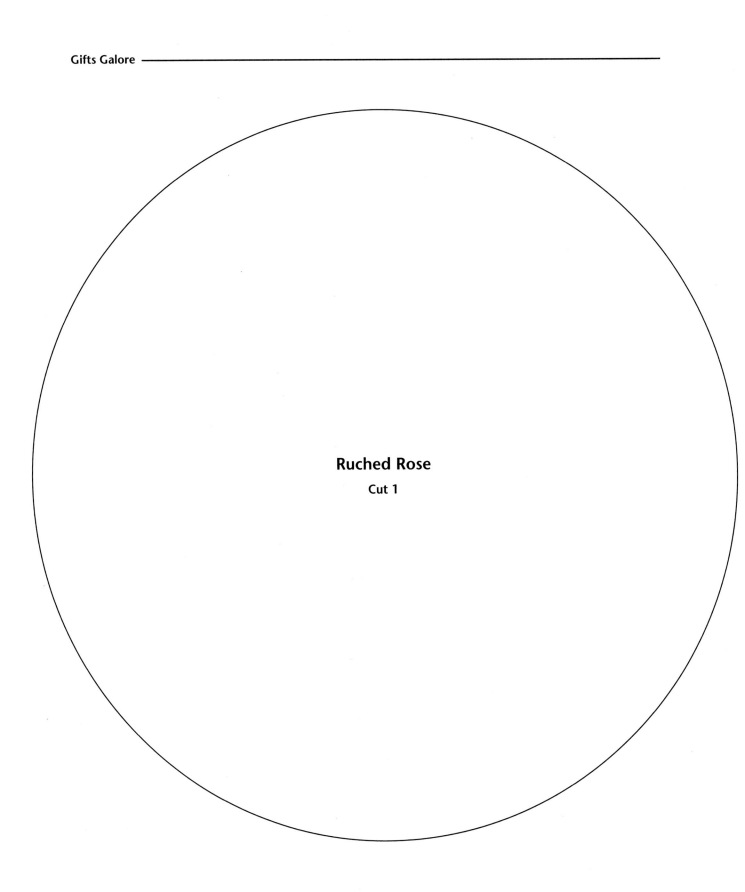

Ruched Rose

Cut 1

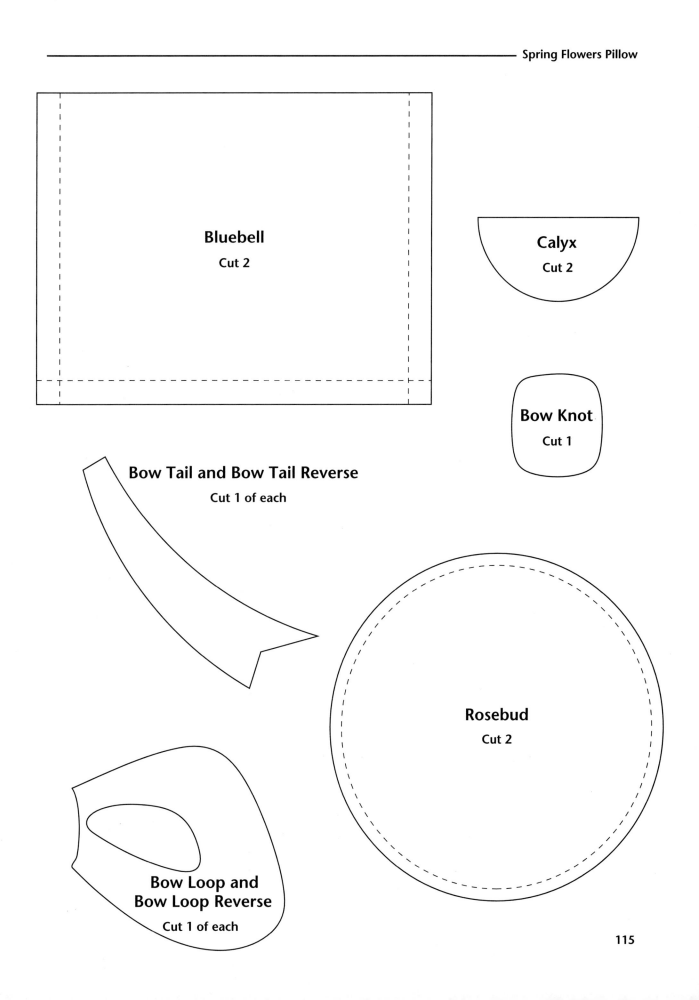

Bluebell

Cut 2

Calyx

Cut 2

Bow Knot

Cut 1

Bow Tail and Bow Tail Reverse

Cut 1 of each

Rosebud

Cut 2

Bow Loop and
Bow Loop Reverse

Cut 1 of each

Snowball and Arrowroot Pillow Quilt

This quilt has a secret! When it's folded up and tucked into a special pocket sewn to the backing, it becomes a patchwork pillow. It can function as an attractive couch cushion at home and double as a lap quilt at outdoor concerts or sporting events.

✦ Size: The pillow pocket is 18 inches square.
   The quilt is 42 × 54 inches.

Fabric Requirements

- 1⅞ yards of medium rose print for the Snowball and Arrowroot blocks, borders, and pocket lining
- 1⅝ yards of medium rose print for the backing
- 1½ yards of burgundy solid for the borders
- ¾ yard of white-on-white print for the Snowball and Arrowroot blocks
- ⅛ yard of medium green print for the stems and leaves
- 6-inch square of rose solid for the Arrowroot block
- 6 strips, each 2½ × 44 inches, of assorted medium blue prints for the Nine-Patch blocks
- 6 strips, each 2½ × 44 inches, of assorted medium and dark blue solids for the Nine-Patch blocks
- 6 strips, each 2½ × 44 inches, of medium rose prints for the Nine-Patch blocks
- 6 strips, each 2½ × 44 inches, of medium and dark rose solids for the Nine-Patch blocks

Other Supplies

- 46 × 58-inch piece of batting for the quilt
- 20-inch square of batting for the pocket
- Template plastic
- Fine-point black permanent marker
- 1 skein of pink pearl cotton
- Thread to match fabrics

Instructions

Note: Each pattern piece includes ¼-inch seam allowances. The appliqué shapes do not include seam allowances. Press the seams toward the darker fabric unless specified otherwise.

Cutting

1. Trace the pattern pieces on pages 124–125 onto template plastic, transferring all markings, and cut out the templates.

2. From the white-on-white print, cut 17 D shapes for the Snowball blocks. Also cut four B triangles and four C shapes for the Arrowroot block.

3. From the 1⅞ yards of medium rose print, cut 68 B triangles, two 4½ × 44½-inch outer border strips, and two 4½ × 56½-inch outer border strips. Also cut four 2½ × 20½-inch border strips for the pocket. From the remaining fabric, cut one 20-inch square for the pocket lining and eight B triangles and five A squares for the Arrowroot block.

4. From the 6-inch square of rose solid, cut four A squares for the Arrowroot block.

5. From the burgundy solid, cut two 2½ × 36½-inch strips and two 2½ × 48½-inch strips for the inner border. Also cut four 1⅞ × 18-inch border strips for the pocket.

6. From the medium green print, cut 12 F shapes and four E shapes, adding an approximately ³⁄₁₆-inch seam allowance to the outside edges of the appliqué shapes as you cut.

Piecing the Nine-Patch Blocks

1. Cut the medium and dark blue print and solid strip into three segments, each approximately 14 inches long. Repeat for each of the medium and dark rose print and solid strips.

2. As shown in **Diagram 1** and the photo on page 117, make one Nine-Patch block by combining the medium blue print strips with the medium blue or dark blue solid strips and the medium rose print strips with the medium rose or dark rose solid strips. Sew strips of these fabrics into strip sets 1 and 2. Press seam allowances toward the darker fabric.

3. From strip set 1, cut two 2½ × 6½-inch rows. From strip set 2, cut one 2½ × 6½-inch row, as shown in **Diagram 2.**

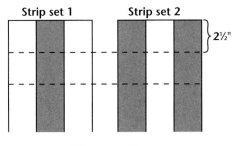

Diagram 2

4. Arrange the rows cut from strip sets 1 and 2 into a Nine-Patch block, as shown in **Diagram 3.** Sew the three rows together, forming the block, and press the block.

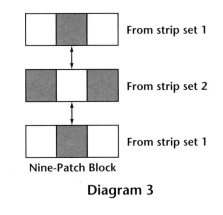

Diagram 3

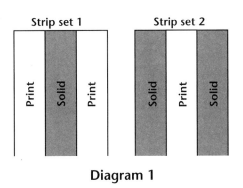

Diagram 1

5. Repeat Steps 2 through 4 to make a total of 12 blue and 6 rose 6-inch-square Nine-Patch blocks.

Piecing the Snowball Blocks

1. Sew a medium rose B triangle to a white-on-white D shape, as shown in **Diagram 4.** Repeat for the other three sides of the D shape, completing one Snowball block.

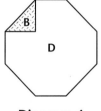

Diagram 4

2. Make a total of 17 Snowball blocks.

Assembling the Quilt

1. Referring to **Diagram 5** and the photograph on page 117, sew the Nine-Patch blocks and Snowball blocks together into rows. In rows 1, 3, 5, and 7, press the seams between blocks to the right. Press the seams between blocks in rows 2, 4, and 6 to the left.

2. Sew the rows of the quilt together and press the completed quilt top.

Adding the Borders

1. Sew the two 4½ × 44½-inch rose border strips to the two 2½ × 36½-inch burgundy border strips, as shown in **Diagram 6.** Press the seams toward the rose borders.

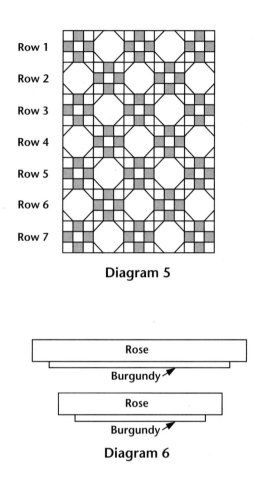

Row 1
Row 2
Row 3
Row 4
Row 5
Row 6
Row 7

Diagram 5

Diagram 6

2. Referring to **Diagram 6,** sew the two 4½ × 56½-inch rose border strips to the two 2½ × 48½-inch burgundy border strips. Again, press the seams toward the rose borders.

3. Place a pin at the midpoint and at each end of the borders to indicate the dimensions of the quilt top. Pin and sew the burgundy border strips to each side of the quilt, beginning and ending each seam ¼ inch in from the corner of the quilt. Press the seam allowances toward the border strips.

4. Starting at one corner of the quilt, place one border strip on top of the adjacent border strip, as shown in **Diagram 7.**

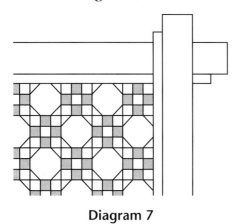

Diagram 7

5. Fold the top border under so that it meets the edge of the other border, forming a 45-degree angle, as shown in **Diagram 8.**

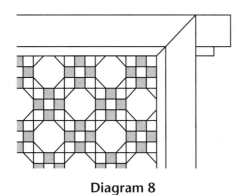

Diagram 8

6. Press the fold in place. With the pressed fold as the corner seam line and the body of the quilt out of the way, sew from the inner corner of the border to the outer corner of the border, as shown in **Diagram 9.** Repeat for each of the other three borders. Trim the corner seams of the borders to ¼ inch and press them open.

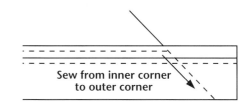

Sew from inner corner
to outer corner

Diagram 9

Piecing the Arrowroot Block

1. Stitch two rose print B triangles to a white-on-white C shape, as shown in **Diagram 10.** Repeat three more times for a total of four B/C units.

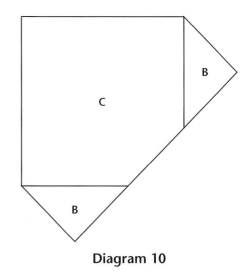

Diagram 10

2. Sew two white B triangles to two of the B/C units, as shown in **Diagram 11.**

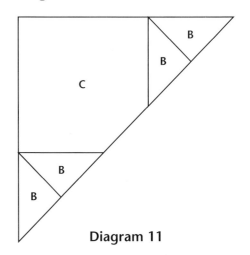

Diagram 11

3. On each of the four B/C units, blindstitch the E stems and F leaves to the white solid C shape, referring to the photograph on page 117 for placement. For more information on hand appliqué, see page 263 in the "General Instructions."

4. To make the center Nine-Patch block, sew five medium rose print A squares and four rose solid A squares into three rows, as shown in **Diagram 12.** Sew the rows together, completing the center Nine-Patch block.

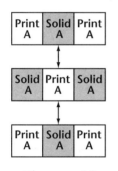

Diagram 12

5. Sew two B/C units to the Nine-Patch block, as shown in **Diagram 13.**

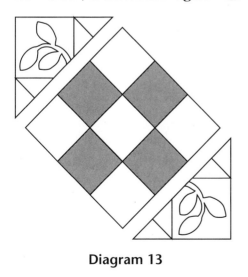

Diagram 13

6. Sew the two remaining B/C units to the other sides of the Nine-

Patch block, as shown in **Diagram 14,** completing the Arrowroot block. Press the block so that all seams lie flat.

Diagram 14

7. Sew the burgundy and medium rose print border strips in the same manner as for the quilt borders, as shown in **Diagram 6** on page 119. Sew each border to the Arrowroot block, mitering and pressing the corner seams as for the quilt. Press the completed block.

Assembling the Arrowroot Pillow Pocket

1. Place the 20-inch square of batting on a flat work surface. Place the pocket lining right side up on top of the batting and the Arrowroot block right side down over the lining.

2. Sew three sides of the pillow pocket together, using a ¼-inch seam allowance. Leave the needle down at the corners, lift the presser foot, pivot, and turn the pillow pocket. Lower the presser foot and continue sewing the seam on the next side. Leave one side open.

3. Trim the seam allowances diagonally at the corners and turn the pillow pocket right side out. Baste the layers of the unstitched side together, but do not turn the raw edges under.

4. Pin baste the layers of the Arrowroot block to prepare for machine quilting. Machine quilt around the center Nine-Patch block and in the ditch of the two borders, as shown in **Diagram 15.**

Diagram 15

Assembling the Pillow Quilt

1. Cut the quilt batting and backing the same size as the quilt top.

2. Place a pin at the midpoint of the top edge of the backing.

3. Find the center of the unstitched side of the Arrowroot block and then mark that midpoint with a pin.

4. Place the Arrowroot block right side down over the right side of the

backing and pin it in place through all layers. Refer to **Diagram 16** to topstitch the pocket to the backing. Beginning at point A, backstitch, then continue sewing to point B. Pivot and stitch to point C and stop. Pivot again and sew to point D and backstitch. Backstitch at the end of the seam. Do not sew from A to D.

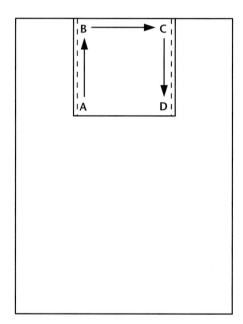

Diagram 16

5. Place the quilt batting on a large, flat work surface. Place the quilt backing right side up over the batting. Place the quilt top right side down over the backing. The Arrowroot pillow pocket will be sandwiched between the two layers. Pin the layers together along each side of the quilt.

6. Sew around all four sides of the quilt through all of the layers, leaving a 12-inch opening on one side for turning.

7. Trim the corner seam allowances diagonally and turn the quilt right side out. Slip stitch the opening closed.

8. With pink pearl cotton, tie the quilt at each corner of the Snowball and Nine-Patch blocks.

Folding the Quilt into the Pillow Pocket

1. Lay the quilt right side up, with the Arrowroot pillow pocket underneath, and fold it into thirds lengthwise, as shown in **Diagram 17.**

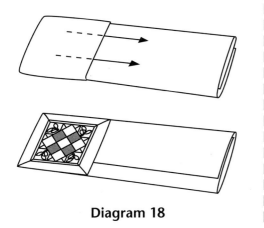

Diagram 17

2. Turn the quilt over, so that the Arrowroot pillow pocket is on top. Placing both hands inside the pocket, grasp the ends of the quilt and pull to turn the pocket right side out, as shown in **Diagram 18.**

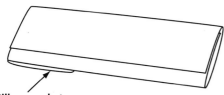

Diagram 18

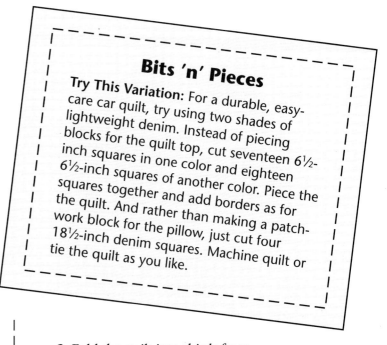

Bits 'n' Pieces

Try This Variation: For a durable, easy-care car quilt, try using two shades of lightweight denim. Instead of piecing blocks for the quilt top, cut seventeen 6½-inch squares in one color and eighteen 6½-inch squares of another color. Piece the squares together and add borders as for the quilt. And rather than making a patchwork block for the pillow, just cut four 18½-inch denim squares. Machine quilt or tie the quilt as you like.

3. Fold the quilt into thirds from the bottom up, as shown in **Diagram 19.**

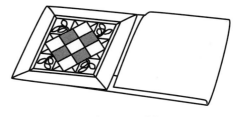

Diagram 19

4. Insert the quilt into the pocket to form the pillow, as shown in **Diagram 20.**

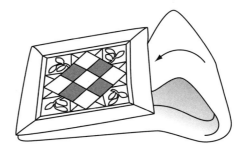

Diagram 20

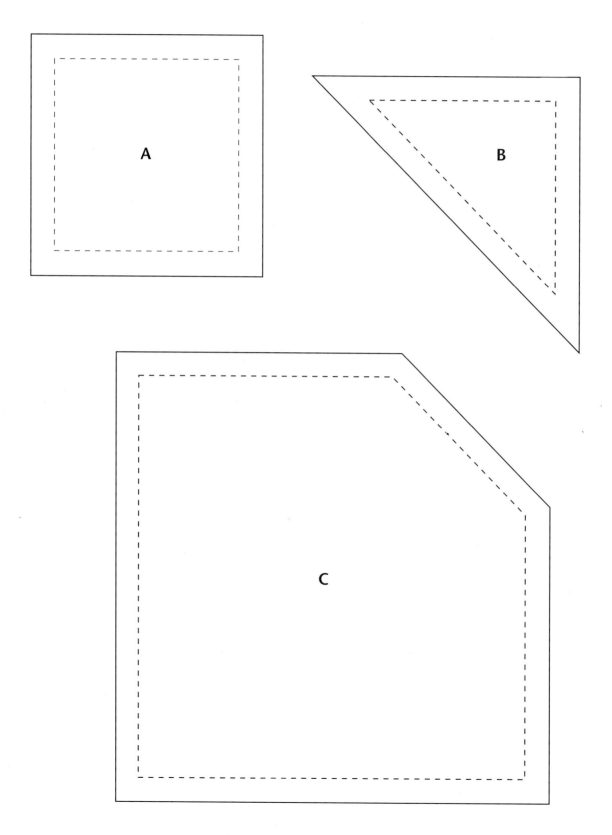

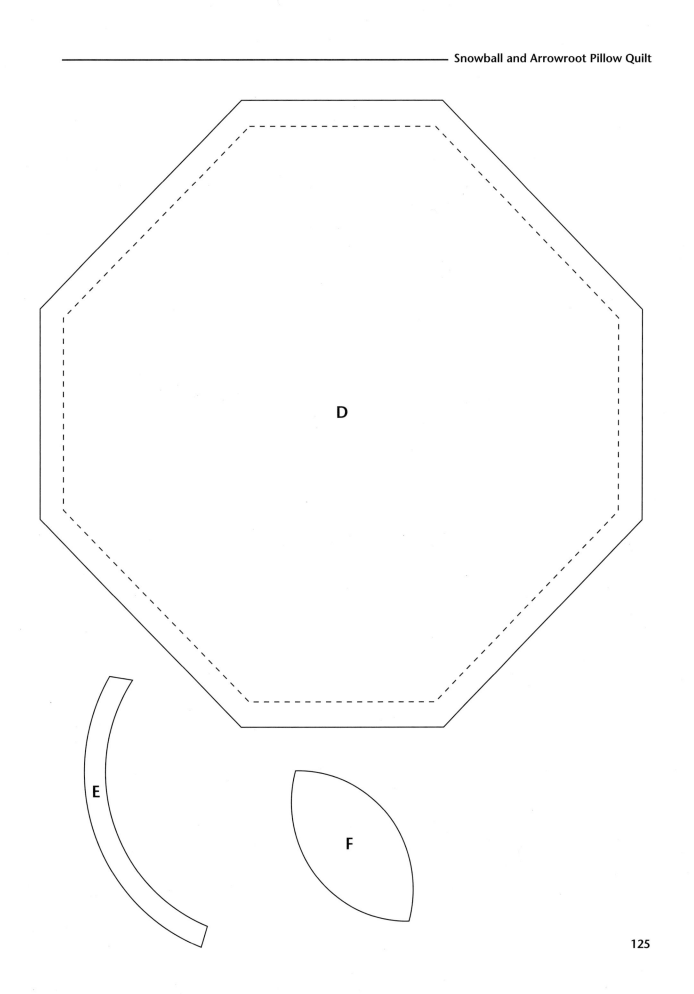

Divine Denim Jacket

Start with a purchased denim jacket and four bold red bandannas, add a dash of creativity, and you'll have a designer original for mere pennies. Make the yoke a focal point with bits of rayon, a few sparkling multifaceted "gems," and touches of fabric paint around the edges. Cut bandanna borders apart to outline the front and lower edges of the jacket, and use individual motifs to add glitz to the pockets.

Supplies

- Purchased hip-length denim jacket with four pockets
- Four 22-inch-square red bandannas
- 2½ yards of heavyweight Heat 'N Bond
- Four 22-inch squares of fusible webbing
- Red-and-gold rayon cording to trim the front and bottom edges of the jacket
- Sewing thread to match the cording
- 7-inch length of ⅜-inch gold grosgrain ribbon
- 7-inch length of ⅜-inch blue grosgrain ribbon
- 20 clear plastic ½-inch gemstones in circle and pear shapes
- Fabric paints in blue, green, pink, white, and metallic gold
- Fabric glue
- Tracing paper
- Hand-sewing needle

Instructions

Cutting and Fusing the Bandanna Pieces

1. Prewash, dry, and press the bandannas and the jacket.

2. Iron fusible webbing onto the wrong side of each bandanna. Use the repeated design along the edges of each bandanna to cut borders for the front and bottom of the jacket. From one bandanna, select two floral motifs to center on the pockets.

3. Cut two 1-inch-wide border strips from one of the bandannas, making sure to include a corner, as shown in **Diagram 1.**

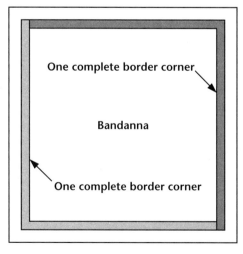

One complete border corner

Bandanna

One complete border corner

Diagram 1

4. Referring to **Diagram 2** on page 128, position one of the bor-

der strips on the front of the jacket so that the border lies ¾ inch in from the bottom edge and 1½ inches in from the side edge. Fuse the border in place. Repeat for the border on the other side of the jacket.

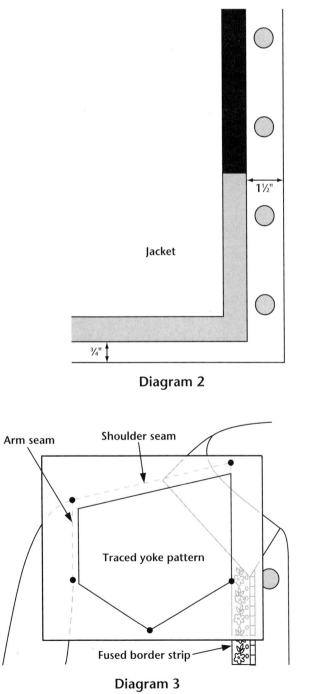

1½"

Jacket

¾"

Diagram 2

Arm seam

Shoulder seam

Traced yoke pattern

Fused border strip

Diagram 3

5. Position and fuse a straight border strip segment over the top edge of the previous one, forming a gentle curve toward the yoke seam. Repeat for the other side of the jacket. In the same way, continue to overlap and fuse border strips around the bottom of the back of the jacket.

6. Trace the yoke pattern on page 131 onto a piece of tracing paper. Lay the tracing paper over the shoulder of your jacket so that one side of the yoke pattern lies next to the fused border strip, as shown in **Diagram 3.** If the yoke pattern does not fit your jacket, you can enlarge or reduce it by marking dots on the tracing paper to indicate the correct size. Then connect the dots with a pencil to custom fit a yoke pattern for your jacket. Cut out the shoulder yoke pattern.

7. Place the yoke pattern on the right side of one bandanna, adjusting the pattern until a motif that pleases you is centered on the yoke. Cut out this yoke. Place the yoke reverse pattern on another bandanna, aligning it to match the print chosen for the other yoke. Cut out the second yoke to match the first one.

8. Fuse the yokes in place (see **Diagram** 4 on the opposite page).

9. Center two floral motifs on the upper left and lower right pockets, as shown in **Diagram** 4. Place two border strips vertically ¼ inch apart on the upper right pocket and two border strips horizontally ¼ inch apart across the top of the lower left pocket. Fuse each of the motifs and strips on the jacket.

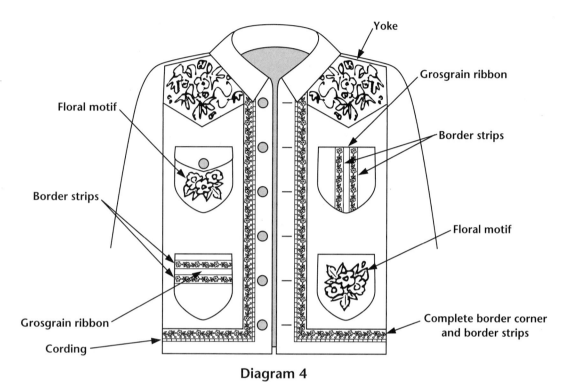

Yoke

Grosgrain ribbon

Floral motif

Border strips

Border strips

Floral motif

Grosgrain ribbon

Cording

Complete border corner
and border strips

Diagram 4

Finishing

1. Measure the width of the lower left pocket. Cut a piece of gold ribbon that length plus ¼ inch. Turn under ⅛ inch on each end of the ribbon and glue it between the two border strips, covering the edge of each border strip.

2. Measure the length of the upper right pocket. Cut a piece of blue ribbon that length plus ¼ inch. Turn under ⅛ inch on each end of the ribbon and glue it between the two border strips, covering the edge of each border strip.

3. Measure the entire jacket border, starting at the upper end of the border next to the collar and measuring down one side of the jacket, around the back of the jacket, and back up to the collar on the other side. Cut a piece of red-and-gold cording that length plus an extra 2 inches as a margin.

4. Using red sewing thread and a sewing needle, couch the cording along the inside front and outer bottom edges of the border strip, as shown in **Diagram 5** on page 130. First, bring the needle to the front of the jacket on the left side of the cording, then take the thread over the cording and insert the needle into the jacket on the right side of the cording. On the inside of the jacket, take a stitch about ½ inch from the first stitch and continue sewing over the cording at ½-inch intervals.

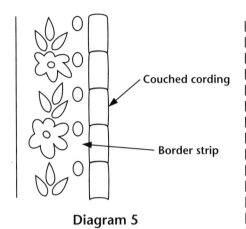

Diagram 5

5. Use the metallic gold paint to outline the edge of the entire border opposite the couched cording. Starting at the collar on one side, paint a thin line of gold all the way around the bottom border of the jacket and up to the collar on the other side. Allow the paint to dry on the front before you begin to paint along the border on the back of the jacket.

6. Use metallic gold paint to outline both yokes. Let the paint dry.

7. Outline the border strips and floral motifs on the pockets in the color you desire. Outline several of the flowers, vines, and leaves in each of the floral motifs and yokes. Allow the paint to dry.

8. To add the gemstones, squeeze dots of paint equal to the diameter of the gemstones onto the yokes and floral motifs. Press the gemstones onto the paint, allowing the paint to come up slightly over the edges of the gemstones as you press. For best results, practice this step on a scrap of fabric before applying gemstones to the actual jacket. When the paint is dry, it will hold the stones in place.

Bits 'n' Pieces

Try This Variation: To decorate a denim jacket with fabric instead of bandannas, you need only ½ yard of a large floral print. The border strips are the only things that must be treated differently. Piece together enough 1-inch strips of fabric to go around the jacket, mitering the corners when you come to them. If you like the look of repeated motifs, experiment with the effects you can achieve with a small coordinating print or striped fabric.

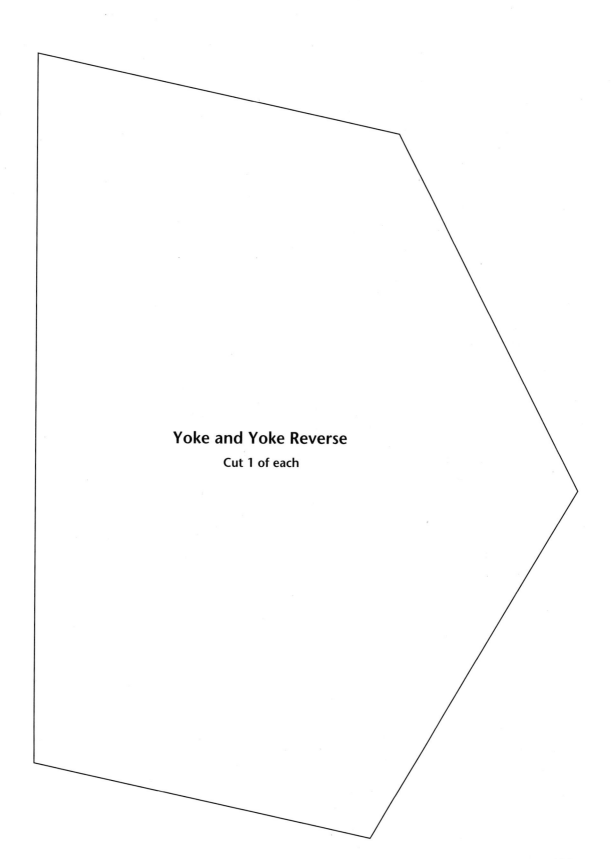

Yoke and Yoke Reverse

Cut 1 of each

Floral Cardigan Sweatshirt

A sweatshirt is no longer just a perfect garment to wear for exercise. By splitting the front and planting a row of bright fabric flowers around the neckline and along the front edges, you can make a sensational cardigan. Add a sprinkling of seed beads and a splash of colorful bias binding. What mom wouldn't enjoy getting one of these for Mother's Day?

Fabric Requirements

+ ⅜ yard of pink print for the bias binding
+ 8-inch squares of purple, blue, yellow, off-white, and pink print for the flower petals
+ 4-inch squares of tan, yellow, turquoise, coral, and rust print for the flower centers
+ ¼ yard of green print for the leaves

Other Supplies

+ 1 large coral crew neck sweatshirt
+ Sewing threads to match the flower petals
+ 5 shades of seed beads for the flower centers
+ Template plastic
+ Fine-point black permanent marker
+ A handful of polyester fiberfill for stuffing 20 flower centers
+ Aleene's Tack it Over and Over glue for placing flower appliqués on the sweatshirt

Instructions

Cutting

1. Cut the front of the sweatshirt down the middle and trim off the neck ribbing.

2. Measure around the neck and down both sides of the front of the sweatshirt. To make the bias binding, cut enough 1½-inch bias strips from pink print to go around the front opening and the neck. Add 2 inches to the length of the bias strip for turning under at the bottom. For more information on making and attaching bias binding, see page 269 in the "General Instructions."

3. Trace the flower petal, flower center, and leaf patterns on page 135 onto template plastic and cut out the templates.

4. Following the flower petal template, draw four flower petals on each of the purple, blue, yellow, off-

white, and pink print squares, and cut them out.

5. Following the flower center template, draw four flower centers on each of the tan, yellow, turquoise, coral, and rust print squares, and cut them out.

6. Following the leaf template, draw 40 leaves on the green print and cut them out.

Assembling the Flowers

1. With a needle and thread, run a line of gathering stitches around one flower center, ⅛ inch from the edge.

2. Pull the thread slightly to gather the flower center. Insert a small amount of polyester fiberfill into the center of the wrong side. Gather the thread tightly to close the flower center.

3. Finger press a ¼-inch hem around the outside edge of the flower petal. With a needle and thread, run a line of gathering stitches ⅛ inch from the folded edge around the circle.

4. Place the stitched side of the flower center on the wrong side of the flower petal and stitch it in place. Pull the gathering stitches to bring the flower petal up loosely around the flower center, then use the gathering thread to sew the flower petal to the flower center.

5. Sew six seed beads in the middle of the flower center, stitching through the entire flower. Pull the thread taut, so that each bead makes an indentation in the flower center.

6. Referring to **Diagram 1,** fold a leaf in half, wrong sides together. Fold the corners down to meet in the center along the raw edges. Sew a line of gathering stitches across the bottom of the triangle and gather the lower edge of the leaf. Repeat for a second leaf.

7. Referring to **Diagram 2,** sew two leaves to the back of each flower, placing the unfolded side of the leaves up.

8. Repeat Steps 1 through 7 to make 20 flowers total.

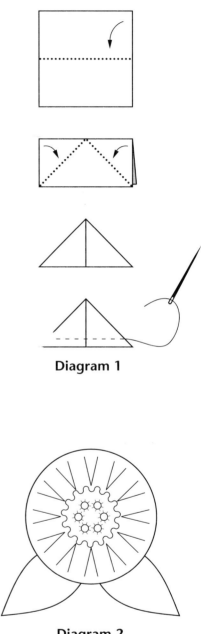

Diagram 1

Diagram 2

Finishing

1. With right sides together, align and pin the bias strip around the front and neck edges of the sweatshirt, stretching the strip slightly around the inner curve of the neckline to make it lie smoothly after it is turned to the wrong side of the sweatshirt. Leave 1 inch of the bias strip free at the bottom edge of each front side. Sew the bias strips to the front edges using a ¼-inch seam allowance.

2. Fold the 1-inch section of bias strip to the wrong side at the bottom of each front and pin it in place. Turn under a ¼-inch hem in the bias strip and pin it. Slip stitch the bias binding in place.

3. On each side of the sweatshirt, pin ten flowers evenly from the bottom knit band to the shoulder seam. Hand sew the flowers in place.

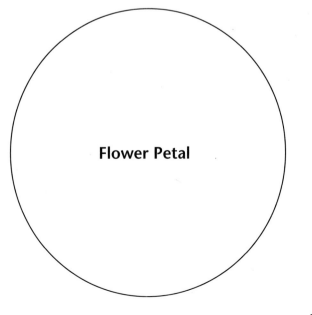

Bits 'n' Pieces

Try This Variation: For a completely different look, try using colorful buttons rather than fabric for the center of each flower.

1. On each flower petal, turn under a ⅛-inch hem twice and sew a line of gathering stitches close to the edge of the hem. Gather the flower petal circle tightly.

2. Make and sew two leaves onto the back of each flower, taking care not to sew through the gathered side of the flower.

3. After binding the front and neck edges of the sweatshirt, position ten flowers on each side of the front. Sew a button to the sweatshirt through the gathered center opening of each flower.

Flower Center

Leaf

Flower Petal

Fabric-Covered Picture Frames

Designing best-sellers for your next bazaar couldn't be easier. Create an elegant setting for a bridal photo by covering a cardboard frame with crazy patchwork in shades of yellow, blue, pink, and green. Round up scraps of burgundy, teal, and lavender synthetic suede to make a frame with a Southwestern flair, or use strip-pieced checks, plaids, and stripes for a homespun look.

✦ *Size: The Crazy Patchwork Frame is 8 × 10 inches.
The Synthetic Suede Frame is 8 × 10 inches.
The Strip-Pieced Calico Frame is 11 × 14 inches.*

Note: The fabric requirements, cutting lists, and piecing instructions for the three frames are provided separately. The assembly instructions that follow are the same for the three frames, with any differences indicated.

Crazy Patchwork Frame

Fabric Requirements

- Ten 5-inch squares of assorted cotton, silk, satin, or velvet for the frame front
- ½ yard of coordinating fabric for the frame back and support
- 10 × 12-inch piece of cotton batiste for the foundation

Other Supplies

- 2 yards of ½-inch rose satin flat braid trim for the border of the frame front and photo opening
- 1 skein each of embroidery floss in rose, blue, yellow, lavender, green, and dark purple
- ½ yard of fleece for padding the frame front
- ½ yard of fusible webbing
- 4-inch length of ½-inch coordinating satin ribbon for the support
- White craft glue
- ¾-inch masking tape
- 8 × 10-inch piece of mat board with a precut 4½-inch oval opening for the frame front
- 8 × 10-inch piece of mat board for the frame back
- 3 × 7-inch piece of mat board for the support
- 2 × 10-inch piece of ¼-inch foam core board
- Craft knife

Cutting

Note: Use ¼-inch seams unless specified otherwise. The batiste is the foundation on which all of the crazy patch pieces are sewn.

1. Center the right side of the frame front on the wrong side of the

136

batiste and trace around the outside edges of the frame, adding ¾ inch. Trace along the inside edge of the oval opening and again ¾ inch inside the oval opening. Remove the frame front.

2. Cut the smaller center oval out of the batiste and discard it.

3. Using a dark sewing thread, machine stay stitch the batiste along the traced line that marks the outside edges of the frame. Then stay stitch along the traced line that marks the oval opening of the frame. This will reinforce the raw edges.

4. Choose one print from the assortment of cotton fabrics and cut a square that measures at least 1½ inches. Cut the rest of the scraps into various angled shapes, making sure to cut enough to cover the entire batiste foundation.

Creating the Crazy Patchwork

Note: The numbers in **Diagrams 1** through **5** indicate only the order of piecing. They do not necessarily coincide with the shapes of the patchwork pieces shown in the illustrations. The joy of crazy patchwork is that it's done randomly, so it is hard to a make a mistake.

1. Referring to **Diagram 1,** place piece 1 right side down on the batiste foundation. Sew one side of piece 1 to the foundation.

2. Fold piece 1 over so that it is right side up. Press it flat, as shown in **Diagram 2.**

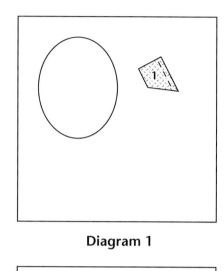

Diagram 1

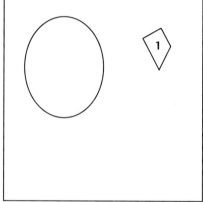

Diagram 2

3. With right sides together, stitch piece 2 to any side of piece 1, as shown in **Diagram 3.**

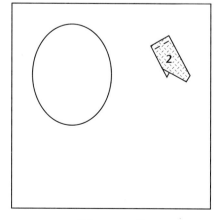

Diagram 3

4. Fold piece 2 over so that it is right side up and press it.

5. With right sides together, stitch piece 3 over the edges of piece 1 and piece 2, as shown in **Diagram 4.**

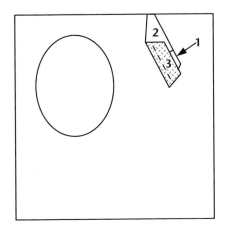

Diagram 4

6. Trim any excess fabric from the seam allowance, turn piece 3 to the right side, as shown in **Diagram 5,** and press the seam flat.

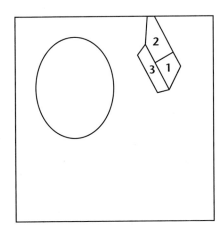

Diagram 5

7. Continue adding pieces to the foundation in the same manner, working clockwise to cover the batiste foundation. For more information about crazy patchwork, see page 261 in the "General Instructions."

Embellishing the Crazy Patchwork

Use various colors of embroidery floss and embroider decorative stitches on the crazy patchwork pieces and between the patchwork seams. Use a satin stitch, lazy daisy stitch, and French knots to create flowers, and use a straight stitch and lazy daisy stitch to make stems and leaves. Add other decorative stitches you like, such as a feather or chain stitch. For more information on embroidery, see pages 273–275 in the "General Instructions."

Synthetic Suede Frame

Fabric Requirements

◆ 10 × 12-inch piece of burgundy synthetic suede for the frame front
◆ 8-inch square of lavender synthetic suede for the large and small diamonds
◆ 4-inch square of teal synthetic suede for the corner squares
◆ ½ yard of coordinating burgundy solid for the frame back and support

Other Supplies

◆ 1 yard of ¼-inch burgundy ribbon
◆ Sewing threads to match fabrics
◆ ½ yard of fleece for padding the frame front
◆ ½ yard of fusible webbing
◆ 4-inch length of ½-inch coordinating satin ribbon for the support
◆ White craft glue

- ¾-inch masking tape
- Tailor's chalk
- 8 × 10-inch piece of mat board with a precut 4½ × 6½-inch rectangular opening for the frame front
- 8 × 10-inch piece of mat board for the frame back
- 3 × 7-inch piece of mat board for the support
- 2 × 10-inch piece of ¼-inch foam core board
- Template plastic or tracing paper
- Fine-point black permanent marker
- Press cloth
- Craft knife

Cutting

1. Trace the pattern pieces for the large diamond, small diamond, and corner square on pages 148–149 onto template plastic or tracing paper, and cut out the templates.

2. Iron an 8-inch square of fusible webbing onto the wrong side of the lavender synthetic suede. Trace two large diamonds and two small diamonds onto the paper side of the fusible webbing. Cut out the four diamonds. Remove the paper backing from the fusible webbing.

3. Iron a 4-inch square of fusible webbing onto the wrong side of the teal synthetic suede. Trace four corner squares onto the paper side of the fusible webbing. Cut out the four squares. Remove the paper backing from the fusible webbing.

4. Center the frame front on the wrong side of the burgundy synthet-

ic suede. Using tailor's chalk, trace around the outside edges of the frame, adding ¾ inch. Trace along the inside edge of the rectangular opening and again ¾ inch inside the rectangular opening. Remove the frame front.

5. Cut along the traced line that is ¾ inch inside of the traced rectangle and discard the center piece of fabric.

Fusing the Pattern Pieces

1. Using a matching sewing thread, machine stay stitch the burgundy synthetic suede along the traced line that marks the outside edges of the frame. Then stay stitch the traced line that marks the rectangular opening of the frame. This reinforces the raw edges.

2. Referring to **Diagram 6,** position and iron the large and small diamonds and corner squares onto the

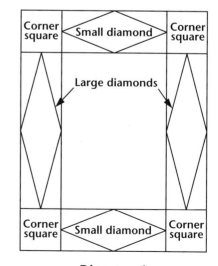

Diagram 6

right side of the burgundy synthetic suede, placing a press cloth over the right side of the synthetic suede pieces to protect the fabric surface.

3. With matching sewing threads, topstitch each shape to the burgundy fabric ¹⁄₁₆ inch from the edges.

Strip-Pieced Calico Frame

Fabric Requirements

♦ Twenty-eight 1 × 18-inch strips of yellow, pink, purple, and blue calico prints
♦ 3 × 10-inch piece of calico print for the corner squares
♦ 13 × 16-inch piece of cotton batiste for the foundation
♦ ½ yard of coordinating fabric for the frame back and support

Other Supplies

♦ 3 yards of ½-inch white satin flat braid trim for the border of the frame front and photo opening
♦ 2 yards of ½-inch white flat lace trim for the border of the frame front
♦ ½ yard of fleece for padding the frame front
♦ ¾ yard of fusible webbing
♦ 5-inch length of ½-inch coordinating satin ribbon for the support
♦ White craft glue
♦ ¾-inch masking tape
♦ 11 × 14-inch piece of mat board with a precut 8 × 10-inch oval opening for the frame front
♦ 11 × 14-inch piece of mat board for the frame back
♦ 4 × 10-inch piece of mat board for the support

♦ 2 × 14-inch piece of ¼-inch foam core board
♦ Craft knife

Cutting

Note: This frame contains seven yellow fabrics, nine pink fabrics, four purple fabrics, and eight blue fabrics. After you cut each fabric into 1 × 18-inch strips, cut each of the strips into three 6-inch segments.

1. From the 10-inch piece of calico print, cut four 2½-inch corner squares.

2. Center the frame front on the wrong side of the batiste and trace around the outside edges of the frame, adding ¾ inch. Trace along the inside edge of the oval opening and again ¾ inch inside the oval opening. Remove the frame front.

3. Cut the smaller center oval out of the batiste and discard it.

4. Using a dark sewing thread, machine stay stitch the batiste along the traced line that marks the outside edges of the frame. Then stay stitch along the traced line that marks the oval opening of the frame. This reinforces the raw edges.

Piecing the Frame Front

Note: Use ¼-inch seams unless specified otherwise. The batiste is the foundation on which all of the corner squares and strips are sewn. The stitching sequence for the calico strips on the frame front begins at each corner and moves toward the midpoint.

1. Referring to **Diagram 7,** baste each corner square right side up in the corners of the batiste foundation.

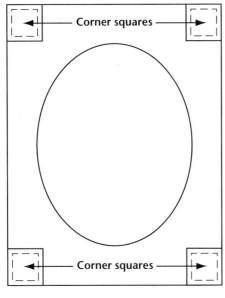

Diagram 7

2. Begin piecing the calico strips by placing one at an angle on top of the left bottom corner square, making sure that right sides are facing, as shown in **Diagram 8.** Sew the calico strip to the corner square. Fold the strip to the right side and finger press the seam.

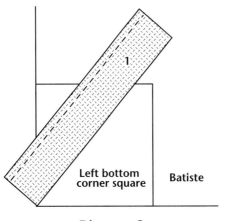

Diagram 8

3. Place a second calico strip at an angle on the other side of the left bottom corner square, as shown in **Diagram 9.** This strip should overlap the first strip at the top. Sew the second strip to the corner square. Fold the strip to the right side and finger press this seam. Treat each corner in the same manner. Continue adding strips alternately on each side of this corner square, making sure that the strips overlap and working toward the center on each side of the frame.

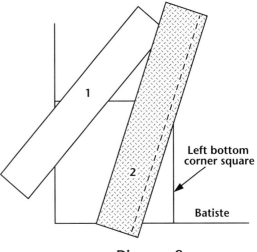

Diagram 9

4. Treat each corner of the frame front in the same manner, making sure to follow the calico strip placement sequence of the other corners, as shown in **Diagram 10** on the opposite page. Strip 1 in each corner was sewn to the corner square first. Strip 2 in each corner was sewn second.

5. Piece strips toward the midpoint of each side of the frame front, as indicated by the arrows in **Diagram 11** on the opposite page.

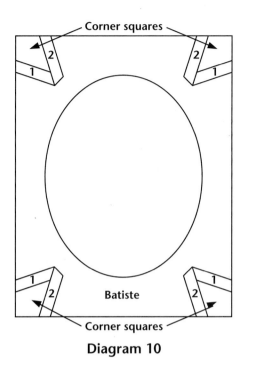

Diagram 10

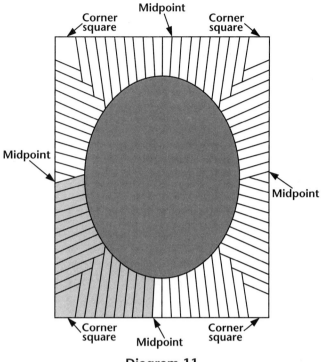

Diagram 11

When you reach the midpoint of each side, turn under ¼ inch on the final strip and blindstitch it in place by hand.

Assembling the Frames

Covering the Frame Front

1. Center the mat board frame front on top of the fleece. Cut one piece of fleece the same size and shape as the frame front, making sure to cut out the center opening. Repeat this step to cut a second piece of fleece.

2. Using thick white glue, secure the two layers of fleece to the mat board frame front, making sure to match up the photograph openings in all three layers.

3. Place the crazy patchwork, synthetic suede, or strip-pieced calico frame fronts on a work surface with

the wrong side facing up. Center the mat board frame front with the fleece side down onto the fabric, making sure the photograph openings line up through all layers.

4. Fold the raw edge of one side of the fabric over one edge of the mat board frame front and glue it in place. As a reinforcement, use several pieces of masking tape to hold the raw edge in place while the glue dries. When dry, remove and discard the masking tape. Repeat for the other three sides of the fabric and mat board frame front.

5. Clip small V-shapes around the photograph opening of the fabric, making sure not to clip through the stay stitching. Fold the fabric to the back of the frame front and glue it in place. Use several pieces of masking tape to hold the raw edge in place

143

while the glue dries. When it is dry, remove and discard the masking tape.

6. For the Crazy Patchwork Frame, measure and cut a piece of rose satin flat braid trim long enough to go around the inside opening and glue it in place. Repeat this step using burgundy ribbon for the Synthetic Suede Frame and white satin flat braid trim for the Strip-Pieced Calico Frame.

7. For the Crazy Patchwork Frame, measure and cut a piece of rose satin flat braid trim long enough to go around the outside edge of the frame and glue it in place. Repeat this step using burgundy ribbon for the Synthetic Suede Frame and white satin flat braid trim for the Strip-Pieced Calico Frame.

8. For the Strip-Pieced Calico Frame, measure and cut a piece of white flat lace trim long enough to go around the outside edge of the frame. Glue ⅛ inch of the lace to the wrong side of the frame front so that the remainder of the lace stands out from the behind the frame.

Covering the Frame Back

1. For the Crazy Patchwork and Synthetic Suede frames, iron a 9 × 11-inch piece of fusible webbing onto the wrong side of the same size piece of coordinating fabric to cover the frame back. For the Strip-Pieced Calico Frame, iron a 12 × 15-inch piece of fusible webbing onto the wrong side of the same size piece of coordinating fabric to cover the frame back. Remove the paper backing from the fusible webbing.

2. With the webbing side down, center and iron the 9 × 11-inch piece of fabric for the Crazy Patchwork and Synthetic Suede frames onto the two 8 × 10-inch frame backs. Again with the webbing side down, center and iron the 12 × 15-inch piece of fabric for the Strip-Pieced Calico Frame onto the wrong side of the 11 × 14-inch frame back.

3. Turn the frame back over so that the right side is facing up. Fold the extended edges of the fabric to the right side of the frame back and iron them in place.

4. For the Crazy Patchwork and Synthetic Suede frames, iron a 7¾ × 9¾-inch piece of fusible webbing onto the wrong side of the same size piece of coordinating fabric to cover the right side of the frame backs. For the Strip-Pieced Calico Frame, iron a 10¾ × 13¾-inch piece of fusible webbing onto the wrong side of the same size piece of coordinating fabric to cover the right side of the frame back. Remove the paper backing from the fusible webbing.

5. With the webbing side down, center and iron the 7¾ × 9¾-inch piece of fabric for the Crazy Patchwork and Synthetic Suede frames onto the two frame backs. Again with the webbing side down, center and iron the 10¾ × 13¾-inch piece of fabric for the Strip-Pieced Calico Frame onto the frame back. These are the insides of the frame backs.

Covering the Frame Support

1. Trace the small support pattern for the Crazy Patchwork and Synthetic Suede frames on page 148 onto template plastic or tracing paper. Repeat for the large support pattern for the Strip-Pieced Calico Frame on page 149. Cut out the templates.

2. Trace the small support pattern onto the 3 × 7-inch piece of mat board and the large support onto the 4 × 10-inch piece of mat board.

3. Using a craft knife, cut the support from the mat board. Using light pressure on the knife, score a line along the dashed line near the top of the support. Reinforce this scored line with a piece of masking tape placed on the other side of the support.

4. For the Crazy Patchwork and Synthetic Suede frames, iron an 8 × 9-inch piece of fusible webbing onto the wrong side of the same size piece of coordinating fabric to cover the small support. For the Strip-Pieced Calico Frame, iron a 10 × 11-inch piece of fusible webbing onto the wrong side of the same size piece of coordinating fabric to cover the large support. Remove the paper backing from the fusible webbing.

5. Center the support on the paper side of the fusible webbing. Referring to **Diagram 12,** draw three supports next to each other. Draw a line ½ inch above the top line of the traced support in the center. Draw another line ½ inch below the bottom line of the traced sup-

port in the center. Cut out the entire support section of fabric including the top and bottom sections of the center support.

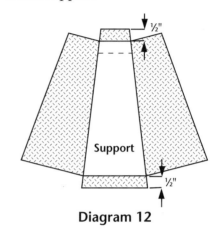

Diagram 12

6. Remove the paper backing from the fusible webbing. Trim one-third of the fabric from the right and left sides of the entire support section of fabric, as shown in **Diagram 13.**

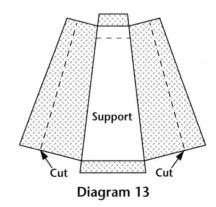

Diagram 13

7. Center the mat board support, with the scored side facing up, on the webbing side of the fabric. Fold the right side of the fabric over the support and iron it in place, then fold the left side of the fabric over the support and iron it in place, as shown in **Diagram 14** on page 146.

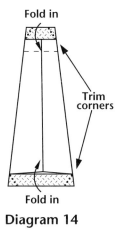

Diagram 14

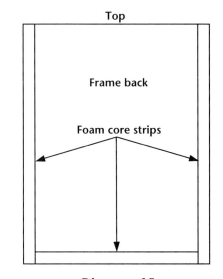

Diagram 15

8. Trim the top and bottom corners, as shown in **Diagram 14.** Fold the bottom fabric up over the edge of the support and iron it in place. Fold the top fabric down over the edge of the support and iron it in place. Turn the support to the right side and iron the fabric on this side in place.

Attaching the Foam Core Board

1. For each of the Crazy Patchwork and Synthetic Suede frames, cut two ½ × 10-inch strips and one ½ × 7-inch strip of foam core board. For the Strip-Pieced Calico Frame, cut two ½ × 14-inch strips and one ½ × 10-inch strip of foam core board.

2. Glue the shortest strip of foam core board to the bottom edge of the frame back, then glue the two longer strips to the sides of the frame back, as shown in **Diagram 15.** Allow the glue to dry.

3. Apply glue to the surface of each of the three strips of foam core board. Place the frame front on top of the strips, making sure to

align all of the edges of the frame front with the frame back. Press the frame front firmly in place. Do not glue the top edge of the frame front and frame back together. The photograph will be inserted through this opening.

Attaching the Support to the Frame Back

Apply glue to the wrong side of the support above the scored bend. Referring to **Diagram 16** on the opposite page, position the support so that the bottom edge is centered along the bottom edge of the frame back, then press the top portion with glue firmly in place. Allow the glue to dry.

Finishing

1. Apply 1 inch of glue along one end of each piece of ribbon for the frame support. Attach the ribbon to the center of the frame back, approximately 2½ inches from the bottom edge, as shown in

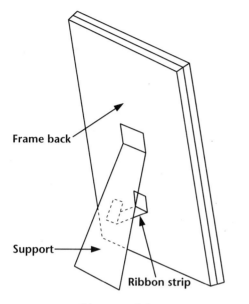

Diagram 16

Diagram 16. Apply 1 inch of glue along the other end of the ribbon and attach it to the center of the support, approximately 2½ inches from the bottom edge. For the Crazy Patchwork and Synthetic Suede frames, there should be 2 inches of ribbon free between the frame back and the support. For the Strip-Pieced Calico Frame, there should be 3 inches of ribbon free between the frame back and the support. Allow the glue to dry.

2. Carefully slide a photograph between the frame front and the frame back through the opening at the top edge of the frame.

Bits 'n' Pieces

Try These Variations: You can magically change the Crazy Patchwork Frame into a sweetheart frame for Valentine's Day. Purchase an 8 × 10-inch piece of mat board with a precut 4½-inch heart opening for the frame front. Then use scraps of red and white cotton, silk, satin, and velvet for the crazy patchwork. Use red and white embroidery floss to embroider decorative stitches on the patchwork.

The Synthetic Suede Frame can easily become a Christmas frame by selecting green, red, and white coordinating yuletide cotton prints or green, red, and white moiré for a bejeweled look. Cut out the diamond shapes in red and the corner squares in white. Machine appliqué each shape with green thread and a medium zigzag stitch.

How about strip piecing baby's first picture frame in soft cotton pastels, pink and blue satin, or bright primary shades? Add a final touch of coordinating satin flat braid trim inside the oval and around the outside border of the frame.

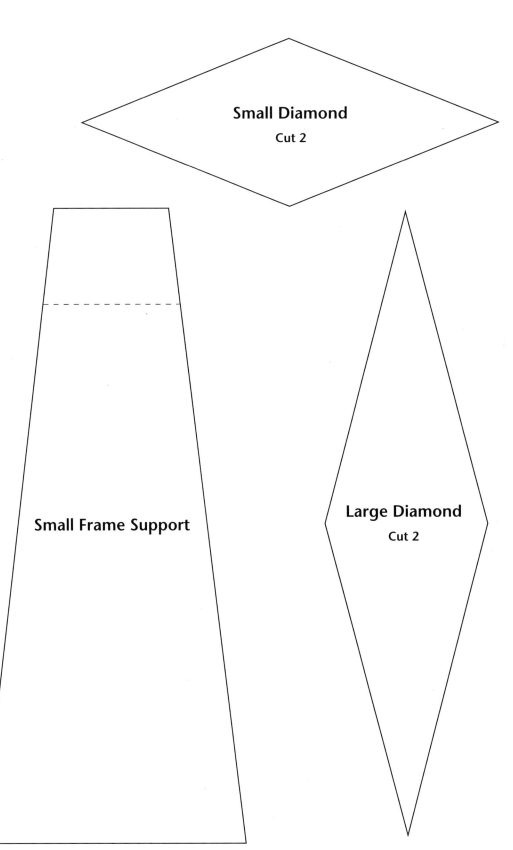

Small Diamond
Cut 2

Small Frame Support

Large Diamond
Cut 2

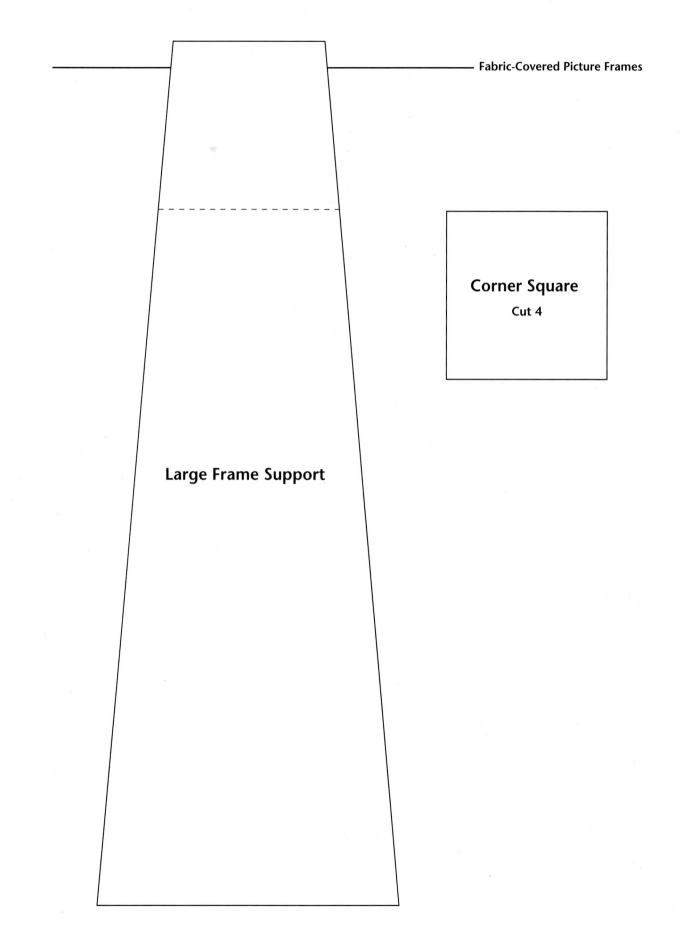

Corner Square

Cut 4

Large Frame Support

Partridge Tableau

Celebrate special occasions like weddings, anniversaries, or births by making a fabulous fabric announcement with the look of German Scherenschnitte. Write names and dates on the heart in calligraphy with a permanent fabric marking pen. The trick to making perfect tiny "cutouts" on the flowers, leaves, heart, and birds' wings is to cut small pieces of background fabric and simply fuse them on the larger design shapes.

✦ *Size: The design area is 9 inches wide × 10½ inches high.*

Fabric Requirements and Other Supplies

- ✦ ⅜ yard of teal solid for the background and the small accent areas
- ✦ One 12-inch piece of light gray print for the design
- ✦ 1 yard of fusible webbing
- ✦ Sharp embroidery scissors
- ✦ Fine-point black permanent marker for calligraphy (optional)
- ✦ Tracing paper

Instructions

Cutting

1. With a black permanent marker, trace the two halves of the pattern on pages 152–153 onto a piece of tracing paper, matching the placement lines. Cut out a 12-inch square of fusible webbing. Trace *only* the outline of the design onto the paper side of the fusible webbing. Do not trace any of the small gray areas at this time.

2. Iron the webbing side of the fusible webbing onto the wrong side of the gray print. Using sharp embroidery scissors, cut along the outline of the design.

3. Cut a 13 × 18-inch piece of teal solid for the background.

4. Cut out a 10-inch square of fusible webbing. Trace the gray areas on the pattern onto the paper side of the fusible webbing.

5. Iron the webbing side of the fusible webbing onto the wrong side of the remaining piece of teal solid. Do not cut out the shapes until you are ready to position them on the gray print.

Assembling the Partridge Tableau

1. Remove the paper backing from the wrong side of the design on gray print.

2. Center the gray print design on the right side of the teal background fabric and fuse the design to the background.

3. Use sharp embroidery scissors to cut out each of the small teal pieces, fusing one to the gray design area before cutting out the next piece.

Partridge Tableau

(section 1 of 2)

Join to section 2

Join to section 1

Partridge Tableau

(section 2 of 2)

Yo-Yo and Button Vest

What better way to use up small scraps of your favorite fabrics than by making and embellishing a one-of-a-kind vest? Start with a purchased pattern for any vest you like. Before you make the vest, cover the individual pattern pieces with an assortment of handmade yo-yos and colorful buttons. If you pack up some colorful fabric circles in a plastic bag and take them with you wherever you go, you'll be ready to stitch at a moment's notice.

◆ *Size: Approximately 180 yo-yos will cover the front of a medium-size vest.*

Fabric Requirements

- Fabric for the vest as specified on the purchased pattern
- Matching fabric for the vest lining as specified on the pattern
- ½ yard of matching fabric for the bias binding
- ⅛ yard of 8 different prints or fabric scraps that are at least 4 inches square for each yo-yo

Other Supplies

- Purchased pattern for a fully lined vest (project photo shows Butterick vest #6488)
- Assorted buttons for the center of each yo-yo
- Pearl cotton in assorted colors for attaching buttons
- Sewing thread to match fabrics
- Template plastic
- Fine-point black permanent marker

Instructions

Cutting

1. Lay out and cut out the pattern pieces for your vest according to the pattern instructions. If your pattern is for an unlined vest, eliminate the facing pieces. If your vest has a matching lining, lay out and cut out the front and back pattern pieces for the lining.

2. Cut the binding fabric into 1½-inch bias strips. Sew the short ends of the strips together to make enough bias binding for the edges of the vest.

3. Trace the large and small yo-yo patterns on page 157 onto template plastic and cut them out.

4. Following the templates, draw approximately 90 large and 90 small yo-yos on the fabric scraps and cut them out. If you are using a different vest pattern than the one used here, cut enough yo-yos to cover both front pieces.

Assembling the Vest

1. Turn under and finger press a ⅛-inch seam along the raw edge of one yo-yo circle and sew a line of

small gathering stitches along the folded edge. To form the yo-yo, pull the thread to gather the stitches, as shown in **Diagram 1,** then secure the thread. The gathered side is the right side of the yo-yo. Repeat for all of the yo-yos.

2. Pin large and small yo-yos randomly on each vest front, avoiding the side seams.

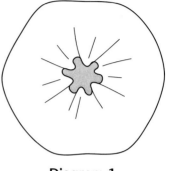

Diagram 1

Bits 'n' Pieces

Try These Variations: Yo-yos make great decorations for other clothing and accessory items. Try out some of the following creative ways to use yo-yos:

• Cluster a few yo-yos with sewn button centers on a pair of canvas tennis shoes. Use fabric glue to attach the yo-yos to the shoes.

• Use an outline stitch to embroider some stems "growing" out of the pocket on a shirt. Add colorful yo-yo "flowers" to the top of each stem. Cut some fabric "leaves" with pinking shears and sew a line through the center of each leaf to attach it to the shirt.

• Use a hot-glue gun to attach yo-yos to a headband or hair clip.

• Make a fabric purse and sprinkle it with matching or contrasting yo-yos.

• Add yo-yos to a denim skirt or jacket.

3. Place a button at the center of each yo-yo and sew the button and yo-yo to the vest front with pearl cotton.

4. Sew the front vest pieces to the vest back at the shoulder seams and side seams. If your vest has lining, assemble the lining in the same manner.

5. Place the lining (if used) inside the vest, wrong sides together and baste the edges. Cut off the seam allowances.

6. Bind the raw edges of the vest with bias binding. For more information on making and attaching bias binding, see page 269 in the "General Instructions."

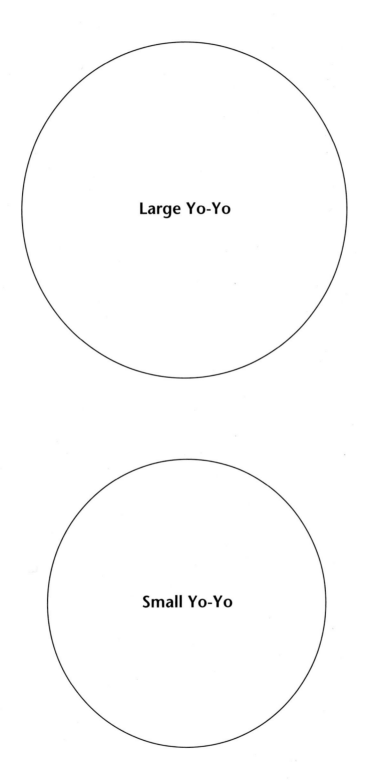

Large Yo-Yo

Small Yo-Yo

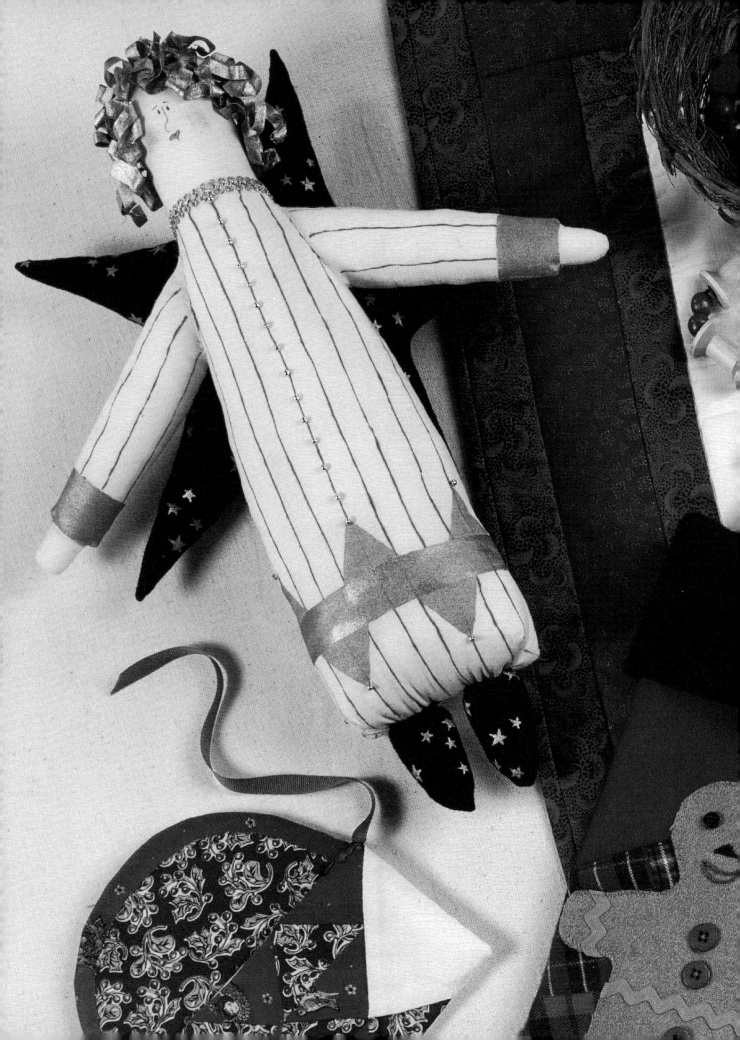

Santa Claus
Is Coming *to* Town

Christmas Card Baskets

Overflowing with glad tidings from friends and loved ones, these pocketed Christmas card baskets hold the season's best wishes. And you can create them in the blink of an afternoon! When the holiday is over, simply fold up the baskets and tuck them into your Christmas memory book.

❈ *Size: Each of the three baskets is 7½ × 22 inches.*

Fabric Requirements

* ⅜ yard of muslin for the back, lining, and basket block
* ⅓ yard of red print for the basket block
* ⅓ yard of green print for the basket block
* ¾ yard of batting

Other Supplies

* 18-inch square of cardboard or plastic
* 1 yard of ⅜-inch or ½-inch red grosgrain ribbon for the bows
* Sewing threads to match fabrics
* Template plastic
* Fine-point black permanent marker
* Pencil or removable marker for tracing templates on fabric

Instructions

Note: Patterns include ¼-inch seam allowances.

Cutting

1. Trace the pattern pieces on pages 164–165 onto template plastic. Transfer all markings and cut out the templates.

2. From the muslin, cut 3 D pieces, 3 C rectangles, 3 B pieces, and 3 B reverse pieces.

3. From the red print, cut 18 A triangles and 3 E pieces.

4. From the green print, cut 15 A triangles and 3 D pieces.

5. From the batting, cut 6 D pieces and 3 C rectangles.

6. From the cardboard or plastic, cut 3 D pieces ⅛ inch inside the seam allowance.

7. Cut four 9-inch lengths of grosgrain ribbon.

Piecing the Baskets

1. Referring to **Diagram 1** on the opposite page, stitch three red print A triangles and two green print A triangles together to make Row 1.

2. To make Row 2, sew two red print A triangles and one green print A triangle together, as shown in **Diagram 1.**

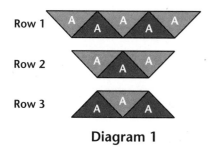

Row 1

Row 2

Row 3

Diagram 1

3. To make Row 3, sew two green print A triangles and one red print A triangle together, as shown in **Diagram 1.**

4. To assemble the basket, first sew Row 1 to Row 2, matching

seams, then sew Row 3 to Row 2, matching seams.

5. Referring to **Diagram 2,** stitch one muslin B piece and one muslin B reverse piece to the sides of the A unit. This forms the pocket unit.

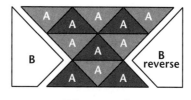

B

B reverse

Diagram 2

6. Baste one batting C rectangle to the back of the pocket unit, stitching in the seam allowance around the bottom and side edges.

7. With right sides together, pin a muslin C rectangle to the top and bottom edges of the pocket unit, then sew along the top and bottom edges of the basket. Turn the pocket unit right side out and press the seams, as shown in **Diagram 3.**

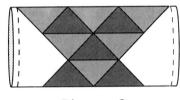

Diagram 3

8. Referring to **Diagram 4,** turn under the seam allowance of the inner curved edge of one red print E handle and baste it in place on the green print D piece, forming the handle unit. Blindstitch the inner curved edge.

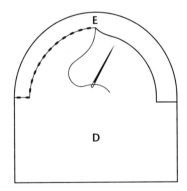

Diagram 4

9. As shown in **Diagram 5,** place the pocket unit over the handle unit so that the handle shows above the basket. Pin the side edges together

and machine baste along each side inside the seam allowance.

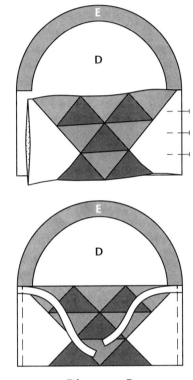

Diagram 5

10. Repeat Steps 1 through 9 to make three baskets.

11. Referring to **Diagram 5,** sew a 9-inch length of ribbon on each side of the pocket unit of one basket, on the left side of the pocket unit of the second basket, and on the right side of the pocket unit of the third basket. Tie the ribbon between the baskets into bows.

12. Referring to **Diagram 6** on the opposite page, place one muslin D piece over the card basket, right sides together. Pin the top and sides together. Sew the pieces together, leaving the bottom edge open. Clip several small V-shapes in the curves so the top edge lies smoothly. Turn the card basket right side out and press the edges. Repeat for the other two baskets.

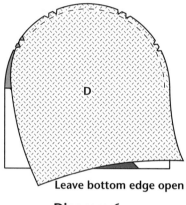

Leave bottom edge open

Diagram 6

Padding the Baskets

1. Referring to **Diagram 7,** place a piece of batting on each side of the cardboard or plastic D pieces. The batting pieces are slightly larger than the cardboard or plastic. Topstitch by machine or whipstitch by hand around all edges.

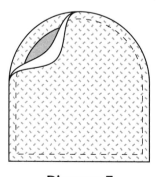

Diagram 7

2. Referring to **Diagram 8,** slip the padded boards inside the pockets.

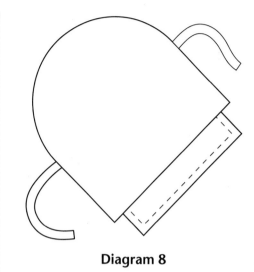

Diagram 8

3. As shown in **Diagram 9,** turn under the remaining edges and blindstitch the bottom edge of each basket closed.

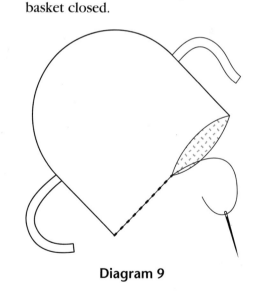

Diagram 9

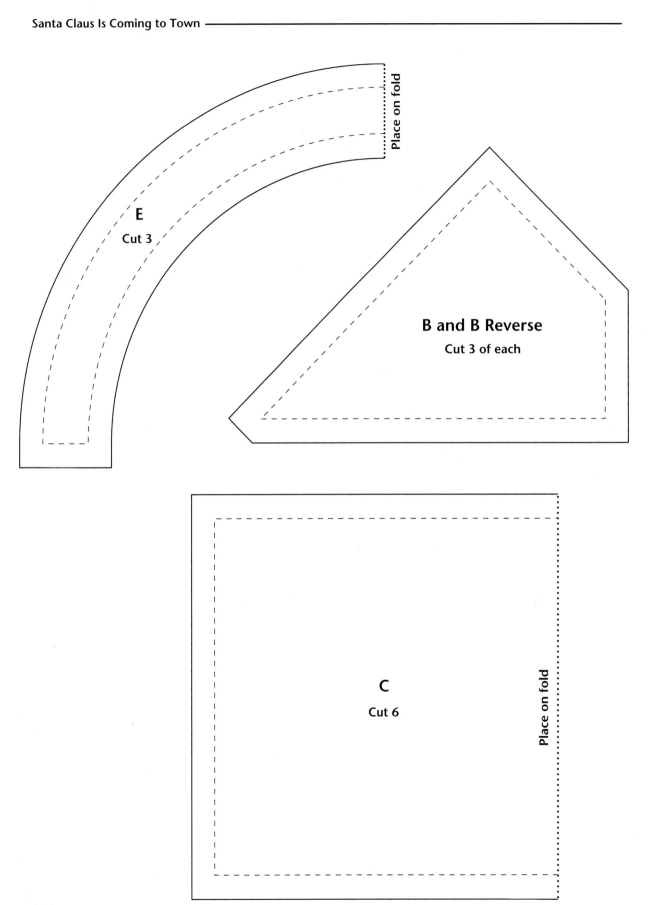

E

Cut 3

Place on fold

B and B Reverse

Cut 3 of each

C

Cut 6

Place on fold

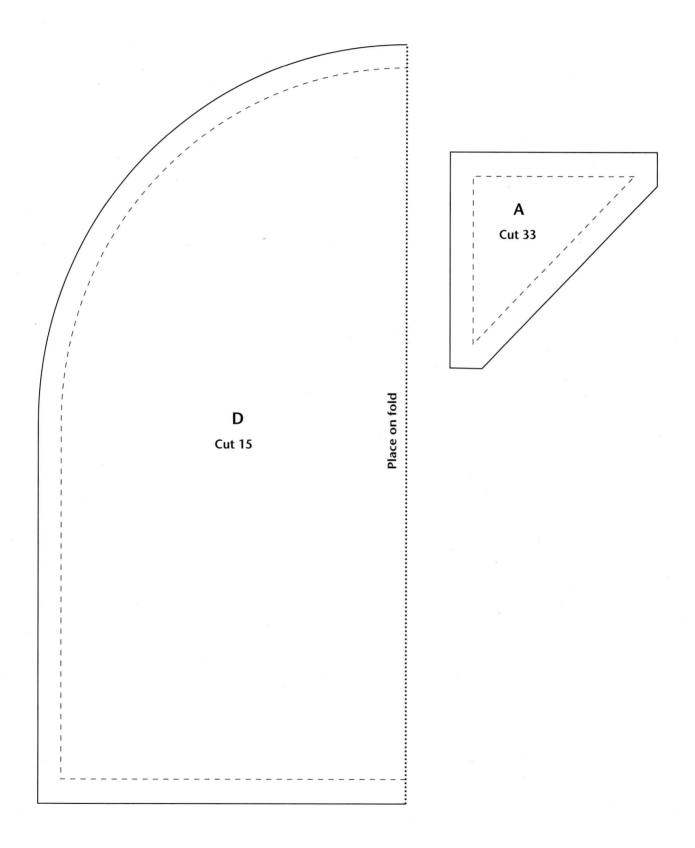

A
Cut 33

D
Cut 15

Place on fold

Christmas Tree Quilt

A jumble of colorful patchwork pine boughs gives this quick-and-easy Christmas quilt old-fashioned charm. Top the tree with a shining golden star and lots of bright red ornaments to make a delightful yuletide door banner for welcoming holiday guests.

❄ *Size: The quilt is 31 × 37 inches.*

Fabric Requirements

* ½ yard of assorted green prints for the tree
* ⅜ yard of white solid for the background
* ¼ yard of assorted tan prints for the floor
* ⅛ yard of assorted red prints for the ornaments
* 6 scraps of brown prints for the trunk
* 3 scraps of assorted gold prints for the star
* 8-inch square of white-on-white print for the starlight
* 1½ yards of green print for the inner and outer borders and the binding
* ⅞ yard of red print for the middle border
* 1¼ yards of fabric for the backing

Other Supplies

* 35 × 40-inch piece of batting
* Template plastic
* Fine-point black permanent marker
* 1 skein of red pearl cotton or embroidery floss for tying the quilt
* Large-eye, sharp needle

Instructions

Note: Prewash and press all of the fabrics. Pattern pieces include ¼-inch seam allowances. All of the border strips are slightly longer than needed and will be trimmed to length after they are stitched to the quilt.

Cutting

1. Trace the pattern pieces on pages 172–173 onto template plastic, transferring all markings, and cut out the templates.

2. From the assorted green prints, cut 108 A shapes.

3. From the white solid, cut three B and three B reverse shapes, four C and four C reverse shapes, four D and four D reverse shapes, four E and four E reverse shapes, and six F and six F reverse shapes.

4. From the tan prints, cut 27 A shapes and four B and four B reverse shapes.

5. From the assorted red prints, cut 28 A shapes.

6. From the brown prints, cut six A shapes.

7. From the gold prints, cut three A shapes.

8. From the white-on-white print, cut seven A shapes.

9. From the green print, cut two 1¾ × 25½-inch strips and two

$1\frac{3}{4} \times 26$-inch strips for the inner border. Cut two $1\frac{3}{4} \times 32$-inch and two $1\frac{3}{4} \times 37$-inch strips for the outer border. Also cut four $1\frac{1}{2} \times 44$-inch strips for the binding.

10. From the red print, cut two $2\frac{1}{2} \times 28$-inch strips and two $3\frac{1}{2} \times 29$-inch strips for the middle border.

Piecing the Quilt Top

Note: This quilt is pieced row by row, starting at the top of the quilt. Use $\frac{1}{4}$-inch seam allowances and press all seams toward the darker fabric.

1. Referring to **Diagram 1,** sew a white F shape, three white-on-white A shapes, and a white F reverse shape together to make Row 1.

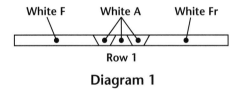

Diagram 1

2. Referring to **Diagram 2,** sew a white F shape, a white-on-white A shape, a gold A shape, a white-on-white A shape, and a white F reverse shape together to make Row 2. Repeat to make Row 3.

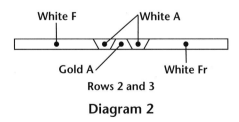

Diagram 2

3. Referring to **Diagram 3,** sew a white F reverse shape, a green A, a gold A, a green A, and a white F shape together to make Row 4.

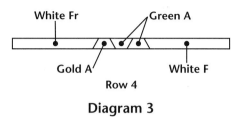

Diagram 3

4. Referring to **Diagram 4,** sew a white F reverse shape, three green A shapes, and a white F shape together to make Row 5. Repeat to make Row 6.

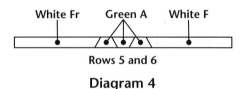

Diagram 4

5. Referring to **Diagram 5,** sew a white E shape, a green A, a red A, a green A, a red A, a green A, and a white E reverse together to make Row 7.

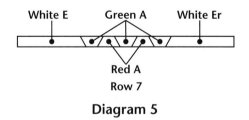

Diagram 5

6. Referring to **Diagram 6,** sew a white E reverse shape, a green A, a red A, a green A, a red A, a green A, and a white E together to make Row 8.

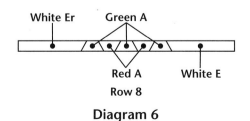

Diagram 6

7. Referring to **Diagram 7,** sew a white E reverse shape, five green A shapes, and a white E shape together to make Row 9. Repeat to make Row 10.

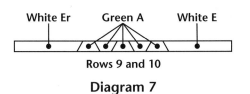

Rows 9 and 10

Diagram 7

8. Referring to **Diagram 8,** sew a white D shape, a green A, a red A, a green A, a red A, a green A, a red A, a green A, and a white D reverse together to make Row 11.

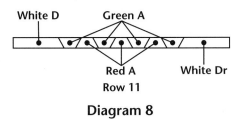

Row 11

Diagram 8

9. Referring to **Diagram 9,** sew a white D reverse shape, a green A, red A, a green A, a red A, a green A, a red A, a green A, and a white D together to make Row 12.

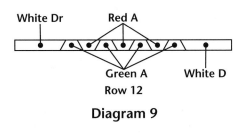

Row 12

Diagram 9

10. Referring to **Diagram 10,** sew a white D reverse shape, seven

green A shapes, and a white D together to make Row 13. Repeat to make Row 14.

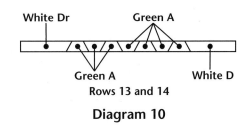

Rows 13 and 14

Diagram 10

11. Referring to **Diagram 11,** sew a white C shape, a green A, a red A, a green A, a red A, a green A, a red A, a green A, a red A, a green A, and a white C reverse together to make Row 15.

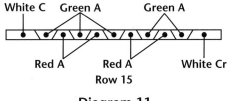

Row 15

Diagram 11

12. Referring to **Diagram 12,** sew a white C reverse, a green A, a red A, a green A, a red A, a green A, a red A, a green A, a red A, a green A, and a white C together to make Row 16.

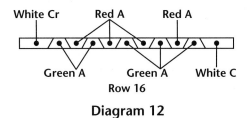

Row 16

Diagram 12

13. Referring to **Diagram 13** on page 170, sew a white C reverse shape, nine green A shapes, and a white C shape together to make Row 17. Repeat to make Row 18.

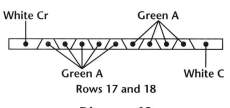

Diagram 13

14. Referring to **Diagram 14,** sew a white B, a green A, a red A, a green A, a red A, a green A, a red A, a green A, a red A, a green A, and a white B reverse together to make Row 19.

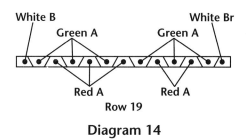

Diagram 14

15. Referring to **Diagram 15,** sew a white B reverse, a green A, a red A, a green A, a red A, a green A, a red A, a green A, a red A, a green A, a red A, a green A, and a white B together to make Row 20.

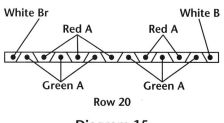

Diagram 15

16. Referring to **Diagram 16,** sew a white B reverse, 11 green A

shapes, and a white B together to make Row 21.

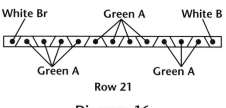

Diagram 16

17. Referring to **Diagram 17,** sew a tan B reverse, 11 green A shapes, and a tan B together to make Row 22.

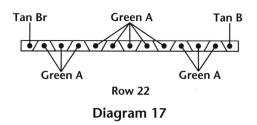

Diagram 17

18. Referring to **Diagram 18,** sew a tan B reverse shape, four tan A shapes, three brown A shapes, four tan A shapes, and a tan B together to make Row 23.

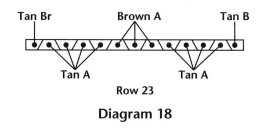

Diagram 18

19. Referring to **Diagram 19** on the opposite page, sew a tan B, four tan A shapes, three brown A shapes, four tan A shapes, and a tan B reverse together to make Row 24.

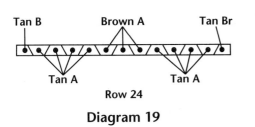

Diagram 19

20. Referring to **Diagram 20,** sew a tan B, 11 tan A shapes, and a tan B reverse together to make Row 25.

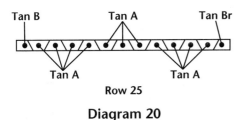

Diagram 20

Assembling the Quilt Top

1. Referring to the photograph on page 167, sew the 25 rows together, starting with Row 1 at the top of the quilt and working to Row 25 at the bottom of the quilt. Take care to center or match the A shapes in each row to the A shapes in the previous row. Press each seam as you work.

2. Trim the sides of the quilt evenly so that it is 22½ inches wide.

Adding the Borders

Note: Press the seams toward the borders unless specified otherwise.

1. Sew the green 1¾ × 25½-inch inner borders to the sides of the quilt top.

2. Sew the green 1¾ × 26-inch inner borders to the top and bottom edges of the quilt.

3. Sew the red 2½ × 28-inch middle borders to the sides of the quilt. Trim the ends of the borders even with the quilt.

4. Sew the red 3½ × 29-inch middle borders to the top and bottom edges of the quilt. Trim the ends of the borders even with the quilt.

5. Sew the green 1¾ × 32-inch outer borders to the top and bottom edges of the quilt, beginning and ending each seam ¼ inch in from the edge of the quilt. Sew the green 1¾ × 37-inch outer borders to the sides of the quilt, beginning and ending the seams ¼ inch in from the edge of the quilt. Trim the excess from the corner seam allowances and press the corner seams open.

Layering and Quilting

1. Layer and baste the backing, batting, and quilt top. For more information on layering and basting, see page 268 in the "General Instructions."

2. Machine quilt in the ditch of the border seams and around each red decorative ornament on the Christmas tree.

Binding the Quilt

1. Fold the four binding strips in half lengthwise, wrong sides together, and press.

2. Trim the batting and backing to ½ inch larger than the quilt top.

3. Pin a binding strip along one edge of the quilt, with right sides together and matching raw edges. Stitch the binding to the quilt through all layers, using a ¼-inch seam allowance. Backstitch at each end of the seam and trim the ends of the binding strip even with the quilt edge. Repeat to bind the opposite side of the quilt.

4. Fold these binding strips around to the wrong side of the quilt and hand stitch them in place, as shown in **Diagram 21.**

Diagram 21

5. Pin a binding strip along the top edge of the quilt, allowing it to extend slightly beyond the previously sewn binding. Sew the binding to the quilt through all layers, using a ¼-inch seam allowance. Backstitch at each end. Repeat at the bottom edge of the quilt.

6. Fold these binding strips to the wrong side of the quilt. Tuck the ends in to make smooth, square corners, then hand stitch the strips in place.

Tying the Quilt

1. Thread a sharp, large-eye needle with approximately 1 yard of red pearl cotton or embroidery floss. Pull the thread to make sure the ends are even. Do not tie a knot at either end of the thread.

2. On the right side of the quilt, insert the needle down through the center of one green A shape. Bring the needle back up through all layers, approximately ¼ inch away. Pull the thread until there is approximately a 3-inch tail and tie a square knot. Trim the threads to ½ inch above the knot. Continue to tie square knots at even intervals over the surface of the Christmas tree.

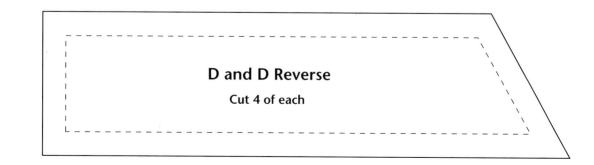

D and D Reverse

Cut 4 of each

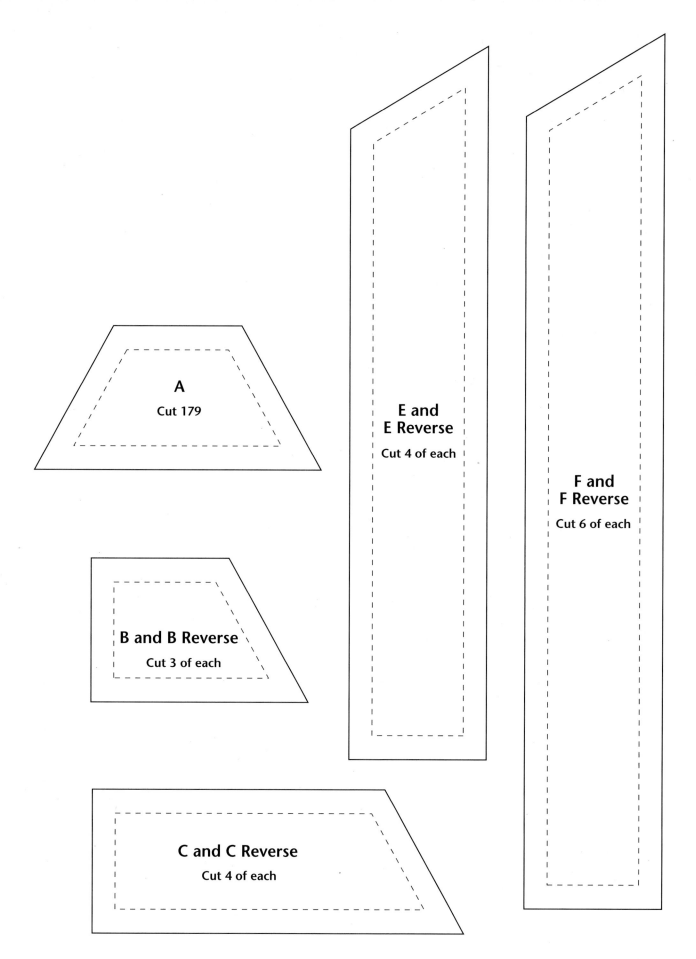

A

Cut 179

**E and
E Reverse**

Cut 4 of each

**F and
F Reverse**

Cut 6 of each

B and B Reverse

Cut 3 of each

C and C Reverse

Cut 4 of each

Agnes the Angel

Agnes the Angel would love to be appointed guardian of your Christmas festivities, and you can create her in just an hour or two. She has a genuine folk art appeal that comes from a profusion of shiny golden curls and a muslin gown embellished with hand-painted stripes and tiny gilt beads. With her whimsical expression and exuberantly outstretched arms, Agnes is guaranteed to delight everyone she meets.

❊ *Size: Agnes is 14 inches tall.*

Fabric Requirements

* 16 × 24-inch piece of muslin for the face, body, hair, and arms
* 14 × 20-inch piece of black-and-gold print for the feet and star

Other Supplies

* 100 percent cotton sewing thread to match each fabric
* Twenty-four 4-mm gold beads
* 6-inch length of ⅜-inch gold braid or trim
* 4-inch length of gold thread
* Fine-point black and gold permanent markers
* Graphite pencil
* Red colored pencil for the cheeks and lips
* Metallic gold acrylic paint
* Small paintbrush
* Fabric draping and stiffening solution
* Metallic gold spray paint
* Fabric glue
* 16-ounce bag of polyester fiberfill
* 4 cups of plastic pellets
* Tracing paper

Instructions

Note: All pattern pieces include ¼-inch seam allowances.

Cutting

1. Trace the patterns on pages 178–181 onto tracing paper, transferring all marks, and cut out the patterns.

2. Place the body pattern on the muslin and use the graphite pencil to draw around it, transferring all marks. Mark the stripes with the gold marker. Mark the eyes, eyebrows, nose, and mouth with the black marker. Shade the cheeks and lips with red pencil. Cut out the front of the body.

3. Place the body pattern on the muslin and draw around it a second time, transferring all marks and omitting the facial features. Mark the stripes with gold marker. Cut out the back body.

4. Draw two arms on the muslin, marking the stripes with gold marker. Reverse the pattern and draw two more arms. Cut them out.

5. Fold the square of black-and-gold fabric in half lengthwise, right sides together, and place the star

pattern on the fold of the fabric, as shown in **Diagram 1.** Draw another star pattern on the fold, creating a second star. Cut out both stars.

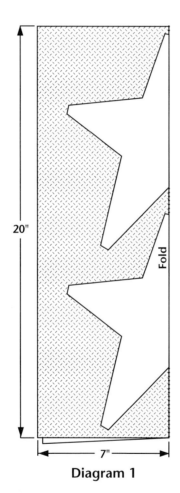

Diagram 1

6. Position the foot pattern on the remaining folded black-and-gold fabric. Draw two foot patterns and cut out four feet.

Assembling the Angel

1. Place the front and back body pieces right sides together and stitch around the body, leaving an opening on the side and the bottom, as shown in **Diagram 2** and on the

pattern. Do not turn the body right side out at this time.

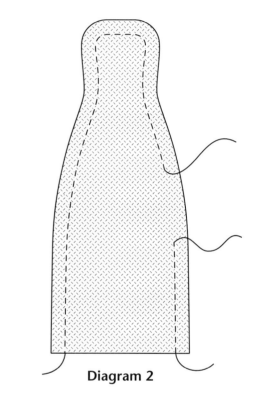

Diagram 2

2. With right sides together, stitch around each matched pair of feet, leaving the tops open, as indicated on the pattern. Turn the feet right side out, lightly stuff them with polyester fiberfill, and stitch across the top opening. Align the raw edges of the feet with the raw edges of the bottom of the back body piece. With the feet sandwiched between the front and back body pieces, stitch across the bottom of the body pieces, catching the feet in the seam.

3. To make the gussets on each side of the body, measure in 1 inch from the bottom corner point of the body. Sew across the bottom corner seam at a 90-degree angle, as shown in **Diagram 3.**

4. Turn the body right side out through the side opening. Stuff the top half of the body firmly with polyester fiberfill. Fill the bottom half of the body with plastic pellets. Whipstitch the opening closed and tack the feet to the body front so they face forward when the doll is standing.

5. Fill in the marked zigzag design at the bottom of the body using the brush and metallic gold paint.

6. Place two arm pieces right sides together and stitch around the arm, leaving the top open for turning. Turn under ¼ inch along the top edge and baste. Repeat to make the second arm. Turn the arms right side out and stuff them firmly with polyester fiberfill. With a strip of masking tape, outline the cuffs, as shown on the arm pattern. Paint the cuffs with metallic gold paint and allow the paint to dry.

7. Pin the arms to the body, placing them along the side seams according to the markings on the body pattern piece. Slip stitch the arms to the body, adding more stuffing at the top of each arm if necessary.

8. Place the two stars right sides together and stitch around the outside edges. Carefully cut a 2-inch slit in the center of one of the star pieces. Clip the inner corners and

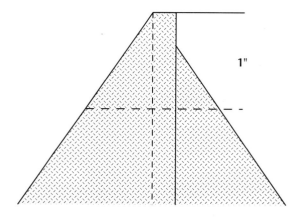

Diagram 3

outer points of the star and turn the star right side out through this slit. Stuff the points of the star firmly with polyester fiberfill, then stuff the remainder of the star. Slip stitch the opening closed.

Bits 'n' Pieces

Try This Variation: Agnes would make a great country-style topper for a Christmas tree. Start by filling the body with polyester fiberfill. Allow the feet to point down, rather than stitching them to the body to make them face forward. Then, to hold the angel in place on the top of a Christmas tree, make a small "pocket" for the back of the body, following the directions below.

1. Cut a 4½ × 7-inch strip of muslin for the pocket. Turn under a ¼-inch hem twice on all four sides of the strip. Stitch the hem in place.

2. Slip stitch the sides and top to the back of the body, leaving the bottom open for the tree branch.

9. Pin the star to the angel so that the slit faces the back body piece. At the center point of the star, tack through the star and into the back of the angel twice.

Making the Hair

1. Cut twelve ¼ × 9-inch strips from the remaining piece of muslin.

2. Following the manufacturer's instructions, pour a cup of draping and stiffening solution into a plastic bag and add one muslin strip. Squeeze the solution through the fabric and take it out of the bag, removing excess solution with your fingertips. Repeat with the other 11 strips.

3. Lay the strips out in twisted fashion on a piece of waxed paper to dry. Remove the strips from waxed paper when they are dry.

4. Place the strips on newspaper, coat them with metallic gold spray paint, and allow the paint to dry.

5. Glue the strips randomly to the top and back of the head, forming curls.

Finishing

1. Glue the 6-inch length of gold braid or trim around the neck.

2. Sew gold beads at each point of the painted gold zigzag at the bottom of the body.

3. Using a ruler and a pencil, measure and mark fourteen ½-inch intervals along the center stripe of the front of the body and sew on 14 gold beads.

4. Form the 4-inch length of gold thread into a loop and sew it to the back of the wings to display Agnes on a wall.

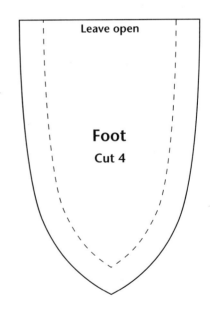

Leave open

Foot

Cut 4

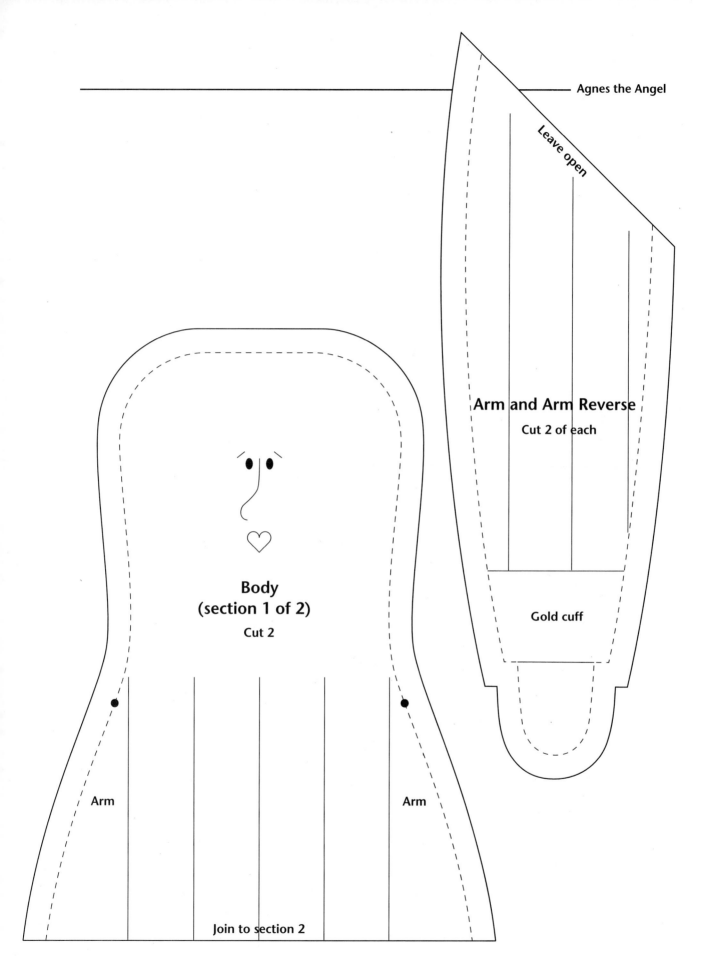

Agnes the Angel

Leave open

Arm and Arm Reverse

Cut 2 of each

Gold cuff

**Body
(section 1 of 2)**

Cut 2

Arm

Arm

Join to section 2

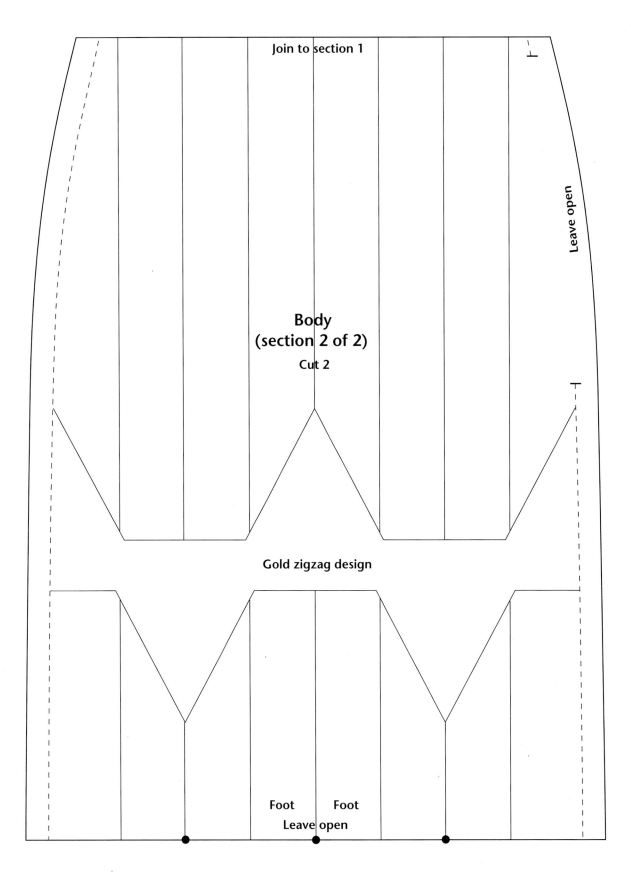

Join to section 1

Leave open

Body
(section 2 of 2)
Cut 2

Gold zigzag design

Foot   Foot

Leave open

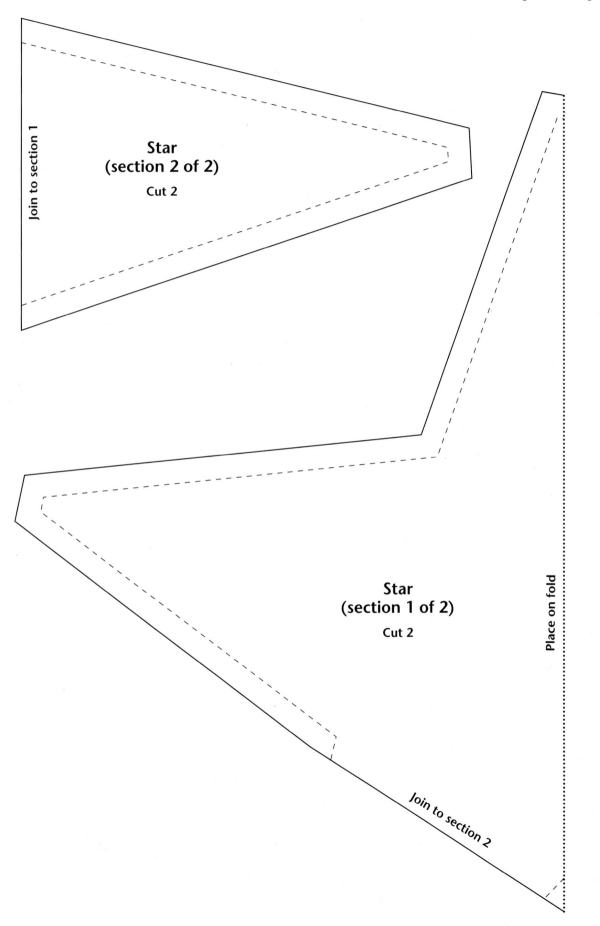

Star
(section 2 of 2)

Cut 2

Join to section 1

Star
(section 1 of 2)

Cut 2

Join to section 2

Place on fold

Elmo the Elf

You can almost hear the hum of the busy workshop where Elmo waits eagerly for Santa's call. He'll soon join the other elves in making toys for all good girls and boys.

❈ *Size: Elmo is 16 inches long and approximately 6 inches high when sitting.*

Fabric Requirements

* 18 × 20-inch piece of dark red print for the body, legs, and arms
* 12-inch square of muslin for the head and hands
* 4 × 8-inch piece of black solid for the shoes
* 10-inch square of medium rose solid for the collar
* 9 × 12-inch piece of medium red print for the hat
* 5 × 8½-inch piece of dark floral print for the tie

Other Supplies

* Sewing threads to match fabrics
* 2 cups of plastic pellets
* Polyester fiberfill
* 1 skein each of rose and black-brown embroidery floss
* Embroidery needle
* 1-inch black pom-pom for the hat
* Powder blusher
* 3-inch length of braided wool roving for the hair
* Two ⅜-inch dark red buttons for the body
* Tracing paper
* Pencil for marking fabric or tracing paper
* Fabric glue

Instructions

Cutting

Note: All pattern pieces include ¼-inch seam allowances.

1. Trace the pattern pieces on pages 187–191 onto tracing paper, transferring all markings. Cut out the patterns.

2. Place the body pattern on the wrong side of the dark red print and mark around it. Repeat for a second body piece and cut out both.

3. From the same dark red print, cut two 3½ × 10-inch strips for the legs and two 2½ × 10-inch strips for the arms. For information about using a rotary cutter, see page 259 in the "General Instructions."

4. Fold the muslin in half with right sides together. Place the head pattern on the muslin and mark around the pattern with a pencil. Cut out two head pieces and mark the facial features on the right side of one head. Mark and cut two hands from the remaining muslin.

5. Fold the black fabric in half lengthwise with right sides together, and place the shoe pattern on the fabric. Mark and cut out two shoes.

6. Fold the medium rose fabric in half with right sides together. Place the fold line of the back collar pattern along the fold of the fabric and mark around the pattern. Place the front collar pattern on the fabric and mark around it. Move the front collar pattern and draw around it again. Cut out one back collar and four front collar.

7. Fold the medium red print fabric in half lengthwise with right sides together. Place the hat pattern on the fabric and mark around it. Cut out two hats.

8. Fold the floral print fabric in half lengthwise with right sides together. Place the tie pattern on the fabric, draw around it once, and cut out two ties.

Assembling Elmo

THE COLLAR, HEAD, AND BODY

1. To make the front collar, place a pair of front collar pieces right sides together. Sew around two sides, leaving the neck and shoulder seams unstitched. Turn the front collar right side out and press. Repeat to make a second front collar.

2. Place each front collar on the right side of the front body, as shown in **Diagram 1.** With right sides together, pin the neck of the front head to the neck of the front body, with the front collar pieces sandwiched between them. Sew the body, collar, and head pieces together. Press the seams and collar toward the body.

3. With wrong sides together, fold the back collar piece in half lengthwise and press. With right sides

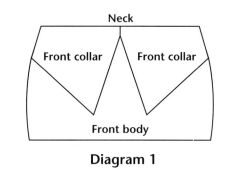

Diagram 1

together, place the long raw edges of the back collar at the neck edge of the back body.

4. With right sides together, pin the neck edge of the back head to the back body so that the back collar is sandwiched between them. With all raw edges aligned, sew the three pieces together at the neck edge. Press the seams and collar toward the body.

5. On the right side of the face, satin stitch the nose using three strands of rose embroidery floss. Embroider French knots for the eyes using three strands of black-brown floss. Using two strands of black-brown floss, embroider a V-shaped mouth with two straight stitches. Refer to the section on embroidery techniques on pages 273–275 in the "General Instructions" for instructions on satin stitching, straight stitching, and making French knots.

6. Sew two dark red buttons to the center of the front of the body according to the markings on the pattern.

THE HANDS, ARMS, SHOES, AND LEGS

1. Pin the short end of one muslin hand piece to the short end of one dark red arm strip, right sides together. Sew along that edge and press the seam toward the dark fabric. Repeat for the second arm.

2. Fold one arm/hand piece in half lengthwise with right sides together. Sew across the short edge of the hand and down the side of the entire arm, leaving the other short end of the arm unstitched. Repeat to make the second arm. Turn the arms right side out.

3. Pin the straight edge of one black shoe piece to the short end of one dark red leg strip, right sides together. Sew along that edge and press the seam toward the shoe piece. Repeat for the second leg. With right sides together, begin at the toe and sew along the length of the shoe and leg. Don't stitch across the short straight end of the leg. Repeat for the second leg.

4. Using either a wooden spoon handle or a chopstick, lightly stuff polyester fiberfill into the shoes of both legs. Tie an overhand knot at the ankle of each leg. Continue to stuff the remainder of both legs lightly, leaving ½ inch unstuffed at the top of each leg. With the leg seam running straight up the center of the back of each leg, sew across the legs 2½ inches above the ankle knot to create a knee. Baste across the top of both legs.

5. Lightly stuff the hands on both arms and tie an overhand knot at the wrist. Continue to lightly stuff the remainder of both arms, leaving 3 inches unstuffed at the top. Tie an overhand knot with the unstuffed end, leaving approximately 1 inch of each arm unknotted to insert into the seam of the body.

Sewing

1. With right sides together, center and pin the top of each leg to the bottom of the front body, as indicated by the large placement dots on the front body. Sew across the top of the legs to secure them, as shown in **Diagram 2.** Position the arms on the front body at the large placement dots. Sew across the top of the arms to secure them, as shown.

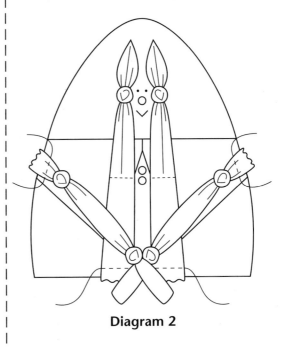

Diagram 2

2. With right sides together, align the back body and the front body,

Bits 'n' Pieces

Try This Variation: You can also use the instructions for Elmo to make a great Santa Claus with the following minor changes:

1. Use red fabrics of your choice for the clothing. Omit the fabric collar pieces and the buttons. Instead, create "fur" trim with 1-inch-wide strips of cotton batting. Sew the batting around the cuffs, down the center of the body, and around the top and bottom edges of the body.

2. Make the legs 3 inches shorter and the shoes 3 inches longer for boots. Sew a 1-inch-wide strip of batting at the top of each boot before you sew the seam along the length of the boot and leg. Knot the boot at the ankle after stuffing only the foot.

3. Sew a 1-inch-wide strip of batting above each hand before you sew the seam along the length of the arms.

4. Make hair and a beard from white braided roving and glue the roving to the head and face, fluffing it out as desired.

5. Trim the bottom of the hat with a 1-inch-wide strip of batting and hand sew the hat to the top of the head.

6. Referring to the diagram below, twist some brass wire into a pair of tiny round spectacles and hand sew them to the face above the nose.

7. Sew around three sides of two 6-inch squares of black fabric, then sew a line of gathering stitches around the top. Fill the bag with polyester fiberfill and insert a few small toys in the top of the bag. Tighten the thread around the toys.

with the arms and legs sandwiched between the two body pieces. Starting at one of the marks at the bottom of the body, sew around the sides and the top of the head, leaving a portion at the bottom of the body open between the marks. Take care to catch only the tops of the arms in the side seams. Turn the body right side out through the opening.

3. Stuff the head and the upper part of the body with polyester fiberfill and fill the lower part of the body with about 2 cups of plastic pellets. Slip stitch the bottom of the body closed.

THE HAT AND TIE

1. With the right sides of the hat pieces together, sew around the sides, leaving the bottom edge unstitched. Turn under and sew a ¼-inch hem at the bottom of the hat. Repeat to create a finished edge. Turn the hat right side out and press. Sew the pom-pom to the tip of the hat.

2. Place the two halves of the floral print tie right sides together. Starting at one of the marks on one long side, sew around the tie, ending at the second mark. Turn the tie right side out through the opening and stitch the opening closed by hand. Press the tie flat.

3. Tie an overhand knot in the center of the tie and tack the knot to the body between collar points at the neck.

Finishing

1. To finish the facial features, apply a smudge of powder blusher to each cheek.

2. Following the manufacturer's instructions, unravel the roving and glue it randomly over the top of the head for hair.

3. Whipstitch the hat to the top of Elmo's head, allowing the fluffy ends of his hair to show.

4. Referring to **Diagram 3,** fold each hand in half and tack it into a fist shape. Sew the fists together as if they are clasped.

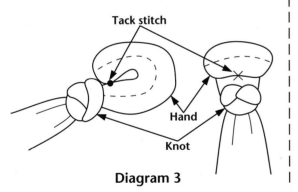

Diagram 3

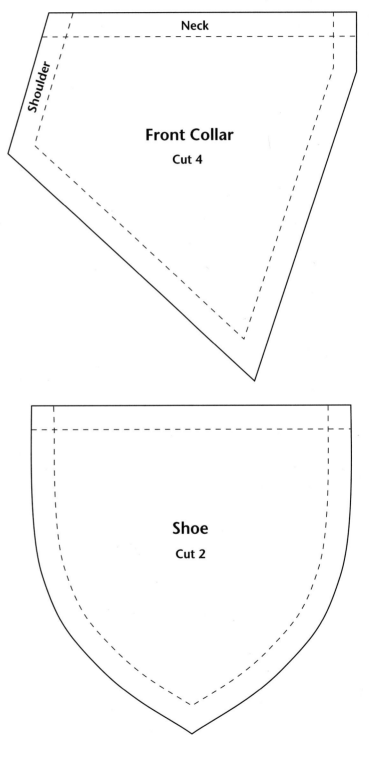

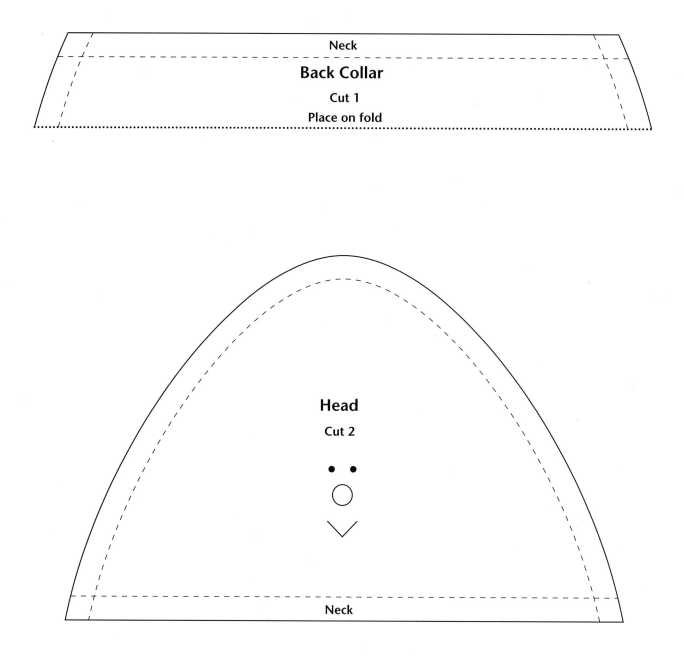

Neck

Back Collar

Cut 1

Place on fold

Head

Cut 2

Neck

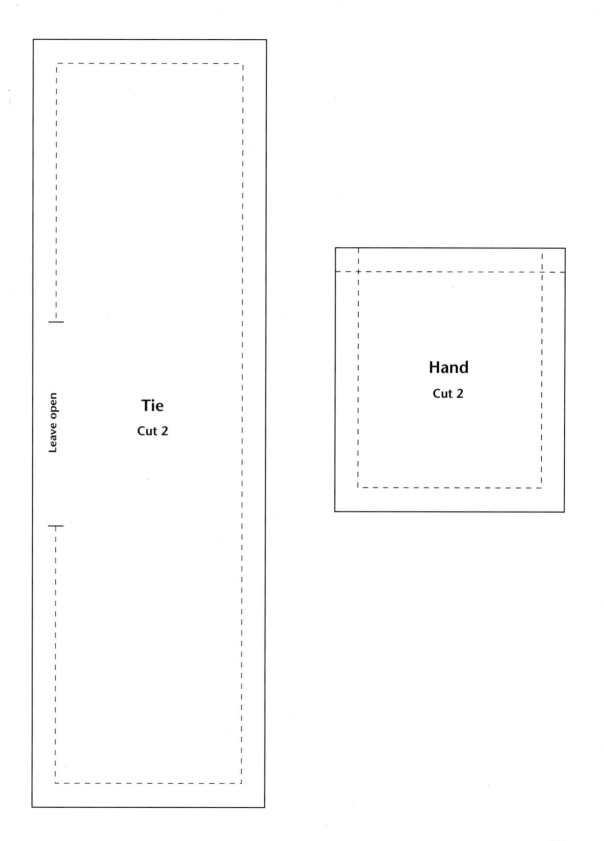

Leave open

Tie

Cut 2

Hand

Cut 2

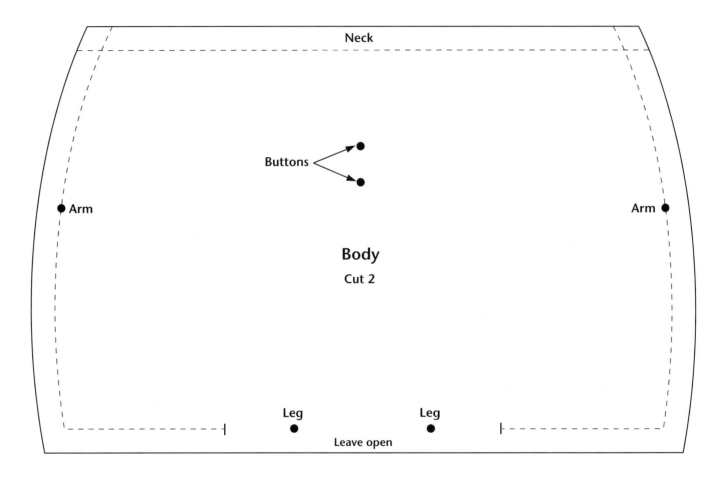

Neck

Buttons

Arm
Arm

Body

Cut 2

Leg
Leg

Leave open

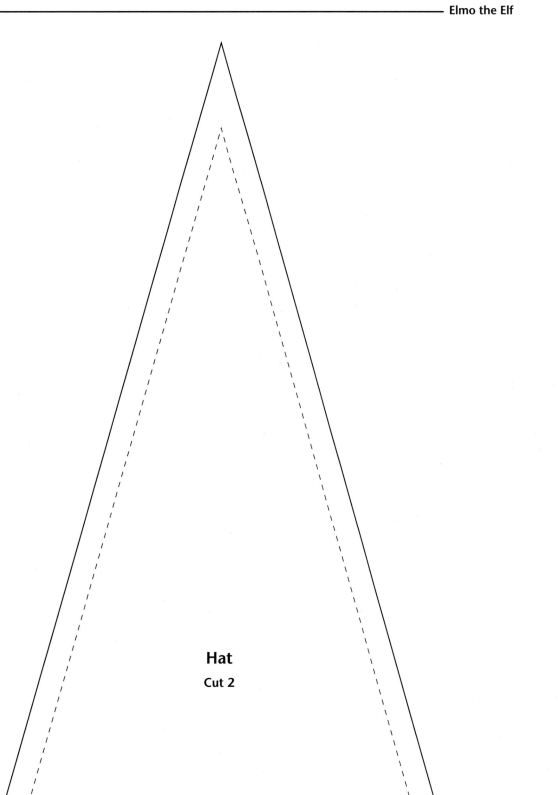

Hat

Cut 2

Christmas Stockings

Even Santa might put these gingerbread boy and girl stockings on his Christmas wish list. Enjoy an afternoon of sewing, sipping hot cocoa, and listening to Christmas carols while you turn some fuzzy fleece and warm wool flannel into a great gift for any little boy or girl.

❊ *Size: The stockings are approximately 16 inches long.*

Fabric Requirements
(for two stockings)

* ½ yard of red fleece for the stockings
* ½ yard of black fleece for the cuffs
* 12-inch square of camel wool flannel for the gingerbread figures
* 12-inch square of red plaid flannel for patchwork
* 12-inch square of green plaid flannel for patchwork
* 12-inch square of blue plaid flannel for patchwork

Other Supplies

* ½ yard of ¼-inch blue rickrack for the gingerbread boy
* ½ yard of ¼-inch pink rickrack for the gingerbread girl
* ¼ yard of ⁷⁄₁₆-inch black grosgrain ribbon for the hanging loops
* One skein of black pearl cotton for the noses and eyelashes
* One skein of red pearl cotton for the mouths
* Four ¼-inch black buttons for the eyes
* Four ½-inch blue buttons for the gingerbread boy
* Two ½-inch green buttons for the gingerbread girl
* ⅓ yard of fusible webbing
* Sewing thread to match fabrics
* Embroidery needle
* Tracing paper or template plastic
* Fine-point black permanent marker
* Pencil or removable marker for tracing templates onto fabric
* Fabric glue
* Transparent tape

Instructions

Note: Sew all seams with a ¼-inch seam allowance. Place each fabric right side up when cutting unless specified otherwise.

Cutting

1. Trace the patterns on pages 199–207 onto template plastic or tracing paper, transferring all markings, and cut out the templates.

2. To make the complete stocking pattern, tape together the three stocking pieces, matching the placement lines indicated.

3. To make the complete cuff pattern, tape together the two cuff pieces, matching the placement lines indicated.

4. From the red fleece, cut two stockings and two reversed stockings.

5. Fold the black fleece lengthwise. Place the cuff on the fold of the fabric and cut out one cuff. Repeat for a second cuff.

6. Iron a 12-inch square of fusible webbing onto the wrong side of the 12-inch square of camel wool flannel. Trace one gingerbread boy and one gingerbread girl onto the paper side of the fusible webbing. Cut out the gingerbread boy and girl.

7. From the red plaid, cut two each of A and F.

8. From the green plaid, cut two each of the B, D, and G shapes.

9. From the blue plaid, cut two each of the C and E shapes.

10. From the blue rickrack, cut four 2-inch lengths for the gingerbread boy's arm and leg trim. Cut one 4½-inch length for the gingerbread boy's waist trim. Cut the same number of pieces from pink rickrack for the gingerbread girl's arm, leg, and waist trim.

11. From the black grosgrain ribbon, cut two 4½-inch lengths for the hanging loops.

Sewing the Patchwork Together

1. With right sides together, sew the bottom edge of one A shape to the top edge of one B shape, as shown in **Diagram 1.** Press this seam open.

2. With right sides together, sew the bottom edge of one C shape to the top edge of one D shape, as shown in **Diagram 1.** Press this seam open.

3. With right sides together, sew the bottom edge of one D shape to the top edge of one E shape, as shown in **Diagram 1.** Press this seam open.

4. With right sides together, sew the A/B unit to the C/D/E unit, as shown in **Diagram 2.** Press this seam open.

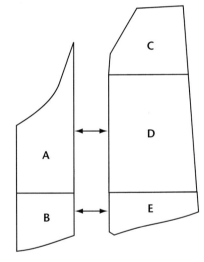

Diagram 2

5. With right sides together, sew one F shape to C/D/E, starting at the top of C and stopping at the, as shown in **Diagram 3** on the opposite page. Press this seam open.

6. With right sides together, sew one G shape to F, as shown in **Diagram 4** on the opposite page. Press this seam open.

7. Repeat Steps 1 through 6 for the second stocking.

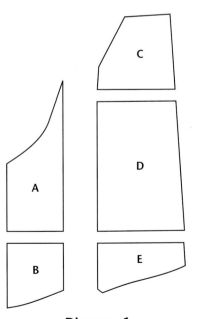

Diagram 1

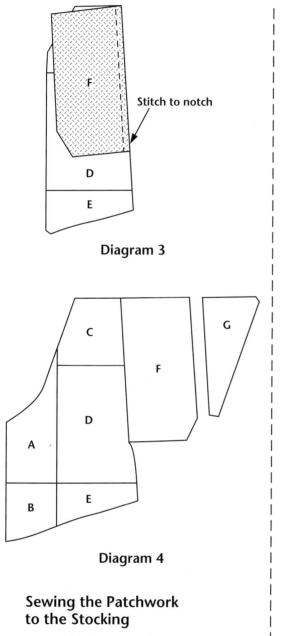

Diagram 3

Diagram 4

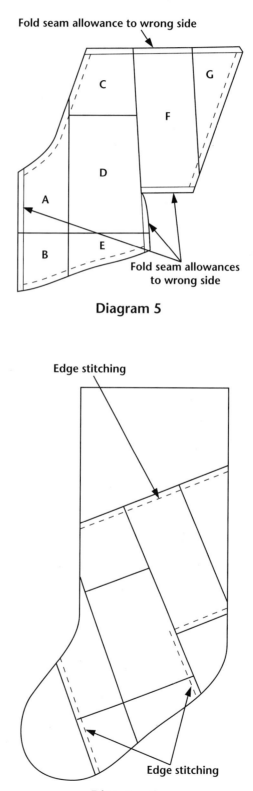

Fold seam allowance to wrong side

Diagram 5

Fold seam allowances
to wrong side

Edge stitching

Edge stitching

Diagram 6

Sewing the Patchwork to the Stocking

1. Fold the outer seam allowances to the wrong side, as shown in **Diagram 5,** and press them in place.

2. Pin the wrong side of the patchwork unit onto the right side of the stocking front. Edge stitch along the indicated lines, as shown in **Diagram 6.**

Bits 'n' Pieces

Try This Variation: To personalize Christmas stockings, use your favorite cookie cutter shapes instead of gingerbread figures. Simply trace a cookie cutter shape onto the paper side of a piece of fusible webbing and iron the webbing onto a colorful piece of felt. Cut out the shape and decorate it with gold and silver sequins, red and green braided trim, or a bevy of beads befitting the season. When you've completed the stocking, use dimensional fabric paint to write the name of a family member on the cuff.

Making the Gingerbread Boy and the Gingerbread Girl

1. Referring to the photograph on page 193, embroider the nose on each gingerbread figure with black pearl cotton using a satin stitch. Embroider eyelashes on the gingerbread girl using an outline stitch.

2. Referring to the same photograph, embroider the mouth on each gingerbread figure with red pearl cotton using an outline stitch. For more information on embroidery, see pages 273–275 in the "General Instructions."

3. Sew the black buttons for the eyes on the face of each gingerbread figure.

4. Sew the blue buttons on the front of the gingerbread boy, as indicated on the pattern.

5. Sew the green buttons on the front of the gingerbread girl, as indicated on the pattern.

6. Referring to **Diagram 7** on the opposite page, use fabric glue to secure the rickrack to the front of the gingerbread boy and girl along the placement lines on the patterns. Allow ¼ inch of rickrack to extend beyond the edges of the figures.

7. Remove the paper backing from each gingerbread figure. Fold and glue the ends of the rickrack to the wrong side of the gingerbread figures to finish the edges. Referring to **Diagram 8** on the opposite page, iron the gingerbread boy on the front of one stocking ⅛ inch in from the edge. Repeat for the gingerbread girl and the other stocking. Top-stitch around both.

Sewing the Stocking and the Cuff Together

1. With right sides together, pin one stocking front to one stocking back. Sew them together, leaving the top open. Referring to **Diagram 9** on the opposite page, clip several small V-shapes in the stocking curves to make the stocking lie flat when turned. Turn the stocking right side out and press.

2. Make a loop from a piece of the black grosgrain ribbon. Pin and baste the loop to the right side of the cuff at the notch, as shown in **Diagram 10** on page 198.

3. As shown in **Diagram 11** on page 198, fold the cuff with right sides together so that the ribbon

Diagram 7

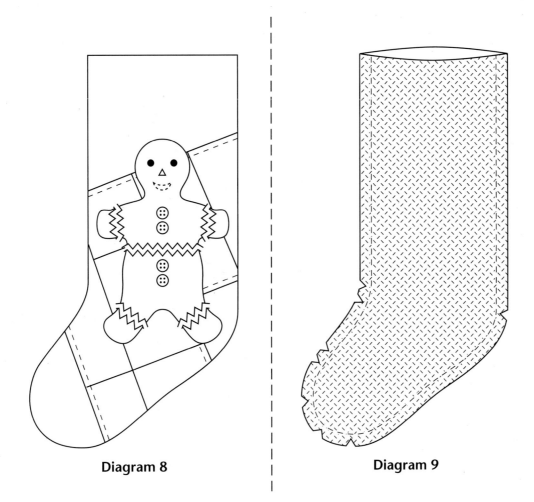

Diagram 8

Diagram 9

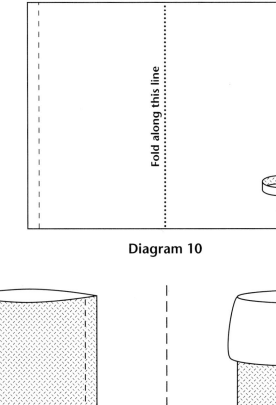

Diagram 10

Diagram 11

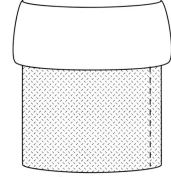

Diagram 12

loop is on the inside. Sew the short ends of the cuff together and press this seam open.

4. Referring to **Diagram 12,** fold the cuff in half, as you would fold a sock cuff. The right side of the fabric will be visible on both the inside and outside of the cuff.

5. With the stocking right side out, place the folded cuff inside the stocking, matching the raw edges. Check to make sure that the ribbon loop is sandwiched between the cuff and the inside of the stocking. Pin the cuff and the stocking together along the upper edge, as shown in **Diagram 13** on the opposite page. Sew the cuff to the stocking, easing the cuff as necessary.

6. Pull out the cuff and fold it down 4 inches over the right side of the stocking.

7. Repeat Steps 1 through 6 for the second stocking.

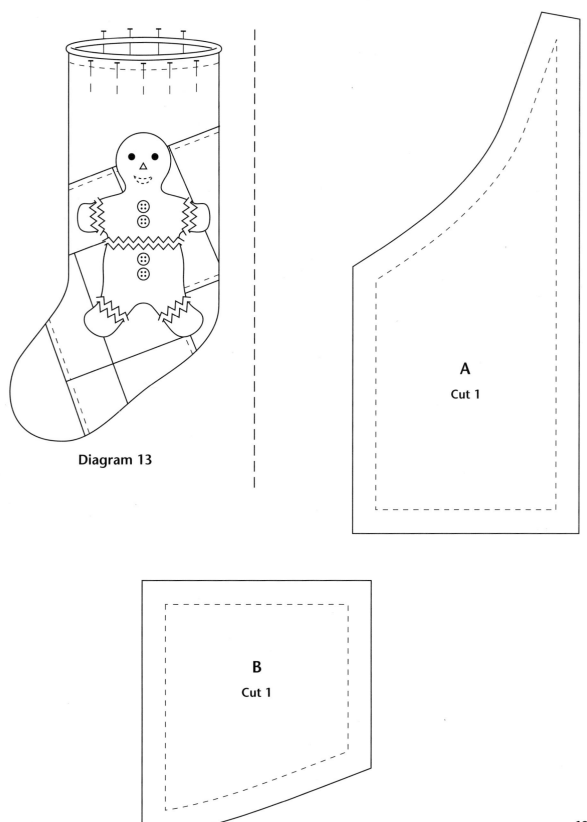

Diagram 13

A
Cut 1

B
Cut 1

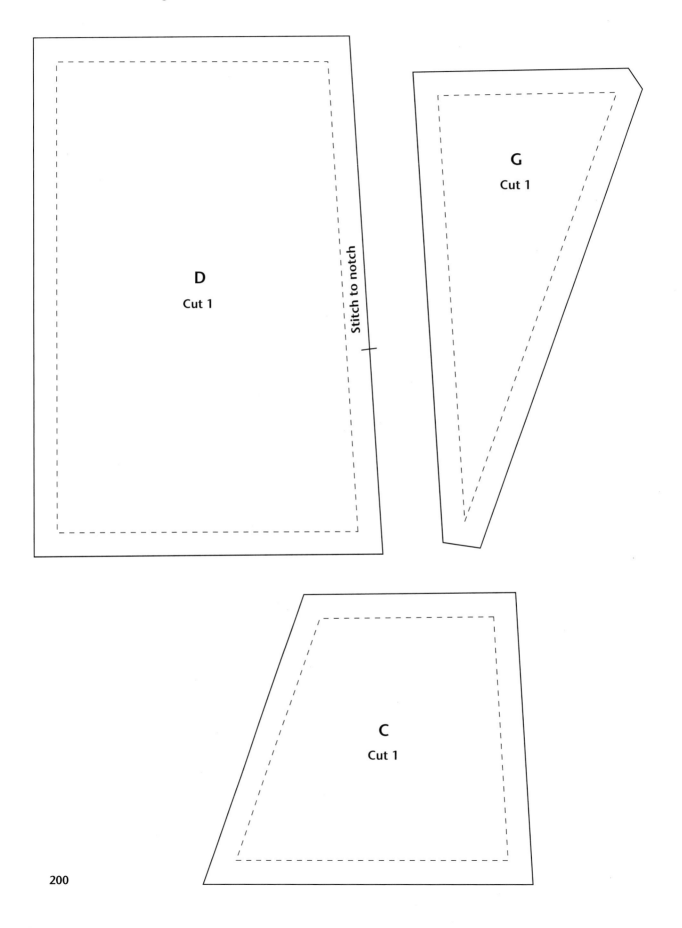

D

Cut 1

Stitch to notch

G

Cut 1

C

Cut 1

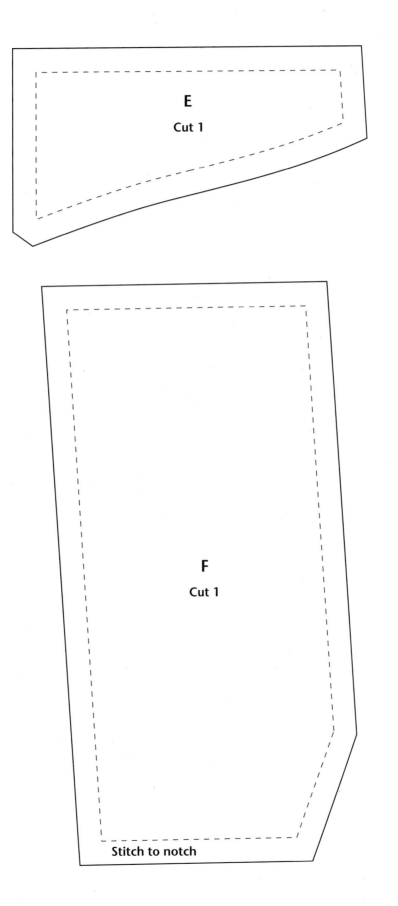

E
Cut 1

F
Cut 1

Stitch to notch

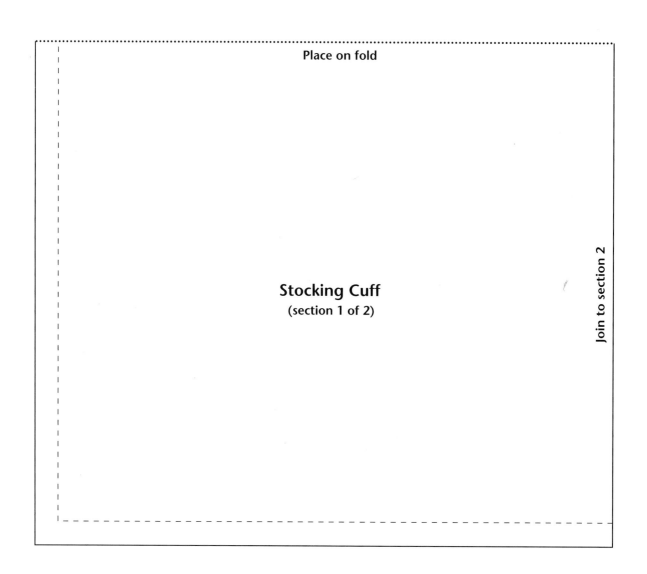

Place on fold

Stocking Cuff

(section 1 of 2)

Join to section 2

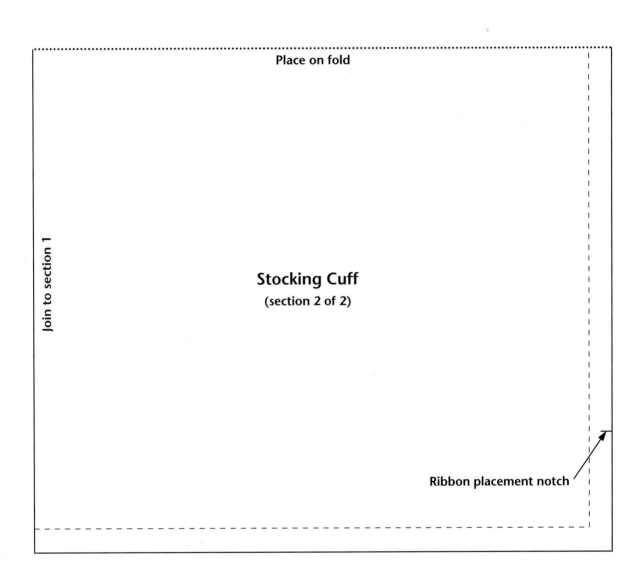

Place on fold

Join to section 1

Stocking Cuff

(section 2 of 2)

Ribbon placement notch

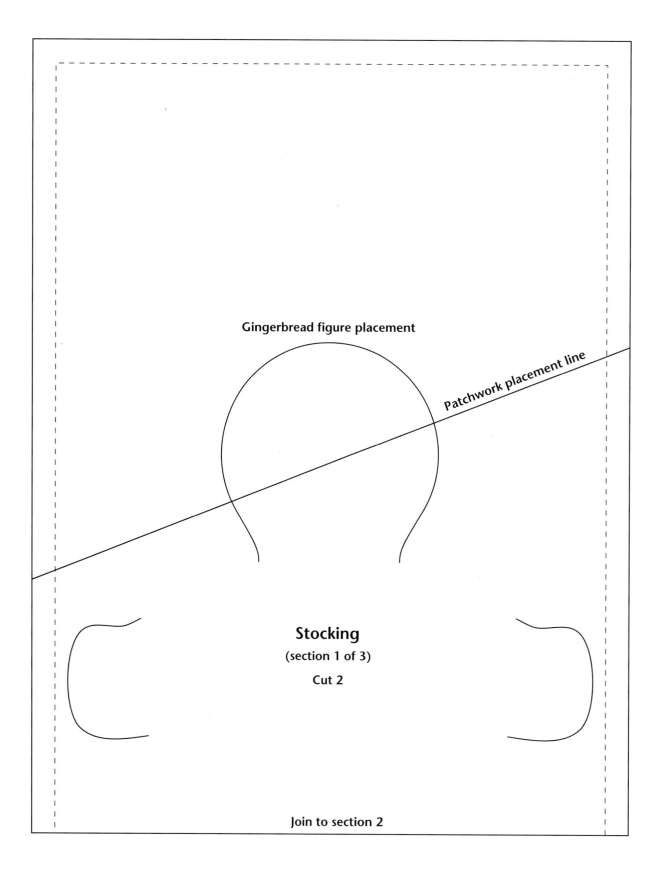

Gingerbread figure placement

Patchwork placement line

Stocking

(section 1 of 3)

Cut 2

Join to section 2

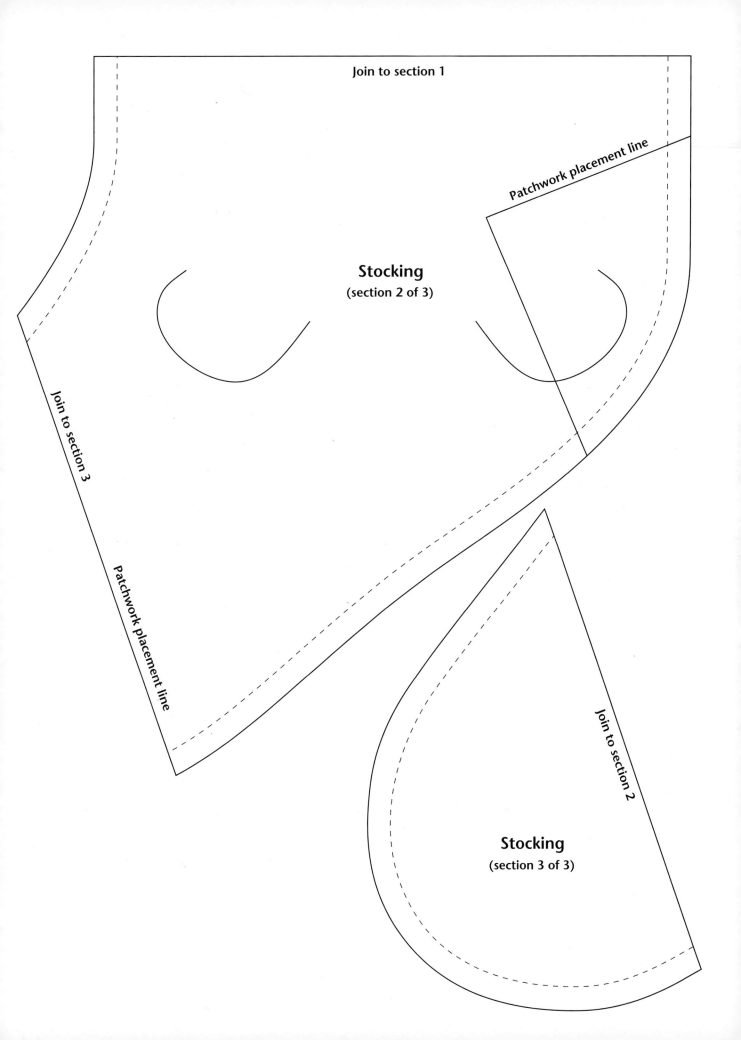

Join to section 1

Patchwork placement line

Stocking
(section 2 of 3)

Join to section 3

Patchwork placement line

Join to section 2

Stocking
(section 3 of 3)

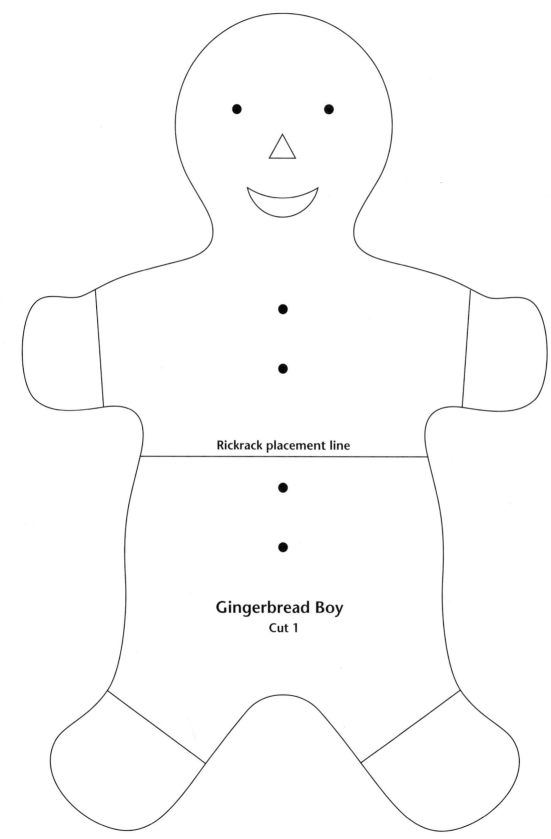

Rickrack placement line

Gingerbread Boy
Cut 1

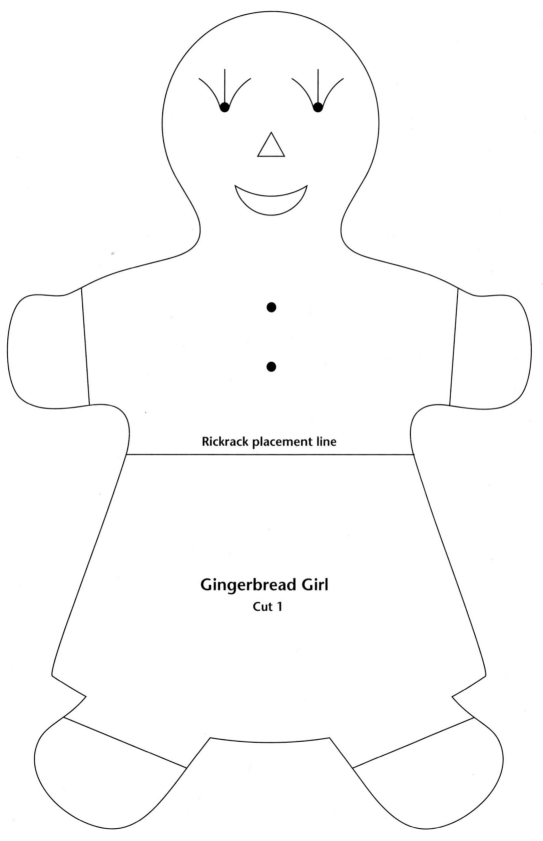

Rickrack placement line

Gingerbread Girl
Cut 1

Holidays
and Special
Occasions

- ★ **Easter Basket Pillow**
- ★ **Folk Art Flag Wallhanging**
- ★ **Halloween Trick-or-Treat Bag**
- ★ **Holiday Kitchen Magnets**
- ★ **Crazy Patchwork Photograph Album Cover**
- ★ **Lace Patchwork Ring Bearer's Pillow**

Easter Basket Pillow

This scrappy holiday pillow has a pieced basket filled with brightly colored machine appliquéd Easter eggs. For a country-style look that you can display year-round, choose background and border colors that go with your decor.

★ *Size: Body of pillow is approximately 16 inches square. Ruffle is 3 inches wide.*

Fabric Requirements

★ ⅛ yard of medium tan print for the basket
★ ¼ yard of medium brown print for the basket and handle
★ ⅛ yard of medium green print for the eggs and corner squares
★ ¼ yard of dark blue print for the eggs and piping
★ ¼ yard of medium aqua print for the piping and one egg
★ ¼ yard of light multicolored print for the bow and one egg
★ ⅜ yard of pale yellow solid for the background
★ 1½ yards of medium pink print for the border strips, pillow back, ruffle, and one egg
★ ⅝ yard of muslin for the pillow form

Other Supplies

★ 17-inch square of fusible interfacing
★ 17-inch square of freezer paper
★ 17-inch square of fleece
★ ½ yard of fusible webbing
★ Sewing threads to match fabrics
★ 6 yards of ⅛-inch-diameter cording for piping
★ Polyester fiberfill
★ Template plastic

★ Fine-point black permanent marker
★ Pencil or removable marker for tracing templates on fabric

Instructions

Note: Patterns include ¼-inch seam allowances, except for the eggs and basket handle, which are machine appliquéd onto the background fabric. When making the pillow, use ½-inch seam allowances for the piping, pillow back, and ruffle. If you hand appliqué the egg and handle, add ⅛-inch seam allowances to the outside edges as you cut them out.

Cutting

1. Trace the pattern pieces on pages 217–219 onto template plastic, transferring all markings, and cut out the templates.

2. From the tan print, cut three C squares and one B triangle.

3. From the brown print, cut two C squares, four B triangles, and one E piece.

4. Iron a 6 × 12-inch piece of fusible webbing onto the wrong side

of a piece of brown print. Trace around the handle template on the right side of the fabric and cut out one basket handle.

5. From the pink print, cut four $2\frac{3}{4} \times 12\frac{1}{2}$-inch border strips, six $4\frac{1}{2} \times 44$-inch strips for the ruffle, and a 17-inch square of fabric for the pillow back.

6. Iron a 5-inch square of fusible webbing onto the wrong side of a piece of pink print. Trace and cut out one half-egg piece.

7. From the green print, cut four F corner squares.

8. Iron a 4×8-inch piece of fusible webbing onto the wrong side of a piece of green print. Trace and cut out two quarter-egg pieces.

9. Iron a 4×8-inch piece of fusible webbing onto the wrong side of a piece of blue print. Trace and cut out two half-egg pieces.

10. From the remaining blue print, cut enough 2-inch bias strips to piece a 2-yard strip for covering the cording at the inner edge of the ruffle.

11. From the aqua print, cut enough 2-inch-wide bias strips to piece a $3\frac{7}{8}$-yard strip for covering the cording at the outer edge of the ruffle.

12. Iron a 5-inch square of fusible webbing onto the wrong side of a piece of aqua print. Trace and cut out one full-egg piece.

13. From the multicolored print, cut one 5×30-inch strip for the bow.

14. Iron a 5-inch square of fusible webbing onto the wrong side of a piece of multicolored print. Trace and cut out one quarter-egg piece.

15. From the yellow, cut one $12\frac{7}{8}$-inch square, then cut it in half diagonally. You'll use one triangle for the top half of the basket block; save the other half for a future scrap project. From the remaining fabric, cut one A triangle, one D piece, and one D reverse piece.

16. From the muslin, cut two 20-inch squares for the pillow form.

Piecing the Basket

Medium   Dark

Fabric Key

1. Referring to **Diagram 1**, stitch one brown B triangle to one tan C square to make Strip 1. To make Strip 2, stitch together one tan C square, one brown C square, and one brown B triangle. Sew Strips 1 and 2 together, matching seams. Stitch one brown B triangle to the adjacent side of Strip 1.

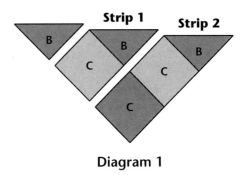

Diagram 1

2. Referring to **Diagram 2**, stitch the D piece to the B/C unit.

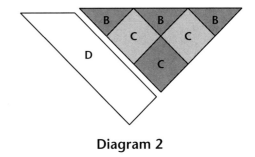

Diagram 2

3. Stitch one tan B triangle and the brown E piece together. Referring to **Diagram 3,** stitch the A triangle to the E piece.

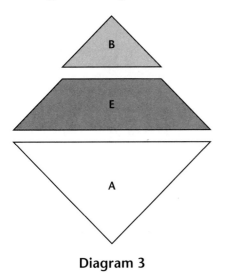

Diagram 3

4. To make Strip 3, stitch one brown C square, one tan C square, and one brown B triangle together. As shown in **Diagram 4,** stitch Strip 3 to the D reverse piece.

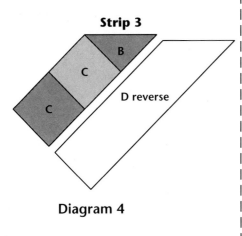

Strip 3

Diagram 4

5. Referring to **Diagram 5,** stitch the B/E/A unit to the B/C/D reverse unit.

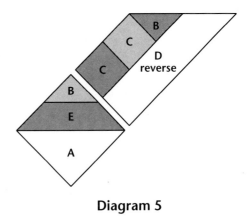

Diagram 5

6. Referring to **Diagram 6,** stitch the unit in **Diagram 2** to the unit in **Diagram 5,** forming the basket.

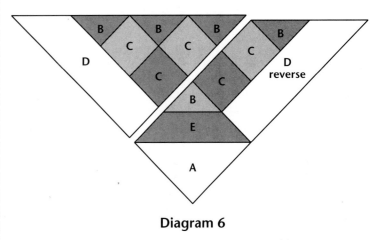

Diagram 6

Appliquéing the Basket Handle and the Eggs

1. Remove the paper from the back of the basket handle, full-egg, quarter-egg, and half-egg pieces to expose the fusible webbing. Referring to **Diagram 7** on page 214, center the basket handle on the right side of the large yellow triangle, positioning the short ends of the handle into the seam allowance on

213

the long side of the triangle. Fuse the handle in position. Arrange and fuse the eggs to the large yellow triangle, making sure to fuse the lower edges of the eggs into the seam allowance.

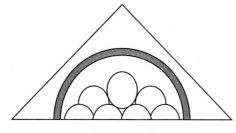

Diagram 7

2. Fuse a piece of freezer paper to the wrong side of the large yellow triangle behind the appliqués. Matching the top thread in your machine to each of the fabrics, satin stitch around each egg and along both sides of the handle. After you have appliquéd each of the eggs and the handle, remove the freezer paper from the back of the triangle.

3. Referring to **Diagram 8,** complete the basket by stitching the appliquéd yellow triangle to the basket half of the block.

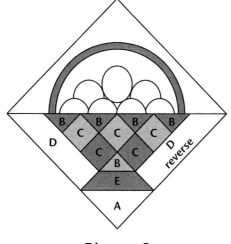

Diagram 8

Finishing the Pillow Top

1. Referring to **Diagram 9,** stitch pink print border strips to two opposite sides of the completed basket block.

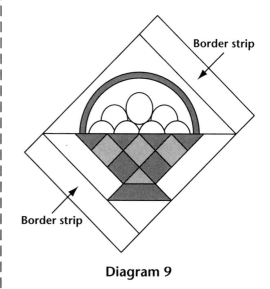

Diagram 9

2. Stitch one green print F corner square to the short ends of the other two border strips. Stitch these border strips with corner squares to the remaining two sides of the basket block, as shown in **Diagram 10.**

Diagram 10

Making the Bow

1. Fold the 5 × 30-inch multicolored bow strip in half lengthwise, with right sides together. To cut the ends of the bow at a 45-degree angle, bring the raw edges of one end of the strip up to the fold. Press a crease in the strip. Cut on the crease line. Repeat for the other end of the strip.

2. Beginning near the center of the strip, stitch along the length of the strip and across the angled edge, ending at the fold.

3. Stitch the other half of the bow strip in the same manner, leaving at least a 3-inch opening for turning the strip right side out.

4. Turn the bow strip right side out through the center opening. Whipstitch the opening closed and press the entire strip flat.

5. Tie a two-loop bow and tack the knot securely in place on the basket handle.

Making the Pillow

1. Stitch a 17-inch square of fleece to the wrong side of the pillow top along all four edges.

2. Cut a piece of cording that measures approximately 68 inches long (or long enough to pipe the entire perimeter of the pillow). Fold the blue print bias strip lengthwise, wrong sides together, and insert the cording between the two layers. Using a zipper foot and a basting stitch, sew as close to the cording as possible. Trim the seam allowance

Bits 'n' Pieces

Try This Variation: If you decorate your home in the country style, it is easy to give this pillow a homey country look. Choose colors like country blue, barn red, mustard yellow, tan, off-white, brown, and green. Whether you love strong or subtle shades, look for tones to complement the colors of the room where you will display the pillow. For the eggs, try using a speckled tan to create the look of country-fresh chicken eggs, or make muslin your choice for eggs with a "store-bought" look. Piece a pretty wicker basket from two patterned muslin and cream fabrics. Add a gaily colored ruffle and bow from a plaid or gingham check to create your own unique country Easter Basket Pillow.

of the piping to ½ inch. Refer to pages 272–273 in the "General Instructions" for more information on how to make piping.

3. Pin the piping to the right side of the pillow top, starting in the middle of one side and aligning raw edges. At each corner of the pillow, clip the seam allowance to ease the piping around the corner. Overlap the ends of the piping. Use a zipper foot to sew the piping to the pillow top, using a ½-inch seam allowance and taking care to stitch as close as possible to the cording.

4. Cut a piece of cording 132 inches long. Fold the aqua print bias strip in half lengthwise, wrong sides together, and insert the cording between the two layers. Using a zipper foot and a basting stitch, sew as close to the cording as possible. Trim the seam allowance of the piping to ½ inch.

5. With right sides facing, stitch together the short ends of three pink print ruffle strips, forming one side of the continuous ruffle, as shown in **Diagram 11.** Repeat with the remaining three pink print ruffle strips to form the other side of the ruffle.

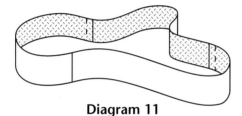

Diagram 11

6. Place the aqua piping on the right side of one ruffle, aligning raw edges and overlapping the ends of the piping. Use a zipper foot and a basting stitch to sew the piping in place, stitching as close as possible to the cording.

7. Pin and sew the ruffles right sides together, using the basting seam line of the piping as a stitching guide.

8. Turn the ruffle right side out and press. Sew a line of gathering stitches ⅜ inch from the raw edges through both layers of the ruffle, as shown in **Diagram 12.** Fold the ruffle in half to find the midpoints and place a pin at these points. Match the midpoints of the ruffle and mark

the quarter points at each end of the ruffle with pins.

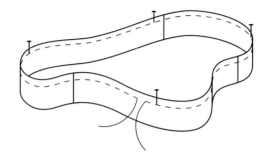

Diagram 12

9. Referring to **Diagram 13,** gather the ruffle and pin it evenly around the edges of the pillow top. Stitch the ruffle to the pillow top, using the seam line of the blue print piping as a stitching guide.

Diagram 13

10. Iron a 17-inch square of fusible interfacing onto the wrong side of the pillow back.

11. Place the pillow top and the pillow back right sides together and sew around the outer edge, using a ½-inch seam allowance. Leave an opening approximately 12 inches long on one side, as shown in **Diagram 14.** Grade the seams to reduce bulk. Turn the pillow right side out.

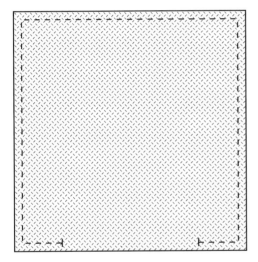

Diagram 14

12. Make a pillow form by stitching the two muslin squares together, leaving a 4-inch opening in one side for turning and stuffing. Turn the pillow form right side out. Stuff firmly; slip stitch the opening closed.

13. Insert the pillow form inside the pillow and use a whipstitch to close the opening along the side of the pillow.

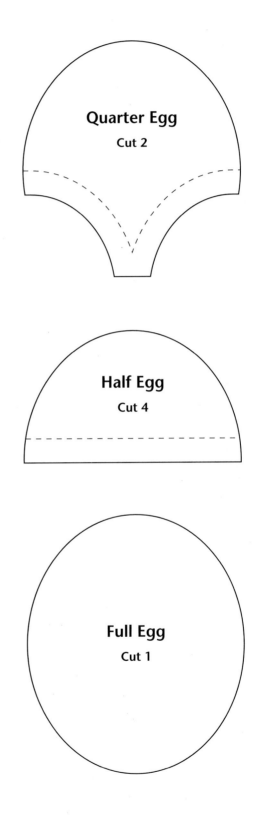

Quarter Egg
Cut 2

Half Egg
Cut 4

Full Egg
Cut 1

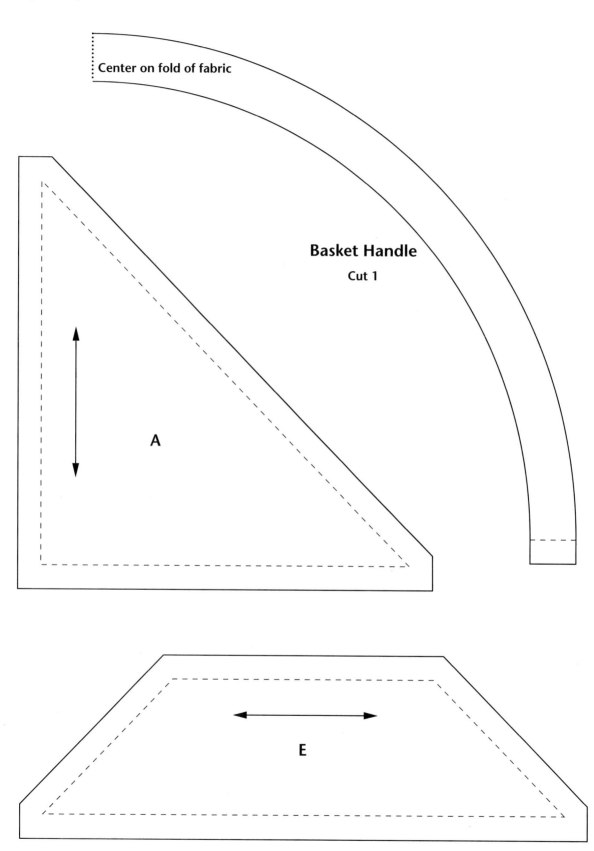

Center on fold of fabric

Basket Handle

Cut 1

A

E

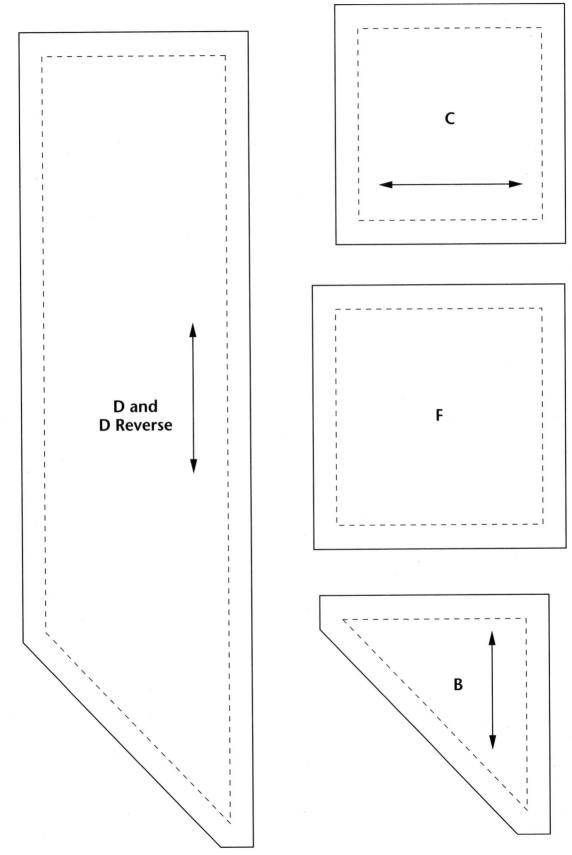

C

**D and
D Reverse**

F

B

Folk Art Flag Wallhanging

Decorate your front door with this folk art American flag to celebrate Independence Day or to make a patriotic statement year-round. The beauty of this quick-and-easy wallhanging comes from a rich variety of reds, blues, golds, and printed muslins. Subtle contrasts in color make the stars twinkle brilliantly against a patchwork background of midnight blues.

★ *Size: The flag wallhanging is 26½ × 37½ inches.*

Fabric Requirements

- ★ Scraps of at least seven assorted red prints *or* ⅝ yard of one red fabric for the stripes
- ★ Scraps of assorted printed muslin fabrics *or* ½ yard of one muslin fabric for the stripes
- ★ Scraps of at least three navy fabrics *or* ½ yard of one navy fabric for the squares and binding
- ★ Scraps of assorted light and dark gold fabrics for the stars
- ★ 1⅞ yards of printed muslin for the backing and rod pocket

Other Supplies

- ★ Template plastic
- ★ Fine-point black permanent marker
- ★ 31 × 41-inch piece of quilt batting
- ★ ⅜ yard of fusible webbing
- ★ Freezer paper
- ★ Yellow-gold, off-white, and navy sewing threads

Instructions

Cutting

Note: All pattern pieces include ¼-inch seam allowances unless specified otherwise.

1. Trace the half diamond pattern on page 223 onto template plastic. Note that the longest and shortest sides have a ⅛-inch seam allowance, while the third side has none. Cut out the traced pattern piece.

2. Draw five half diamonds on several dark gold scraps and five on several light gold scraps. Cut out five from each color scrap for one star. Repeat for a total of nine stars.

3. If you wish to piece the seven red stripes in the flag, cut 65 to 70 assorted red print pieces. Each piece should be 2½ inches wide; length can

vary from 2½ inches to 5½ inches. If you wish to make the stripes from a single fabric, cut four 2½ × 37½-inch strips and three 2½ × 25-inch strips.

4. If you wish to piece the six muslin stripes in the flag, cut 60 to 65 assorted muslin pieces. Each piece should be 2½ inches wide, and the length can vary from 2½ inches to 5½ inches. If you wish to make the muslin stripes from a single fabric, cut three 2½ × 37½-inch strips and three 2½ × 25-inch strips.

5. From a large scrap of navy fabric, cut enough 1½-inch-wide strips to form a 132-inch-long binding strip. If you don't have enough of a single scrap, piece together several

assorted navy scraps to create the length needed. From the remaining navy scraps, cut nine 4½-inch squares.

6. From the printed muslin, cut a 31 × 41-inch backing piece. If you want to hang the quilt horizontally, cut a 3¼ × 37-inch strip for the rod pocket. If you wish to hang the quilt vertically, cut a 3¼ × 25½-inch strip for the pocket.

Assembling the Flag

Note: Press each seam toward the darker fabric, unless specified otherwise.

1. If you're piecing the red print strips, sew together enough to make four strips that measure 2½ × 37½ inches and three strips that measure 2½ × 25 inches.

2. If you're piecing the muslin strips, sew together enough to make three strips that measure 2½ × 37 inches and three strips that measure 2½ × 25 inches.

3. Referring to the photograph on page 221, sew the six 25-inch strips together, starting with a red strip, then alternating the red and muslin. Beginning and ending with a red strip, sew the seven long strips together, alternating the red and muslin strips.

4. Sew three 4½-inch navy squares together into one row.

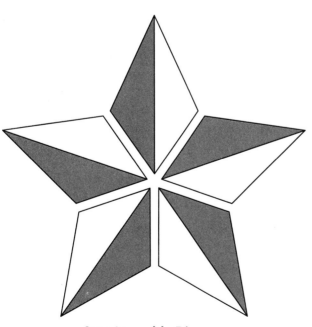

Star Assembly Diagram

Repeat to make the remaining two rows of navy squares. Sew the three rows together.

5. Referring to the **Star Assembly Diagram,** sew together five pairs of light and dark half diamonds. Sew these five pairs of half diamonds together to complete one star. Repeat to make the other eight stars. Iron fusible webbing onto the wrong side of each star and trim any excess webbing from the outside edge.

6. Position and fuse a star in the center of each navy square. Iron the shiny side of a piece of freezer paper onto the wrong side of the star unit. Using yellow-gold thread and a narrow zigzag stitch, machine appliqué around each star and remove the freezer paper.

7. Referring to the **Flag Assembly Diagram** on the opposite page, sew the star unit to the left side of the short stripes.

8. Referring to the **Flag Assembly Diagram,** sew the top half of the flag to the bottom half of the flag.

Quilting

1. Place the backing wrong side up on a flat surface. Layer the batting on the backing, then the quilt top on the batting, right side up. Baste the layers together.

2. Machine quilt in the ditch of each stripe and each navy square.

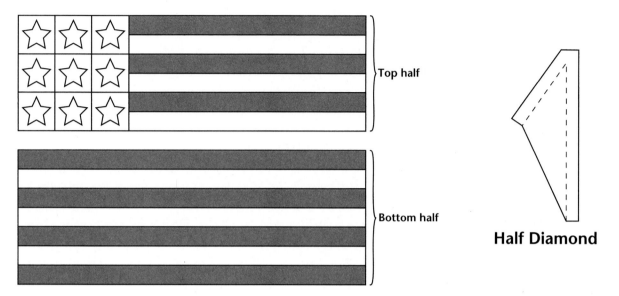

Half Diamond

Flag Assembly Diagram

Finishing

1. Trim the excess backing and batting even with the edges of the top.

2. Turn under ¼ inch twice at the short ends of the rod pocket strip and machine stitch the hems. With wrong sides together, fold the rod pocket strip in half lengthwise and press a crease in the fold. Align the raw edges of the rod pocket with the edge of the quilt and pin it in place. Machine sew the rod pocket to the quilt inside the ¼-inch seam allowance. Blindstitch the folded edge of the rod pocket to the quilt backing, making sure the rod pocket lies flat against the backing.

3. Fold the binding strip in half lengthwise, wrong sides together, and press a crease in the fold. Using a ¼-inch seam allowance, machine sew the strip around each side of the quilt top. Miter each corner and overlap the ends of the binding strips. For more information on making and attaching binding, see page 269 in the "General Instructions."

4. Fold the binding to the back of the wallhanging and blindstitch it in place by hand, mitering each corner.

Halloween Trick-or-Treat Bag

This not-so-scary treat bag will take your favorite little goblin through many Halloween goody hunts. Just start with a purchased canvas shopping bag and fuse an orange piece of fabric on one side. Throw in a purple house of horrors, a hissing black cat, a luminous yellow moon, and a smattering of bats and ghouls. Add a couple of squiggly black lines to make the ghosts grin, and you'll have a "boo"-tiful bag of tricks.

★ *Size: The design area is 9 × 12 inches.*

Fabric Requirements

- ★ 9 × 12-inch piece of orange solid for the background
- ★ 7-inch square of black solid for the roof, windows, cat, and bats
- ★ 6-inch square of yellow solid for the moon
- ★ 6-inch square of white solid for the ghosts
- ★ 4 × 6-inch piece of purple solid for the house
- ★ Small scrap of dark red print for the chimney

Other Supplies

- ★ Purchased canvas shopping bag
- ★ 1 yard of Heat 'N Bond heavy-weight fusible webbing
- ★ 1 bottle of dimensional fabric paint in black, white, yellow, purple, and orange
- ★ Fine-point black permanent marker

Instructions

Note: The pattern for each piece is presented wrong side up. When you trace each piece onto the paper side of a piece of fusible webbing, it will be right side up when it's fused onto the purchased canvas shopping bag.

Cutting

1. Iron the wrong side of the orange rectangle onto the fusible webbing and cut it out.

2. Trace the patterns on pages 227–229 onto the paper side of the remainder of the fusible webbing and cut them out.

3. Iron the lower house, cat, bat 1, and bat 2 onto the wrong side of the black fabric. Iron the large and small ghosts onto the wrong side of the

white fabric. Iron the moon onto the wrong side of the yellow fabric. Iron the upper house onto the wrong side of the purple fabric. Iron the chimney onto the scrap of red print. Cut out all the pieces.

Assembling the Bag

1. Remove the paper from the wrong side of the orange rectangle. Center and fuse the rectangle onto one side of the canvas shopping bag.

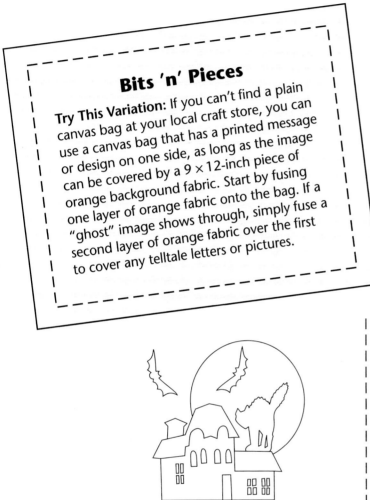

Bits 'n' Pieces

Try This Variation: If you can't find a plain canvas bag at your local craft store, you can use a canvas bag that has a printed message or design on one side, as long as the image can be covered by a 9 × 12-inch piece of orange background fabric. Start by fusing one layer of orange fabric onto the bag. If a "ghost" image shows through, simply fuse a second layer of orange fabric over the first to cover any telltale letters or pictures.

Diagram 1

2. Remove the paper from the wrong sides of the design pieces. Position the pieces on the orange rectangle using **Diagram 1** as a placement guide. Layer the pieces in the following order: moon, lower house, chimney, upper house, cat, bat 1, bat 2, large ghost, and small ghost. Place the left edge of the small ghost over the right edge of the the large ghost. When everything is in the proper position, fuse the pieces in place.

Finishing

1. Outline the lower part of the house with purple paint, including the windows and the door.

2. Outline the top of the roof, the base of the door, the bats, and the cat with black paint. Also use black to fill in the ghosts' eyes and to outline their mouths.

3. Outline the moon with yellow paint.

4. Outline the chimney and the entire orange rectangle with orange paint.

5. Outline each ghost with white paint. After the eyes have dried, add a dot of white to each.

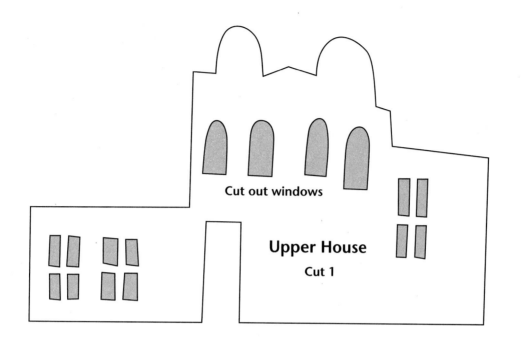

Cut out windows

Upper House

Cut 1

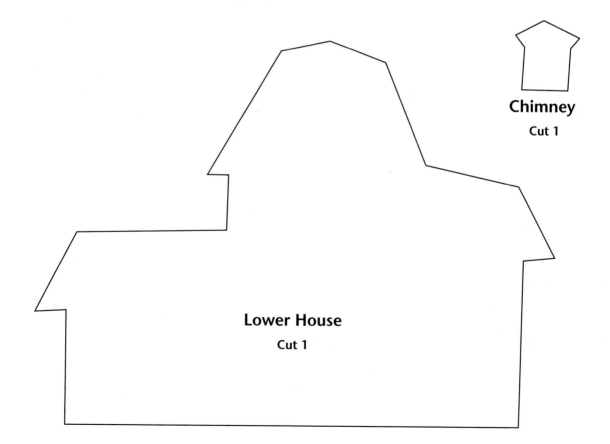

Chimney

Cut 1

Lower House

Cut 1

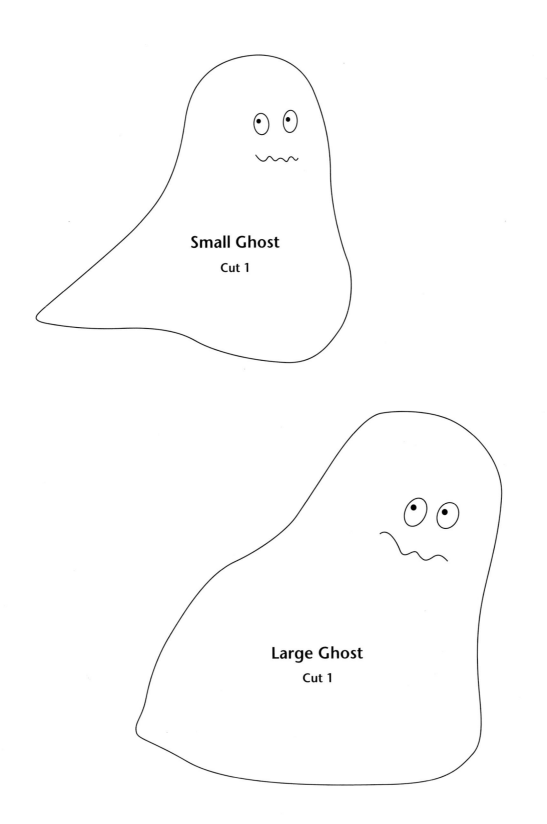

Small Ghost

Cut 1

Large Ghost

Cut 1

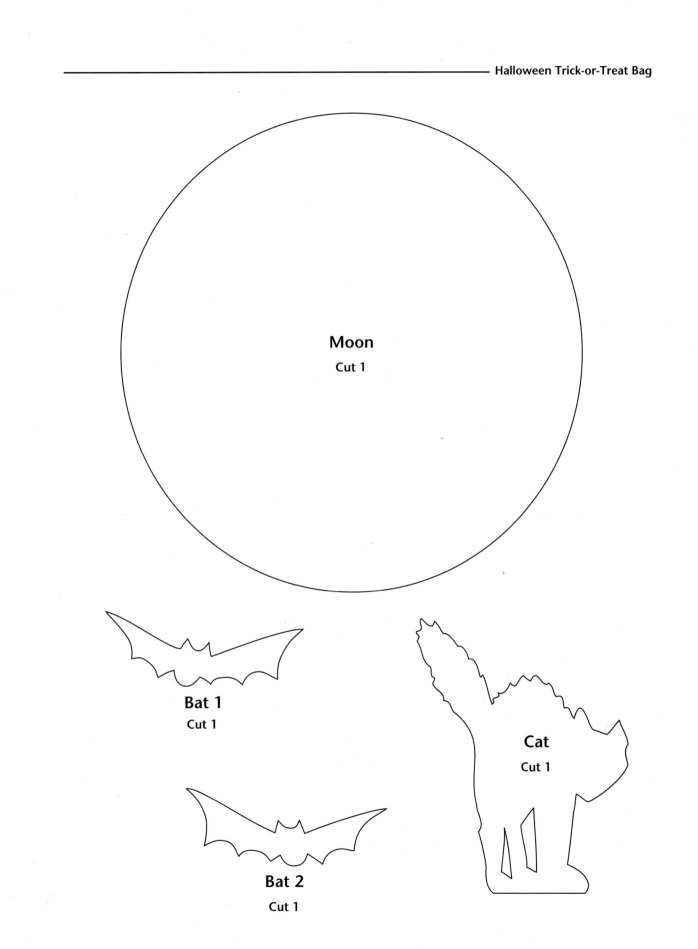

Moon

Cut 1

Bat 1

Cut 1

Bat 2

Cut 1

Cat

Cut 1

Holiday Kitchen Magnets

Add a splash of whimsy to your refrigerator door with an array of no-sew magnets for special occasions like Easter, Thanksgiving, and Independence Day. Browse through your fabric collection to find the perfect oranges for the jack-o'-lantern and a feathery brown print for Tom Turkey. Whatever fabrics you choose, you'll find these eight delightful designs a piece of cake to make.

★ *Size: Each magnet is 2¼ inches square.*

Note: The fabric requirements, cutting lists, and piecing instructions for the eight magnets are provided separately. The assembly instructions for all eight magnets then follow.

St. Patrick's Day Four-Leaf Clover

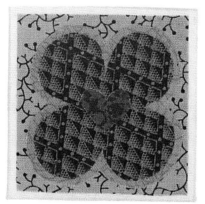

Fabric Requirements

★ 6-inch square of yellow solid for covering the magnet
★ Scraps of dark green and turquoise prints for the clovers

★ Scrap of pink print for the foundation square
★ Scrap of red print for the heart

Other Supplies

★ 9-inch square of foam core board
★ ½ yard of fusible webbing
★ Fabric stiffener
★ 1 package of magnet tape
★ Elmer's glue or fabric glue
★ Sharp scissors
★ Template plastic
★ Fine-point black permanent marker
★ Pencil or removable marker for tracing templates

Cutting

1. Trace the pattern pieces on page 241 onto the template plastic and cut out the templates.

2. Cut a 2¼-inch square of foam core board.

3. Draw around the templates on fusible webbing and cut them out.

4. Cut the following fabrics and fuse the appropriate pattern pieces to them.

★ From the yellow solid, cut a 3-inch square and a magnet back square.

★ From the turquoise, cut one large clover.
★ From the green print, cut one small clover.
★ From the pink print, cut one foundation square.
★ From the red print, cut one heart.

Birthday Cake

Fabric Requirements

★ 6-inch square of light yellow print for covering the magnet
★ Scrap of medium yellow print for the cake
★ Scrap of medium purple print for the icing
★ Scrap of dark purple print for the foundation square
★ Scrap of turquoise print for the foundation square

Other Supplies

★ 9-inch square of foam core board
★ ½ yard of fusible webbing
★ Fabric stiffener
★ 1 package of magnet tape
★ Elmer's glue or fabric glue
★ Sharp scissors
★ Template plastic
★ Fine-point black permanent marker
★ Pencil or removable marker for tracing templates
★ Iron

Cutting

1. Trace the pattern pieces on page 241 onto the template plastic and cut out the templates.

2. Cut a 2¼-inch square of foam core board.

3. Draw around the templates on fusible webbing and cut them out.

4. Cut the following fabrics and fuse the appropriate pattern pieces to them.
★ From the light yellow print, cut a 3-inch square and a magnet back square.
★ From the medium yellow print, cut two cake pieces.
★ From the medium purple print, cut one icing piece.
★ From the dark purple print, cut one foundation square.
★ From the turquoise print, cut one foundation square.

Independence Day Heart

Fabric Requirements

★ 6-inch square of red print for covering the magnet
★ Scraps of red print and white solid (or a red-and-white striped fabric) for the heart and stars

- ★ Scrap of medium orange print for the foundation square
- ★ Scrap of blue print for the heart

Other Supplies

- ★ 9-inch square of foam core board
- ★ ½ yard of fusible webbing
- ★ Fabric stiffener
- ★ 1 package of magnet tape
- ★ Elmer's glue or fabric glue
- ★ Sharp scissors
- ★ Template plastic
- ★ Fine-point black permanent marker
- ★ Pencil or removable marker for tracing templates
- ★ Iron

Cutting

1. Trace the pattern pieces on page 242 onto the template plastic and cut out the templates.

2. Cut a 2¼-inch square of foam core board.

3. Draw around the templates on fusible webbing and cut them out.

4. Cut the following fabrics and fuse the appropriate pattern pieces to them.
- ★ From the red print, cut a 3-inch square and a magnet back square.
- ★ From the red print, cut one upper, center, and lower stripe.
- ★ From the white solid, cut one heart and two stars.
- ★ From the orange print, cut one foundation square.
- ★ From the blue print, cut one quarter heart.

Valentine's Day Heart

Fabric Requirements

- ★ 6-inch square of red print for covering the magnet
- ★ Scraps of several prints in assorted colors for the heart
- ★ 6-inch square of light yellow print for the foundation square

Other Supplies

- ★ 9-inch square of foam core board
- ★ ½ yard of fusible webbing
- ★ Fabric stiffener
- ★ 1 package of magnet tape
- ★ Elmer's glue or fabric glue
- ★ Sharp scissors
- ★ Template plastic
- ★ Fine-point black permanent marker
- ★ Pencil or removable marker for tracing templates
- ★ Iron

Cutting

1. Trace the pattern pieces on page 241 onto the template plastic and cut out the templates.

2. Cut a 2¼-inch square of foam core board.

3. Draw around the templates on fusible webbing and cut them out.

4. Cut the following fabrics and fuse the appropriate pattern pieces to them.
★ From the red print, cut a 3-inch square and a magnet back square.
★ From the assorted scraps, cut enough small squares and rectangles to cover the heart shape.
★ From the yellow print, cut one foundation square.

Easter Basket

Fabric Requirements

★ 6-inch square of purple print for covering the magnet
★ Scrap of brown print for the basket
★ Scraps of several prints in assorted colors for the eggs
★ Scrap of turquoise print for the foundation square

Other Supplies

★ 9-inch square of foam core board
★ ½ yard of fusible webbing
★ Fabric stiffener
★ 1 package of magnet tape
★ ½ yard of ⅛-inch yellow rickrack
★ Elmer's glue or fabric glue
★ Sharp scissors
★ Template plastic
★ Fine-point black permanent marker
★ Pencil or removable marker for tracing templates
★ Iron

Cutting

1. Trace the pattern pieces on page 242 onto the template plastic and cut out the templates.

2. Cut a 2¼-inch square of foam core board.

3. Draw around the templates on fusible webbing and cut them out.

4. Cut the following fabrics and fuse the appropriate pattern pieces to them.
★ From the purple print, cut a 3-inch square and a magnet back square.
★ From the brown print, cut one basket.
★ From the assorted scraps, cut several small ovals for the eggs.
★ From the turquoise print, cut one foundation square.

Halloween Jack-o'-Lantern

Fabric Requirements

★ 6-inch square of dark purple print for covering the magnet
★ Scrap of orange solid for the face
★ Scraps of two orange prints for the jack-o'-lantern sides
★ Scrap of turquoise print for the leaves

★ Scrap of medium purple print for the foundation star
★ Scrap of brown print for the stem
★ Scrap of black solid for the facial features

Other Supplies

★ 9-inch square of foam core board
★ ½ yard of fusible webbing
★ Fabric stiffener
★ 1 package of magnet tape
★ Elmer's glue or fabric glue
★ Sharp scissors
★ Template plastic
★ Fine-point black permanent marker
★ Pencil or removable marker for tracing templates
★ Iron

Cutting

1. Trace the pattern pieces on page 243 onto the template plastic and cut out the templates.

2. Cut a 2¼-inch square of foam core board.

3. Draw around the templates on fusible webbing and cut them out.

4. Cut the following fabrics and fuse the appropriate pattern pieces to them.

★ From the dark purple print, cut one 3-inch square and a magnet back square.
★ From the orange solid, cut one pumpkin front.
★ From two orange prints, cut two pumpkin sides.
★ From the turquoise print, cut two leaves.
★ From the medium purple print, cut one foundation star.
★ From the brown print, cut one stem.
★ From the black solid, cut two eyes, one nose, and one mouth.

Thanksgiving Turkey

Fabric Requirements

★ 6-inch square of turquoise print for covering the magnet
★ Scrap of brown print for the turkey body
★ Scrap of red print for the wattle
★ Scraps of white and blue solid for the eyes
★ Scrap of yellow print for the foundation square and beak
★ Scrap of fuschia print for the tail feathers

Other Supplies

- ★ 9-inch square of foam core board
- ★ ½ yard of fusible webbing
- ★ Fabric stiffener
- ★ 1 package of magnet tape
- ★ ½ yard of ⅛-inch yellow rickrack
- ★ Elmer's glue or fabric glue
- ★ Sharp scissors
- ★ Template plastic
- ★ Fine-point black permanent marker
- ★ Pencil or removable marker for tracing templates
- ★ Iron

Cutting

1. Trace the pattern pieces on page 243 onto the template plastic and cut out the templates.

2. Cut a 2¼-inch square of foam core board.

3. Draw around the templates on fusible webbing and cut them out.

4. Cut the following fabrics and fuse the appropriate pattern pieces to them.
- ★ From the turquoise print, cut a 3-inch square and a magnet back square.
- ★ From the brown print, cut one body.
- ★ From the red print, cut one wattle.
- ★ From the white solid, cut two ⅛-inch circles for the eyes.
- ★ From the blue print, cut two ⅛-inch circles for the eyeballs.
- ★ From the yellow print, cut one foundation square and one beak.
- ★ From the fuschia print, cut one tail feather.

Christmas Tree

Fabric Requirements

- ★ 6-inch square of light yellow print for covering the magnet
- ★ Scrap of dark green print for the tree
- ★ Scrap of brown-and-beige striped fabric for the tree trunk
- ★ Scrap of medium yellow print for the tree skirt
- ★ Scrap of dark red pindot for the foundation square

Other Supplies

- ★ 9-inch square of foam core board
- ★ ½ yard of fusible webbing
- ★ Fabric stiffener
- ★ 1 package of magnet tape
- ★ Scrap of gold paper
- ★ Elmer's glue or fabric glue
- ★ Sharp scissors
- ★ Template plastic
- ★ Fine-point black permanent marker
- ★ Pencil or removable marker for tracing templates
- ★ Iron

Cutting

1. Trace the pattern pieces on page 242 onto the template plastic and cut out the templates.

2. Cut a 2¼-inch square of foam core board.

3. Draw around the templates on fusible webbing and cut them out.

4. Cut the following fabrics and fuse the appropriate pattern pieces to them.
★ From the yellow print, cut a 3-inch square and a magnet back square.
★ From the green print, cut one tree.
★ From the brown striped, cut one tree trunk.
★ From the yellow print, cut one tree skirt.
★ From the red pindot, cut one foundation square.

Assembling the Magnets

1. Fuse the fusible webbing to the wrong side of each 3-inch square of fabric, then remove the paper backing from the webbing. Fuse the foam core board square to the center of each fabric square.

2. Referring to **Diagram 1,** cut out each corner of the fabric beyond the foam core square.

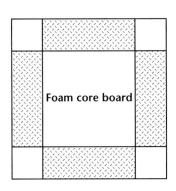

Diagram 1

3. Fold the fabric over the sides of the foam core and iron them in place, as shown in **Diagram 2.**

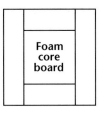

Diagram 2

4. Referring to the assembly diagrams on pages 238–240, fuse the fabric pieces to the fabric-covered foam core, making sure to fuse each piece in the order indicated in the diagrams.

Bits 'n' Pieces
Try These Variations:

1. Cookie cutters open up a whole world of creative magnet designs. Simply trace the outline of a cookie cutter onto a piece of Heat 'N Bond. Then cut out the shape and fuse it to a scrap of fabric. Follow the directions for cutting the shape out of fabric, assembling the magnet, and decorating it. Add some sequins, small beads, feathers, or tiny buttons for a finishing touch to your original design!

2. Turn this project into a playful, yet meaningful gift for young children who are learning to spell. Use alphabet cookie cutters to create magnets that can help build a child's vocabulary.

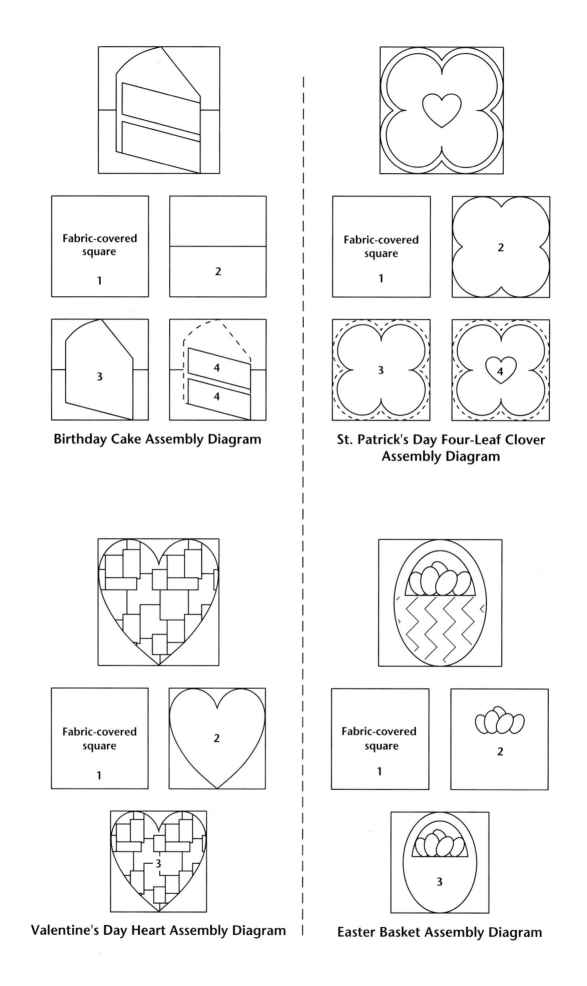

Birthday Cake Assembly Diagram

St. Patrick's Day Four-Leaf Clover Assembly Diagram

Valentine's Day Heart Assembly Diagram

Easter Basket Assembly Diagram

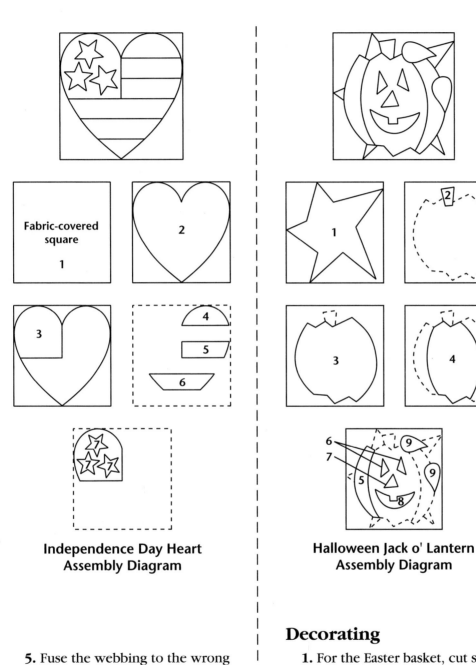

**Independence Day Heart
Assembly Diagram**

**Halloween Jack o' Lantern
Assembly Diagram**

5. Fuse the webbing to the wrong side of the magnet back squares. The fabric for each magnet back square should match the fabric that covers each square of foam core board. Remove the paper backing from the fusible webbing and fuse the magnet back square on the back of the foam core.

Decorating

1. For the Easter basket, cut strips of yellow rickrack and glue them to the basket front.

2. For the Thanksgiving turkey, glue the white eyes to the face. Then glue the blue eyeballs to the eyes. Cut strips of yellow rickrack and glue them to the tail feathers.

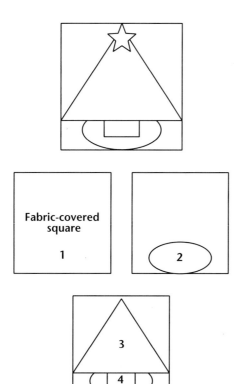

Christmas Tree Assembly Diagram

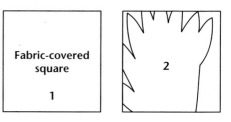

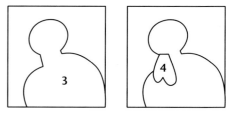

Thanksgiving Turkey Assembly Diagram

3. For the Christmas tree, cut out a star from the gold paper and glue it at the top of the tree.

Finishing

1. Coat each magnet with fabric stiffener to protect it from spills and stains. Let the fabric stiffener dry completely.

2. Cut a 2-inch strip of magnet tape for each square. Peel off the paper backing and affix it to the back of the magnet.

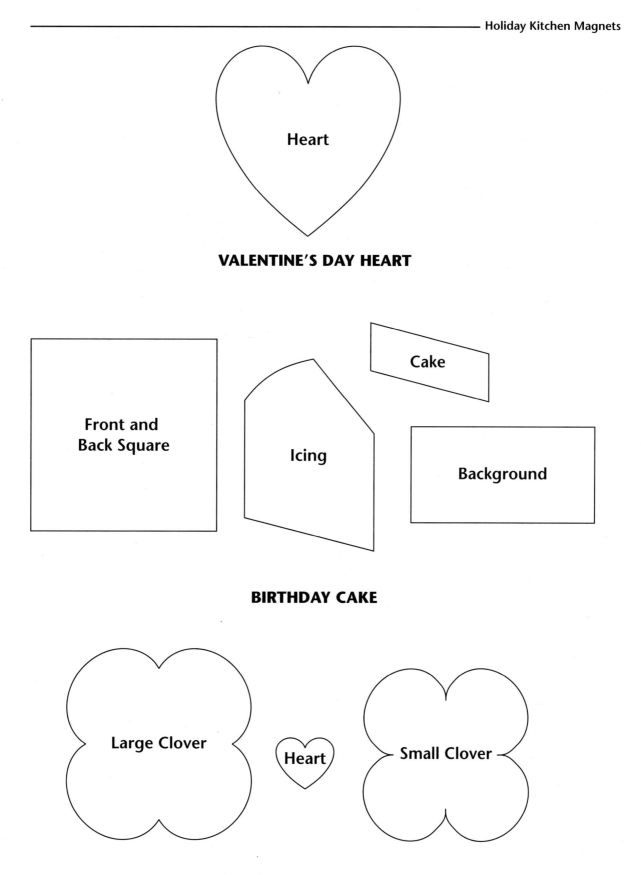

VALENTINE'S DAY HEART

BIRTHDAY CAKE

ST. PATRICK'S DAY FOUR-LEAF CLOVER

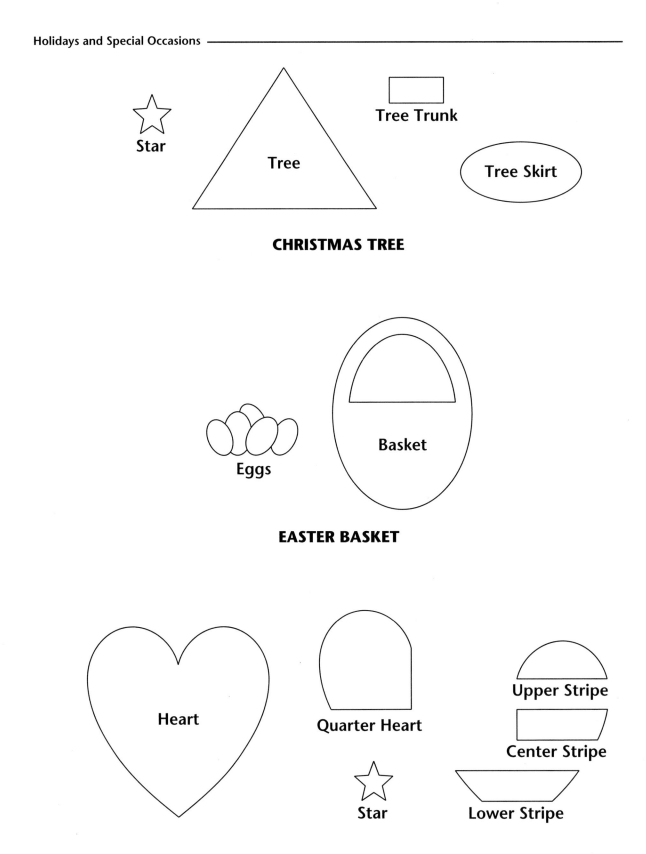

CHRISTMAS TREE

EASTER BASKET

INDEPENDENCE DAY HEART

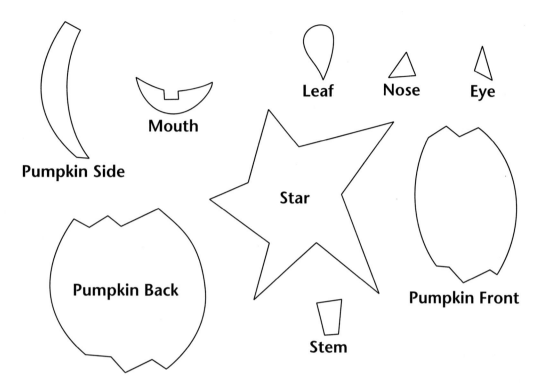

Pumpkin Side

Mouth

Leaf

Nose

Eye

Star

Pumpkin Back

Pumpkin Front

Stem

HALLOWEEN JACK O' LANTERN

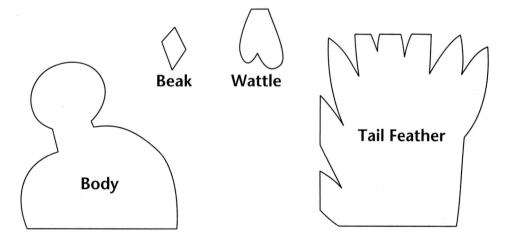

Beak

Wattle

Tail Feather

Body

THANKSGIVING TURKEY

Crazy Patchwork Photograph Album Cover

Slip into the romantic moments of your past as you hand piece bits of taffeta, velvet, and lace. It's a cinch to stitch this Victorian-style album cover for displaying cherished wedding or anniversary pictures.

★ *Size: The album cover will fit an 8 × 9½-inch photograph album.*

Fabric Requirements

- 10¼ × 18¾-inch piece of cotton batiste for the foundation
- 10¼ × 18¾-inch piece of fusible fleece for the underlining
- ½ yard of white polished cotton for the lining and cover sleeves
- Scraps of lace, satin, taffeta, polished cotton, and velveteen for the album cover

Other Supplies

- 2 yards of ⅜-inch white flat lace
- 30-inch length of white-tasseled drapery cording
- Sewing thread to match fabrics
- Metallic gold thread for embroidery
- 1 skein each of pink, peach, and white embroidery floss
- Assorted beads, ribbon flowers, and pearls

Instructions

Note: Sew all seams with a ¼-inch seam allowance. If using wide lace trim for the crazy patchwork cover, back each piece with satin or taffeta.

Cutting

1. From polished cotton, cut one 10¼ × 24¼-inch rectangular lining. Cut two 6 × 10¼-inch cover sleeves.

2. From the assortment of lace, satin, taffeta, polished cotton, and velveteen scraps, cut one five-sided piece that is about 2½ inches wide. Cut the rest of the scraps into various angled shapes, making sure to cut enough to cover the batiste foundation.

Crazy Quilting the Album Cover

1. With right sides together, sew one side of the five-sided piece (piece 1) to the batiste foundation, as shown in **Diagram 1.**

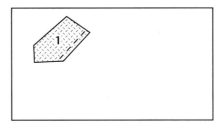

Diagram 1

2. Turn piece 1 right side up and finger press it flat, as shown in **Diagram 2.**

3. With right sides together, stitch piece 2 onto any side of piece 1, as shown in **Diagram 3** on page 246. Turn piece 2 right side up and press.

Diagram 2

245

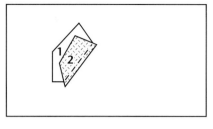

Diagram 3

4. With right sides together, stitch piece 3 onto the batiste foundation, covering the edges of pieces 1 and 2, as shown in **Diagram 4.**

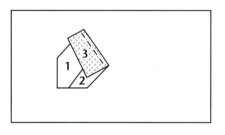

Diagram 4

5. Turn piece 3 right side up and finger press it flat, as shown in **Diagram 5.** If necessary, trim excess fabric from the seam allowance.

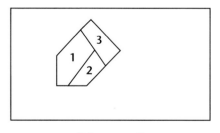

Diagram 5

6. Continue adding fabric pieces in this manner, working clockwise and outward from the center. The crazy patchwork should extend a lit-

tle beyond the edge of the batiste foundation. As the sides of the fabric pieces begin to lengthen, it's helpful to join several fabrics together before stitching them as one piece onto the foundation.

Embellishing the Album Cover

1. Referring to **Diagram 6,** use metallic gold thread to embroider over the seams between pieces, using the feather stitch, lazy daisy stitch, and French knots. For more information about embroidery stitches, see page 273 in the "General Instructions."

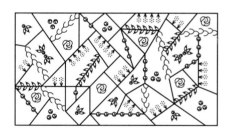

Diagram 6

2. Use metallic gold thread and pink, peach, and white floss to embroider flowers on the patchwork pieces. Use French knots for petals and straight stitches for stems and leaves.

3. Tack beads, ribbon flowers, and pearls randomly over the surface to embellish the crazy-quilted album cover.

Lining the Album Cover

1. Iron the fusible fleece lining onto the wrong side of the crazy-quilted foundation.

2. With right sides together, pin the ⅜-inch white flat lace to the edge of the crazy-quilted foundation. Make sure to match the pattern where the ends of the lace overlap and to baste inside the seam allowance, as shown in **Diagram 7.**

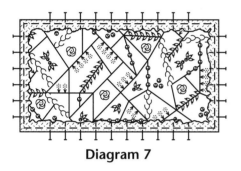

Diagram 7

3. Sew a ½-inch hem along one long side of each cover sleeve.

4. With right sides together, pin three sides of one sleeve at the end of the patchwork foundation (see **Diagram 8**). Do not pin the hemmed edge that faces the center of the foundation. Sew the sleeve and foundation together along three sides; repeat for the remaining sleeve. Do not turn the sleeves right side out.

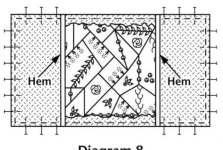

Diagram 8

5. With right sides together, pin the polished cotton lining to the top and bottom of the crazy patchwork foundation, as shown in **Diagram 9.** Sew the pieces together along the top and bottom only. Clip the corners and trim the seam allowance. Turn the lining and the sleeves right side out.

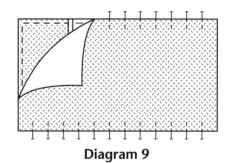

Diagram 9

Finishing

1. Slip the sleeves over the front and back of a photograph album cover.

2. Fold a length of white-tasseled drapery cording in half and place the folded end inside the album cover. Bring the tassels to the inside of the album cover and thread them through the loop of the other end, so that the tassels hang below the edge of the album cover.

Lace Patchwork Ring Bearer's Pillow

Satin, lace, and ribbons are the perfect finishing touch to an elegant wedding. A time-honored tradition guaranteed to turn into a treasured keepsake, this romantic ring bearer's pillow will give you reason to smile every stitch of the way.

★ *Size: The ring bearer's pillow is 8 × 9 inches. The ruffle with lace trim is 4 inches.*

Fabric Requirements

★ Eight to ten 4-inch scraps of lace, taffeta, satin, and velvet for the heart foundation
★ Two 9 × 10-inch pieces of ecru satin for the pillow front and back
★ Three 9 × 10-inch pieces of white cotton batiste for the pillow lining and heart foundation
★ Two 6 × 45-inch strips of ecru satin for the ruffle

Other Supplies

★ 2¾ yards of 1½-inch white flat lace for the ruffle
★ 3 yards of ⅛-inch ecru ribbon
★ 1 yard of ½-inch white flat lace for the pillow
★ ¾ yard of ½-inch white flat lace for the heart
★ 2 gold-tone heart and ribbon charms
★ 1 spool of metallic gold thread
★ 1 skein of white embroidery floss
★ 1 skein of ecru embroidery floss
★ Embroidery needle
★ 16-ounce bag of polyester fiberfill
★ Template plastic or tracing paper
★ Fine-point black permanent marker

Instructions

Note: Sew all seams with a ¼-inch seam allowance. If you use wide lace in the crazy patchwork heart, back each piece with satin or taffeta.

Cutting

1. Trace the heart foundation pattern on page 255 onto tracing paper and cut it out.

2. From the cotton batiste, cut one heart foundation.

3. From an assortment of wide lace trim scraps, taffeta, satin, and velvet scraps, select one fabric for piece 1 and cut out out a five-sided piece that is 2½ inches in diameter. Cut the rest of the scraps randomly into various angled shapes.

Making the Crazy Quilted Heart

Note: The numbers in **Diagrams 1** through **5** indicate only the order of piecing. They do not necessarily coincide with the shapes of the patchwork pieces shown in the illustrations. The joy of crazy quilt piecing is that it's done randomly, and it's hard to a make a mistake!

1. Referring to **Diagram 1,** place piece 1 right side down on the batiste heart foundation. Sew one side of piece 1 to the heart foundation.

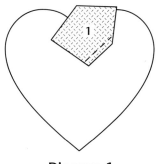

Diagram 1

2. Fold piece 1 over so that it is right side up. Press it flat, as shown in **Diagram 2.**

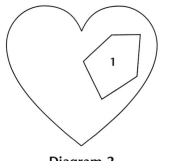

Diagram 2

3. With right sides together, stitch piece 2 onto any side of piece 1, as shown in **Diagram 3.**

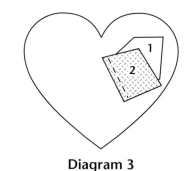

Diagram 3

4. Fold piece 2 over so that it is right side up and press it.

5. With right sides together, stitch piece 3 onto the adjacent side of piece 1. This piece must be large enough to cover the edges of both piece 1 and piece 2, as shown in **Diagram 4.**

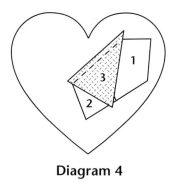

Diagram 4

6. Trim excess fabric from the seam allowance, turn piece 3 to the right side, as shown in **Diagram 5** on the opposite page, and press the seam flat.

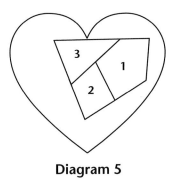

Diagram 5

7. Continue adding pieces to the heart in the same manner, working from the center outward to cover the batiste heart foundation.

Embellishing the Crazy Quilted Heart

1. Referring to **Diagram 6,** use gold thread to embellish the seams between patchwork pieces. Use the feather stitch, lazy daisy stitch, and French knots.

2. Referring to **Diagram 6** and to the photograph on page 249, use gold thread and white and ecru embroidery floss to embroider flowers on the patchwork pieces. Use French knots for the petals and

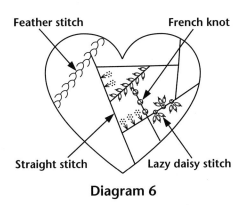

Diagram 6

straight stitches for the stems and leaves. For more information on embroidery stitches, see pages 273-275 in the "General Instructions."

Sewing the Heart to the Pillow

1. Pin a batiste lining piece to the wrong side of the pillow front. Baste inside the ¼-inch seam allowance, as shown in **Diagram 7.** Repeat for the pillow back.

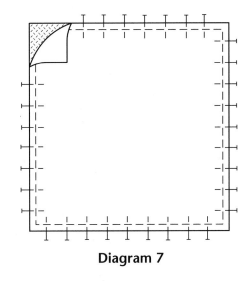

Diagram 7

2. Pin the crazy quilted heart at the center of the satin pillow front and baste inside the ¼-inch seam allowance, as shown in **Diagram 8** on page 252.

3. Starting at the inner point of the heart, pin the ½-inch white flat lace you've chosen for the heart around it, matching the ends, and topstitch it in place, as shown in **Diagram 9** on page 252.

Diagram 8

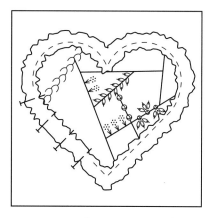

Diagram 9

Bits 'n' Pieces

Try These Variations: First-time weddings need not be the only reason for making a romantic ring bearer's pillow. With a touch of metallic silver thread, you can transform this pillow into a perfect gift for a couple who wants to renew their wedding vows on their 25th anniversary. Embellish the pillow with tiny bells or ribbon roses in silver.

For a completely different look, use pink or blue satin to create a pillow for a baby shower. Use matching ribbons to tie a simple but elegant silver rattle to the crazy-quilted heart.

Sewing the Ruffle

1. With right sides together, sew the short ends of the ruffle together, as shown in **Diagram 10.** Press both of the seams open.

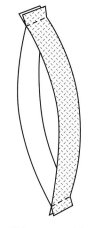

Diagram 10

2. With wrong sides together, fold the ruffle in half lengthwise and press.

3. Referring to **Diagram 11,** sew the 1½-inch white flat lace to the fold on the underside of the ruffle, making sure to match the pattern where the ends of the lace overlap.

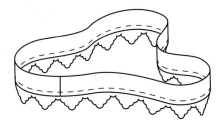

Diagram 11

4. Referring to **Diagram 12,** sew a running stitch through both layers of the raw edge of the ruffle, leaving two long threads on either side of each seam for gathering.

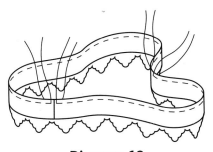

Diagram 12

Sewing the Pillow

1. Referring to **Diagram 13,** pin the ½-inch white flat lace to the edges of the pillow front, right sides together. Baste inside the ¼-inch seam allowance.

Diagram 13

2. Referring to **Diagram 14,** pin the ruffle to the edges of the pillow front, right sides together. Pull the basting threads to gather the ruffle to fit the pillow. Baste inside the ¼-inch seam allowance.

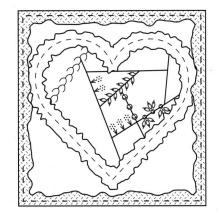

Diagram 14

3. With right sides together, pin the pillow back to the pillow front. Sew the pieces together, leaving a 4-inch opening along the bottom edge, as shown in **Diagram 15.** Turn the pillow right side out.

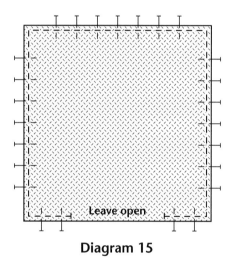

Diagram 15

Finishing

1. Stuff the pillow firmly with polyester fiberfill and blindstitch the opening closed.

2. To make the bows, cut six pieces of ⅛-inch ecru satin ribbon, each 18 inches long.

3. Fold three strands of ribbon in half and tack them on one side of the crazy-quilted heart. Fold the remaining three strands of ribbon in half and tack them on the other side of the crazy-quilted heart. Tie each group of ribbons into a bow, as shown in the photograph on page 249.

4. Tack the heart and ribbon charms to the crazy-quilted heart beneath each bow.

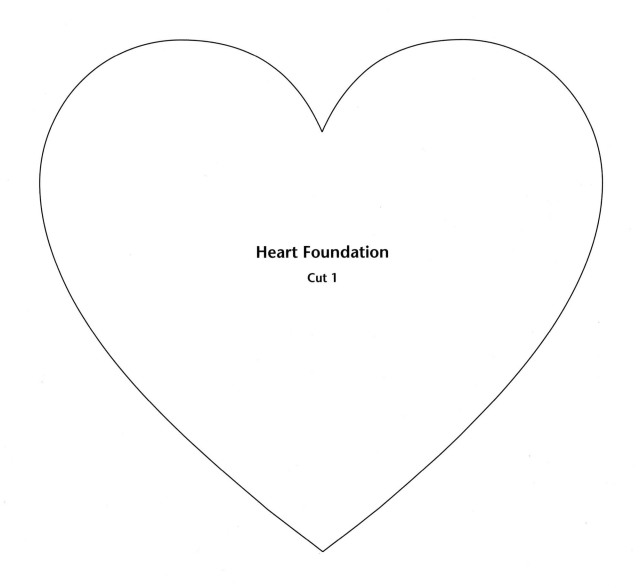

Heart Foundation

Cut 1

General Instructions

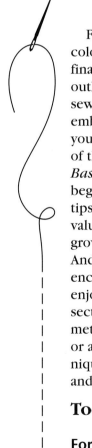

From creating dynamic color schemes to taking the final stitches, this chapter outlines all of the basic sewing, quilting, and embroidery techniques you'll need for making each of the projects in *Scrap Basket Crafts.* If you're a beginner, you'll find these tips, tricks, and helpful hints valuable for expanding your growing repertoire of skills. And if you're an experienced stitcher, you may enjoy reading through this section to brush up on methods you've already used or add a few new techniques to your list of tried-and-true favorites.

Tools and Supplies

For Sewing and Quiltmaking

Many of the same tools and supplies are used for both sewing and quiltmaking. The following supplies are staples in a well-stocked sewing room/quilting studio.

- *Straight pins:* Long pins (1½ inches) with glass or plastic heads are easy to use, especially for pinning multiple layers of fabric together. Do not use burred or rusty pins, which can leave marks in fabric.
- *Scissors:* Use a sharp pair of dressmaker's shears for cutting fabric. A pair of small, sharp embroidery scissors is helpful for trimming threads and seam allowances. And it's a good idea to reserve one pair of scissors for cutting only paper, template plastic, and cardboard.
- *Iron and ironing board:* Pressing is one of the most important steps in accurate sewing and piecing. To increase efficiency, keep an iron-ing board and iron close to your sewing area.
- *Sewing machine:* It's a good idea to clean your sewing machine regular-ly. After approximately every four hours of sewing time, take a few minutes to clean and oil it to keep it in good working condition.
- *Thread:* Use high-quality 100 percent cotton or cotton-covered poly-ester thread for sewing and piecing. For hand quilting, choose quilt-ing thread. For machine quilting, select either high-quality sewing thread or nylon thread for the top and machine embroidery-weight cotton thread for the bobbin.
- *Needles:* Sharps are specifi-cally made for hand sewing and appliqué and betweens are for hand quilting. A good

rule of thumb is to start with a large-size needle and move to a smaller one as you gain experience in stitching. For both sharps and betweens, the larger the number, the smaller and shorter the needle. Experiment with different-size needles to see which are most comfortable in your hand and which are easiest to manipulate through fabric. Embroidery or crewel needles have long oval eyes, which will accommodate several strands of embroidery floss or wool yarn. Beading needles are long and fine, with small round eyes that go through tiny beads easily. Soft sculpture needles range from 3½ to 6 inches long and are perfect for assembling doll bodies.

- *Seam ripper:* This handy two-pronged tool allows you to remove stitches in a seam without damaging the fibers of the fabric.
- *Glue stick:* A glue stick is helpful for basting seam allowances together before sewing a seam.
- *Fusible webbing:* Use ⅛-inch strips of fusible webbing to baste

trims. Wider fusible webbing is useful for stabilizing and basting appliqué patches on background fabrics.

- *Liquid seam sealant:* This liquid seals the edges of fabric, stopping them from fraying. It will also prevent knots in threads from coming undone. One common brand is Fray Check.

For Quiltmaking

In addition to the tools and supplies mentioned previously, the following tools and supplies are especially helpful for quiltmaking.

- *Rotary cutter and cutting mat:* For greater speed and accuracy, you can often cut border strips and other pieces with a rotary cutter rather than with shears. You may wish to use a large rotary cutter for making long, straight cuts and a smaller cutter for making shorter cuts and for cutting curves. Along with either-size cutter, use a self-healing mat designed to protect a work surface and keep fabrics from slipping. One of the most versatile mat sizes is 18 × 24 inches. For more information on how to use a rotary

cutter, refer to "Tips on Rotary Cutting" on page 259.

- *See-through ruler:* The indispensable companion to a rotary cutter and self-healing mat is a see-through plastic ruler. This is available in several sizes and shapes. One of the most useful sizes is a 6 × 24-inch ruler marked in 1-inch, ½-inch, ¼-inch, and ⅛-inch increments, with 45-degree angle lines for mitering. Ruled plastic squares that are 12 inches square or larger are also helpful.
- *Template plastic or cardboard:* Templates are master patterns used to mark patchwork and appliqué shapes on fabric. Although thin, semitransparent plastic, available in sheets at quilt and craft shops, is ideal, cardboard can also be used for making templates.
- *Plastic-coated freezer paper:* Quilters have discovered many uses for freezer paper, such as stabilizing fabric by ironing freezer paper onto the wrong side. Look for high-quality freezer paper, such as Reynolds, in grocery stores.

Selecting and Preparing Fabrics

Coordinating Colors

The instructions indicate the colors used for each project, making it easy to create the same look in your own project. If you wish to change colors, try experimenting with a color wheel to try out various colors and combinations and decide which ones you prefer (see **Diagram 1.**) On the color wheel, warm colors include red-violet, red, red-orange, orange, yellow-orange, and yellow. Cool colors are violet, blue-violet, blue, blue-green, green, and yellow-green. Neutral colors are black, white, and varying shades of gray, which are used to add tints, tones, and shades to change the intensity of any color. Whether you are planning to use odds and ends from your scrap basket or purchase new fabrics, here are some helpful hints on using a color wheel to help choose successful color schemes.

• A monochromatic color scheme is based on one color or hue, which is then varied by the addition of white, gray, or black. For example, combining red with white produces a shade of pink. Adding black to the red results in a burgundy shade, and adding gray to red will create an ash rose.

• Complementary colors are located directly opposite each other on the color wheel. Red and green, yellow and violet, and orange and blue are complementary colors.

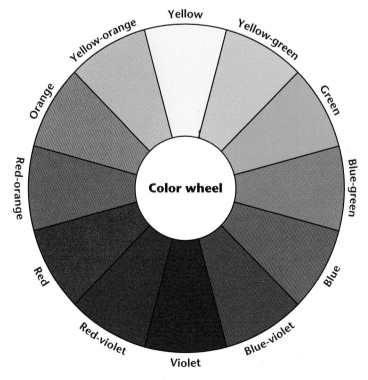

Diagram 1

- Triadic colors are three colors evenly and equally spaced from each other on the color wheel. An example of a triadic color scheme is yellow, blue, and red.
- An analogous color scheme consists of three to six colors that are adjacent to the main color. All of the colors have one color in common. For example yellow-green, green, blue-green, blue, blue-violet, violet, and red-violet all share blue as the common color.

Fabric Type and Quality

Since fabric is the most essential element in a quilt or scrap project, it's always a good idea to buy the best you can afford. You'll be far happier with the results that come from working with high-quality materials. Most quilters and crafters prefer 100 percent cotton broadcloth or dress-weight fabric because it presses well and handles easily, whether you sew by hand or machine. If you have scraps left over from other sewing projects, try to combine fabrics that are similar in weight. If there is a quilt shop or fabric store in your area, the sales staff there can help you coordinate suitable cotton fabrics.

Purchasing Fabric

The yardages in this book are based on a 44- to 45-inch fabric width. They have been double-checked for accuracy and are a bit generous to provide a margin for error. When you purchase fabric, however, remember that the actual width can sometimes be narrower than the size listed on the bolt and that anyone, no matter how experienced, can make a mistake in cutting.

Prewashing Fabric

For best results, it's a good idea to prewash, dry, and press fabrics before using them, especially for quilt-making. Prewashing shrinks fabric and removes any finishes or sizing, softening it and making it easier to handle. Prewashing also allows you to determine whether fabrics are colorfast before using them.

Use warm water and a mild detergent in an automatic washing machine to prewash fabrics, and dry them in an electric clothes dryer set on medium. If you form the habit of washing fabrics immediately after purchasing them, they'll be ready whenever you're ready to start a new project. If you prefer the crispness of unwashed fabric for certain types of projects, however, you may wish to leave fabrics untreated until you are ready to use them. Machine quilters sometimes like to use unwashed fabric and launder a quilt after it is completed, in order to create a crinkled and old-fashioned look in the quilt. The risk in this situation is that the fabric dyes may bleed and damage the look of a finished quilt.

Setting Fabric Dyes

While many fabrics are colorfast, some dyes, especially reds, purples, and dark blues, may bleed. To test a fabric for colorfastness, soak a small scrap of it in warm water. If any color seeps into the water, soak the whole piece of fabric in a solution of 3 parts cold water to 1 part vinegar. Rinse the fabric in warm water two or three times to remove the excess dye. There is also a product called Retayne, manufactured by ProChem in Somerset, Massachusetts, which is made especially to lock dye molecules onto a fabric surface, making it permanently colorfast.

Tips on Rotary Cutting

A rotary cutter can speed up the process of cutting and allow you to finish quilts and other projects more quickly than ever before. And it's a safe and effective piece of equipment when used with caution. Following these simple guidelines will make the rotary cutter become one of your favorite tools.

- Store the rotary cutter out of the reach of children. The blade is extremely sharp and could injure a child very easily.
- Always cut away from yourself.
- Slide the blade guard into place each and every time you lay the rotary cutter down, even if only for a moment.
- To make sure that the left side of your folded fabric is square before you begin to cut, place a ruled square on the fold and a 6 × 24-inch ruler against the side of the square, as shown in **Diagram 2.** Then hold the ruler in place, remove the ruled square, and cut along the right edge of the ruler. If you are left-handed, reverse this and work from the other end of the fabric.
- When cutting strips or rectangles, cut on the crosswise grain, as shown in **Diagram 3** , unless instructed otherwise. Cut the strips into

6" × 24" ruler

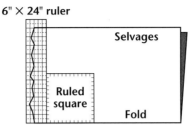

Diagram 2

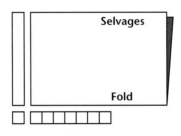

Diagram 3

squares or rectangles, as needed.
- Check periodically to make sure that your cut strips are straight, rather than angled, as shown in **Diagram 4.** If your strips are uneven, refold the fabric, square off the edge, and begin cutting again.

Diagram 4

- The project instructions will tell you when to cut a square of fabric into two triangles by making one diagonal cut or into four triangles by making two diagonal cuts, as shown in **Diagram 5.**

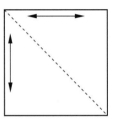

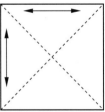

Diagram 5

Tracing and Preparing Patterns and Templates

All of the patterns in this book are full size (except for the background block for the Spring Flowers Pillow, which can be easily enlarged on a photocopier). Transfer each pattern piece onto tracing paper or template plastic. For quilts, template plastic or cardboard is a better choice than tracing paper for making templates. For sewing patterns, you may prefer to use tracing paper for making pattern pieces. To make a plastic template, place a piece of template plastic over a page in this book and trace the appropriate pattern pieces. If you decide to make cardboard templates, first trace the patterns onto tracing paper, then glue them onto the cardboard before cutting out the template.

A few of the sewing patterns are too large to present on a single book page. These patterns have been split into sections and are marked with solid placement lines and instructions to help match the appropriate portions of each pattern. If there are several sections that make up one large pattern piece, you'll also find a visual "map" showing how the various sections fit together.

To create one of these large pattern pieces, place a sheet of tracing paper over one portion of the pattern and trace that section. Then move the tracing paper to the appropriate page, aligning the placement lines on the pattern. Trace the second portion of the pattern. Continue tracing each portion of the pattern piece in this manner, matching the placement

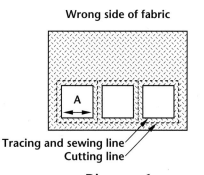

Wrong side of fabric

Tracing and sewing line
Cutting line

Diagram 6

lines, until the pattern is complete.

Most of the patterns in the book have inner dashed lines indicating the seam allowance and outer solid lines as the cutting lines. Pattern pieces for patchwork quilts include ¼-inch seam allowances, unless specified otherwise. Patterns for appliqué shapes do not include any seam allowances.

Transfer all important pattern markings, such as seam lines, body openings, cutting lines, placement lines, and facial features onto your pattern pieces or templates.

For hand-pieced projects, draw around the templates or patterns on the wrong side of the fabric, as shown in **Diagram 6,** leaving at least ½ inch between lines. The lines you draw will be the exact sewing lines. Then add the ¼-inch seam allowances before cutting out the fabric pieces.

The cutting instructions list the correct number of pieces to cut for each project. Each pattern piece is also marked with this information. You may wish to try a combination of cutting techniques, such as using scissors and templates for the smaller or curved pattern pieces and a rotary cutter for longer, straight pieces such as borders and bindings.

For some projects, no templates are necessary. In these cases, the instructions call for either measuring and cutting squares or rectangles directly from the fabric or sewing strips together into strip sets and then cutting them into specific pattern units.

Patchwork Basics

Precise Seam Allowances

Accurate ¼-inch seam allowances are a must for precision patchwork. Even a discrepancy as slight as

1/16 inch in several seam allowances can make a big difference in the width or length of a quilt. Measure the distance from the needle to the outside of the presser foot on your sewing machine to see whether it is actually 1/4 inch. If it is not exactly 1/4 inch, measure 1/4 inch from the needle and place a piece of masking tape at that point. If you like guiding seams against a raised edge, try gluing a piece of Dr. Scholl's Molefoam on the arm of your machine to create a precise 1/4-inch seam allowance.

Follow these guidelines for making patchwork blocks with straight seams. Setting in pieces at an angle should be done only when it is impossible to sew straight seams.

• Combine smaller pieces to make larger units.
• Join larger units into rows or sections.
• Join rows or sections together to complete a quilt.

Machine Piecing

Templates and rotary-cut strips for machine piecing include seam allowances. Use a stitch length of 10 to 12 stitches per inch and choose a neutral thread that blends well with the fabrics in your project.

To join two patchwork pieces, sew from raw edge to raw edge and press the seam to one side. To press a seam, bring the iron down gently and firmly on the fabric from above, rather than rubbing the iron over the surface. Whenever possible, press the seam allowance toward the darker fabric, which prevents the darker seam from "shadowing," or showing through the lighter fabric in a finished quilt. When you sew several blocks together to form a row, press the seam allowances in alternating directions. That way, when you assemble the rows of a quilt top, it's easy to match the seams between blocks, as shown in **Diagram 7.**

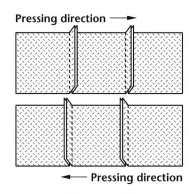

Pressing direction ⟶

⟵ Pressing direction

Diagram 7

Chain piecing is helpful for sewing together many pairs of pieces or larger units. To chain piece, feed pairs of pieces through the sewing machine without cut-

ting the thread between them, as shown in **Diagram 8.** After all of the pieces are sewn together, simply snip them apart and press the seam allowances. You can make use of the same assembly line technique for sewing other pieces to these units.

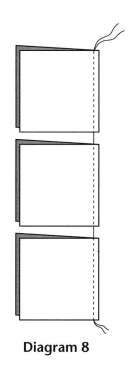

Diagram 8

Machine Appliqué

Machine appliqué is used for projects such as the Babushka Doll Trio on page 38, the Paper Doll Sweatshirt on page 66, and the Hungry Chicks Place Mats on page 34. It's easy, quick, and durable, which makes it ideal for any project that will need to be laundered frequently.

Satin stitch machine appliqué can be done on any sewing machine that has a zigzag stitch setting. Use an open-toe appliqué foot or a presser foot with a channel on the bottom that allows a ridge of stitching to feed evenly. Insert a size 70 universal needle into the sewing machine. Match the top thread in your sewing machine to the appliqué pieces and use a fine, machine embroidery-weight cotton thread in the bobbin. Set the machine on a medium-width zigzag and a very short stitch length. It's helpful to test this stitch on a scrap of fabric. The stitches should be ⅛ to ³⁄₁₆ inches wide and form an even band of color. If necessary, loosen the top tension slightly, so that a tiny amount of top thread will be pulled through to the wrong side of the fabric. Here are some general guidelines and step-by-step instructions for doing smooth satin stitch machine appliqué.

1. To prepare the appliqué shapes, press Wonder-Under or a similar paper-backed fusible webbing onto the wrong side of the fabric, following the manufacturer's instructions. For most products, the procedure is the same. Trace the appliqué

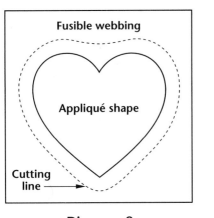

Diagram 9

Diagram 10

shapes onto the paper side of the webbing and roughly cut out the designs, as shown in **Diagram 9.**

2. Cut out the appliqué shapes along the traced lines, as shown in **Diagram 10.** If one shape will be layered over another, allow approximately ¼ inch underlap on the lower shape. Peel off the paper backing, position the appliqué shapes on the background fabric, and fuse them in place with an iron on the Wool setting.

3. Stabilize the background fabric by fusing a piece of freezer paper or commercial fabric stabilizer, such as Tear-Away, on the wrong side of the background fabric in the stitching areas.

4. Match the thread color to the appliqué shapes and machine satin stitch around the edges of the shapes, covering the raw edges. After you finish stitching, carefully remove the freezer paper or stabilizer from the wrong side.

Hand Appliqué

Hand appliqué is used in projects such as the Spring Flowers Pillow on page 106 and the Snowball and Arrowroot Pillow Quilt on page 116. One of the more popular techniques for hand appliqué is the basted method, in which the seam allowances are turned under and secured with basting stitches before the appliqué shapes are sewn onto the background fabric. Another popular technique is needle-turn appliqué, in which the appliqué shapes are first pinned onto the background fabric and then the seam allowances are turned under as you stitch, using the tip of the needle as a guide. For both methods, you will need to use a long, thin needle, such as an 11 or 12 sharp, and thread that matches the color of the appliqué shapes. Stitch the shapes onto the background fabric with a blind hem stitch, as shown in **Diagram 11.**

Begin by bringing the needle through the fold of the appliqué shape. Insert the needle into the background fabric just under the fold, as close as possible to the point at which the thread comes out of the fabric. Bring the needle back up through the background fabric approximately ⅛ inch to the left, or closer, catching just the very edge of the fold on the appliqué shape. Continue

stitching in this manner to create nearly invisible hand appliqué stitches.

Basted Appliqué

1. Make a finished-size template for each appliqué shape. Draw around the templates on the right side of the appropriate fabrics with a pencil or a fabric marker. These will be the turning lines.

2. Cut out the appliqué shapes, allowing a generous ⅛-inch seam allowance around the outside of the turning lines.

3. For each appliqué shape, turn the seam allowance under and baste close to the fold with white or natural thread. Clip concave curves and inner points before basting, as shown in **Diagram 12.** Do not baste the edges that will be covered by another appliqué shape.

4. Pin the appliqué shapes in place and stitch them to the background fabric with a blind hem stitch. If one appliqué piece will be overlapped by another, appliqué the underneath piece first. Remove the basting threads after the stitching is complete.

5. To press your work, place the block face down on a terry-cloth towel. Spritz it lightly with water and press it gently from the wrong side.

Needle-Turn Appliqué

1. Make finished-size templates for each appliqué shape and draw around them lightly on the right side of the appropriate fabrics with a pencil or fabric marker to mark the turning lines.

2. Cut out the appliqué shapes, allowing a generous ⅛-inch seam allowance around the outside of the turning lines.

3. Pin the appliqué shapes to the background fabric. Using the tip and shank of an appliqué needle, turn under ½-inch sections of seam allowance at a time, pressing it flat with your thumb and stitching it in place with a blind hem stitch. Clip concave curves and inner points

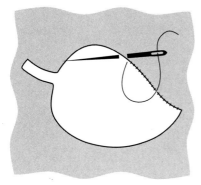

Diagram 11

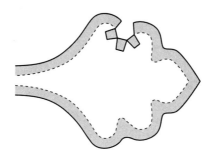

Diagram 12

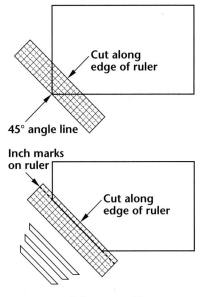

Diagram 13

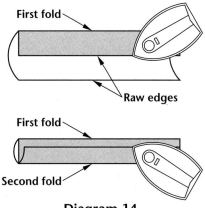

Diagram 14

before turning under the seam allowance.

4. To press your work, place the block face down on a terry-cloth towel. Press it gently on the wrong side of the background fabric.

Bias Vines and Stems

Fabric strips cut on the bias have more give and are easier to manipulate than strips cut on the straight grain. This makes them ideal for creating curved appliquéd stems and vines. Follow these easy steps to make perfect bias strips for hand appliqué.

1. To cut bias strips, use a see-through ruler marked

with 45-degree angle lines. Straighten the left edge of the fabric as described on page 260. Align the 45-degree angle line on the ruler with the bottom edge of the fabric, as shown in **Diagram 13,** and cut along the edge of the ruler to trim off the corner. Move the ruler across the fabric and cut parallel bias strips in whatever width you need.

2. For bias strips that are ¾ inch wide or more, fold and press them in thirds to prepare them for appliqué. Start by placing the bias strip wrong side up on an ironing board, as shown in **Diagram 14.** Fold over a

third of the strip width and press it with the tip of an iron. Fold the second third of the strip over the first and press it with the tip of the iron.

3. Turn the strip over to the right side and press both folds once more. The bias strip is now prepared for appliqué.

4. To appliqué vines and stems, baste the prepared bias strips in position on the background fabric and stitch them in place along both folds. If the stems or vines are curved, appliqué the inner curves before stitching the outer curves.

Assembling a Quilt

Setting patchwork or appliqué blocks together and adding borders is easy with these basic guidelines.

Setting Blocks Together

1. To assemble a quilt with a straight set, start by laying out all of the pieced or appliquéd blocks as they will appear in the quilt, with sashing strips or corner setting blocks between them if there are any.

2. Pin and sew the blocks together into horizontal or vertical rows (or into diagonal rows for diagonally set quilts), alternating the direction in which you press the seams.

3. Sew the necessary number of rows of sashing strips and corner setting blocks, alternating the direction in which you press the seams.

4. Sew the rows of the quilt together, abutting the seam allowances so that the block seams will match. Press the assembled quilt top, working from the wrong side and pressing the seams carefully. Clip and remove stray threads. Then turn the quilt top over and press it from the right side, making sure all seams lie flat.

Attaching Straight Borders

1. As a general rule, it's a good idea to cut border strips longer than necessary, just to be safe. Measure the width and length of your completed quilt top through the center in both directions rather than along the edges. Use these measurements to determine the exact length needed for the border strips. Use a pencil or removable fabric marker to mark each border strip with the correct finished dimensions before sewing it to the quilt top.

2. Fold one of the border strips in half crosswise and press it lightly to mark the midpoint. Align the midpoint of the border with the midpoint on one side of the quilt. With right sides together, pin the border to the quilt top.

3. Sew the border to the quilt top. Press the seam allowance away from the body of the quilt and trim the excess fabric from the border. Repeat for the borders on the other three sides of the quilt.

Mitering Borders

1. To miter the corner seams of the borders, start by sewing each of the four borders to the quilt top,

beginning and ending the seams ¼ inch in from the edge of the quilt top.

2. Press the border seams flat from the right side of the quilt. Starting at one corner of the quilt, place one border strip on top of the adjacent border strip. Fold the top border under so that it meets the edge of the other border, forming a 45-degree angle, as shown in **Diagram 15** on the opposite page.

3. Press the fold in place and bring the top border down, so that the edges of the borders are aligned. With the pressed fold as the corner seam line and the body of the quilt out of the way, sew from the inner corner to the outer corner of the border, as shown in **Diagram 16** on the opposite page.

4. Open the border and check the corner seam to make sure it lies flat. Trim the excess fabric from the border strips so that the corner seam has a ¼-inch seam allowance. Press this seam open.

Marking Quilting Designs

Beautiful quilting is the element that makes every quilt a one-of-a-kind creation. Follow these guidelines for marking quilting designs on a quilt.

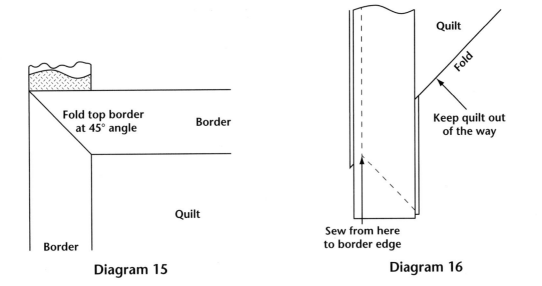

Diagram 15

Diagram 16

Light Fabrics

To mark a quilting design directly onto light fabrics, start by photocopying the design you like or tracing it onto a piece of plain paper. Darken the lines with a black fine-point permanent marker. Place the design under the quilt top and carefully mark the designs on the fabric, drawing a thin, continuous line that will be covered by quilting thread. Use a silver or white quilter's pencil or a mechanical pencil with thin (0.5 mm), medium (B) lead.

Dark Fabrics

A light box will allow you to trace directly onto darker fabrics using the method described above. If you do not have access to a light box, it's still possible to mark dark fabrics from the right side. Make or cut a plastic stencil of the design you've chosen and draw thin lines around it on the quilt top with a silver or white quilter's pencil. To mark long, straight lines of quilting, use a ruler. You can also use masking tape to quilt straight lines, without marking them on the fabric.

Selecting Batting

When you purchase batting, take time to think about the appearance you wish to create in the finished quilt. Experiment with different batts to find the look you like and to discover which type of batting will best achieve that look. No matter what kind of batting you choose, it's helpful to let it "relax" overnight before layering a quilt. Here are some of the most popular batting choices.

Polyester

One hundred percent polyester batting is lightweight, durable, and warm. It launders without shrinking and needles easily. One disadvantage of polyester batts is that the fibers tend to migrate through the fabric of the quilt top, creating a tiny white "beard" on the surface. Many polyester batts are bonded, or coated to reduce bearding, making the batting a bit more difficult to needle. Polyester batting is manufactured in many different lofts, which makes it a good choice for everything from quilted clothing and home accessories to puffy, tied comforters.

Cotton

Unlike polyester, cotton fibers do not beard. Some hand quilters believe that cotton batting is harder to needle than polyester, and some all-cotton batts need to be quilted at intervals of ¼ to ½ inch in order to prevent lumping. Cotton batts tend to shrink when they are laundered, which wrinkles the fabric around the lines of quilting, instantly creating the look of an antique quilt.

Cotton/Polyester Blends

Cotton/polyester batting combines the low-loft, sculpted look of cotton with the durability of polyester. This type of batt is easier to needle than an all-cotton batting, and it can be quilted at wider intervals. The fibers are bonded, or coated, to reduce bearding. Presoaking this type of batting will break down the coating and make it easier to needle.

Preparing to Quilt

When you have marked a quilt top, prepared the backing, and selected the batting, you're ready to layer and baste the quilt sandwich together. Follow these steps to prepare a quilt for quilting.

Layering

1. With wrong sides together, fold the quilt backing in half lengthwise and press it to mark the center line. Open up the backing and place it wrong side up on a flat work surface. Use masking tape at the corners to hold the backing in place.

2. Fold the batting in half lengthwise and place it on top of the quilt backing, aligning the fold with the pressed centerline in the backing. Smooth the batting carefully over the backing, patting out wrinkles as you work from the center toward the outer edges.

3. With right sides together, fold the quilt top in half lengthwise and align this fold with the center of the batting. Unfold the top and smooth it outward from the center, removing any loose threads. Make sure that the backing and batting are at least 2 inches larger than the quilt top on all four sides.

Basting with Thread

If you plan to hand quilt, thread basting is a good choice for holding the layers of the quilt sandwich together. Use a long darning needle and white sewing thread to baste the layers of the quilt sandwich together. The basting lines should be

approximately 4 inches apart. Begin basting at the center of the quilt and work outward in a radiating pattern, or baste in a grid of horizontal and vertical lines, using the seams that join the blocks as guidelines.

Basting with Pins

Pin basting is a good choice for machine quilting because pins hold the layers of a quilt together more securely than thread. Choose nickel-plated, rust-proof brass safety pins in size 0 or 1, which will not leave large holes in fabric. Starting at the center and working outward, place rows of pins approximately 3 inches apart, taking care to avoid seam allowances and quilting areas as much as possible.

Quilting

Hand Quilting

- Use a hoop or quilting frame to hold the quilt layers taut and smooth while you quilt.
- Use quilting betweens in size 9, 10, or 12. (Remember, the higher the number, the smaller the needle.)
- Use quilting thread, 100 percent cotton if possible, rather than regular sewing thread.
- To begin quilting, thread a needle with an 18-inch

length of quilting thread and knot the end. Insert the needle through the quilt top only, then into the batting approximately ½ inch away from where you will take the first quilting stitch. Bring the thread through and tug on it gently to pop the knot through the top and bury it in the batting, as shown in **Diagram 17**.

• Quilt small running stitches about ⅛ inch long through all three layers, as shown in **Diagram 18**. As you take each stitch, hold your left hand underneath the quilt and use the tip of a finger to feel the needle as it penetrates the quilt backing. Guide the needle gently back up

through the layers of the quilt and take the next stitch. As you continue to gain experience, you may find that you like taking two, three, or even four stitches on the needle at one time. Make your stitches as straight and even as possible, keeping the spaces between stitches the same length as the stitches themselves.

Machine Quilting

• Use a walking foot or even feed foot in the sewing machine for machine quilting straight lines. Use a darning or machine embroidery foot for free-motion quilting.

• To secure the thread at the beginning and end of a quilting design, back-

stitch or take several very short stitches.

• For free-motion quilting, disengage the sewing machine feed dogs to make it easier to manipulate the quilt freely. Choose continuous-line quilting designs to avoid frequent stops and starts. Guide the quilt with both hands, working at an even pace in order to make the stitches consistent.

Binding

Cutting Binding Strips

The most common edge finish for a quilt is binding. Straight-grain binding works well for quilts that have straight edges, while bias binding is needed for quilts with curved or angled edges. The projects in this book are bound with straight-grain

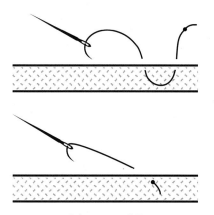

Diagram 17

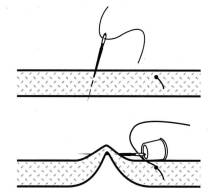

Diagram 18

binding. Follow these steps to make and attach binding to a quilt.

1. Cut the number of binding strips indicated in the project instructions. Cross-grain binding strips are cut from selvage to selvage. If you have enough fabric, you may also cut binding strips on the lengthwise grain.

2. Sew the short ends of the binding strips right sides together with diagonal seams, as shown in **Diagram 19**. Trim the seam allowances to ¼ inch and press them open.

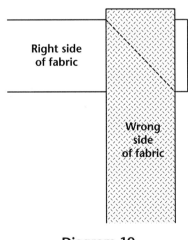

Diagram 19

Right side of fabric

Wrong side of fabric

3. Turn under approximately ½ inch at one short end of the binding strip to create a fold. Fold the entire binding strip in half lengthwise, wrong sides together, and press the fold.

Attaching the Binding

1. Place the folded end of the binding strip on the right side of the quilt top, aligning the raw edges with the edge of the quilt top.

2. Beginning a couple of inches from the corner on one side of the quilt, leave approximately 3 inches of the binding free and start sewing the binding to the quilt. Stitch through all layers with a ¼-inch seam allowance.

3. When you reach a corner, stop stitching exactly ¼ inch in from the raw edge of the quilt top. Backstitch and remove the quilt from the sewing machine, clipping the thread.

4. Fold the binding up and away from the corner, forming a 45-degree fold, as shown in **Diagram 20**. Then fold the binding strip back down and align the raw edges with the adjacent side.

5. Referring to **Diagram 20,** begin the stitching on

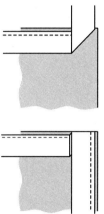

Diagram 20

the next side ¼ inch in from the corner. This provides the fullness necessary to bring the binding to the back side of the quilt. Miter all four corners in this manner.

6. As you approach the point where you began stitching, stop, backstitch, and clip the thread. Overlap the folded beginning of one binding strip with the end of the other binding strip, as shown in **Diagram 21** on the opposite page. Sew across this overlapped section to complete the seam, allowing the end of the binding strip to extend approximately ½ inch beyond the beginning of the binding strip.

7. Trim the excess batting and backing even with the seam allowance.

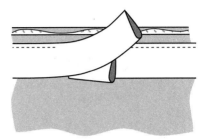

Diagram 21

8. Bring the binding to the back of the quilt and blindstitch the folded edge in place, covering the machine stitches. At each corner, fold in the adjacent sides of the binding and take several stitches in the miter, as shown in **Diagram 22**. In the same manner, add several stitches to the mitered corners on the front of the quilt.

Making a Sleeve

If you wish to display your quilt on a wall, it's easy to add a 4-inch sleeve to the backing when you attach the binding to the quilt. When you're ready to hang the quilt, insert a rod or dowel into the sleeve and place nails or hooks on the wall to support it.

1. Cut a strip of muslin or other fabric that is 8½ inches wide and 1 inch shorter than the width of the finished quilt.

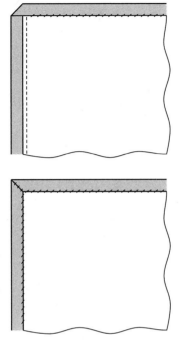

Diagram 22

2. To machine hem the short ends of the sleeve, turn under ½ inch on each end of the strip and press the fold. Turn under another ½ inch and stitch next to the pressed fold.

3. Fold and press the strip in half lengthwise, wrong sides together, aligning the long raw edges.

4. Align the raw edges of the sleeve with the top edge on the back of the quilt, centering the sleeve on the quilt. The binding should already be stitched on the right side of the quilt. Pin the sleeve in place.

5. Working from the right side of the quilt, sew the sleeve to the back of the quilt, stitching over the seam that attaches the binding to the quilt.

6. Bring the binding to the back of the quilt and hand stitch it to the back of the quilt, covering the raw edge of the sleeve, as shown in **Diagram 23**. If the binding seems to be too bulky in the area of the sleeve, trim away a bit more batting and backing fabric from the seam allowance before stitching the binding in place.

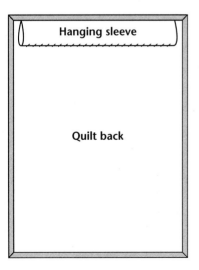

Hanging sleeve

Quilt back

Diagram 23

7. Stitch the bottom edge of the sleeve in place on the back of the quilt, taking care not to sew through to the front of the quilt.

Piping

Making Piping

Piping adds a colorful finishing touch to the edge of a pillow or cushion. Here are the basic steps for making and attaching covered piping.

1. Sew together the short ends of the bias strips in the same manner as for straight-grain binding strips and press the seams open.

2. With wrong sides together, fold the bias strip in half lengthwise, and insert the cording.

3. Align the raw edges of the bias strip. With a zipper foot, machine baste the cording inside the bias strip, stitching as close as possible to the cording, as shown in **Diagram 24.** Trim the seam allowance to ½ inch.

Attaching Piping

1. Beginning away from a corner point, pin the covered piping on the right side of the pillow top or other project, aligning the raw edges. At the pillow corners, clip the seam allowance of

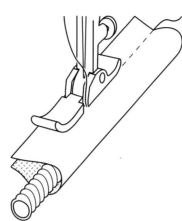

Diagram 24

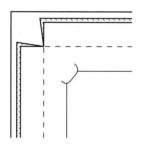

Diagram 25

the piping, as shown in **Diagram 25,** to help ease it around the angles.

2. Leaving approximately 2 inches free at both the beginning and the end of the piping, sew it to the pillow. To join the ends of the piping, trim the ends of the cording and butt them together, as shown in **Diagram 26.**

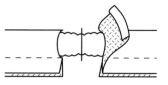

Diagram 26

3. Turn under ½ inch on one bias strip and fold it over the cording and the other end of the bias strip, as shown in **Diagram 27.** Finish sewing the remainder of the seam.

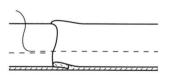

Diagram 27

Shirring Piping

1. Cut cross-grain strips for making shirred piping. Sew the strips together in the same manner as for binding and press the seams open.

2. Fold the strip in half lengthwise with wrong sides together, inserting the cording. Stitch across the end, as shown in **Diagram 28** on the opposite page. Sew the cording into the piping for several inches and stop.

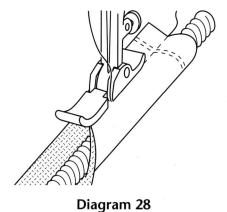

Diagram 28

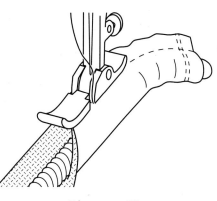

Diagram 29

3. Pull on the cording, shirring the piping strip, as shown in **Diagram 29.** Continue stitching and stopping until you have the necessary length of shirred piping. Finish the ends of the strips and attach the shirred piping to the project by first sewing the piping to the pillow. Then join the ends of the piping, trim the cording, and butt the ends together. Finally, turn under and fold the strip over the cording. Finish the seam.

Embroidery and Hand-Sewing Stitches

Several basic embroidery and hand-sewing stitches are used in the Crazy Patchwork Photograph Album Cover on page 244 and the Lace Patchwork Ring Bearer's Pillow on page 248. To work the stitches in the diagrams on pages 274–275, thread a needle with embroidery floss and follow the stitching order given in each of the diagrams.

Embroidery and Sewing Stitches

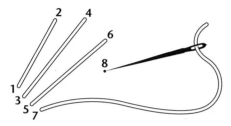

Straight Stitch

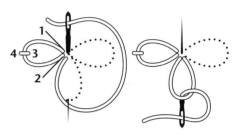

Lazy Daisy Stitch

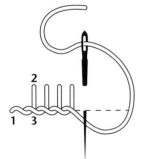

Buttonhole Stitch

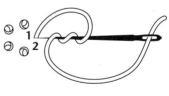

French Knot

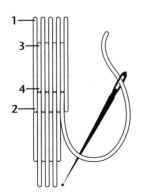

Long and Short Stitch

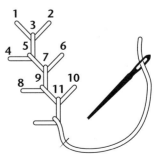

Feather Stitch

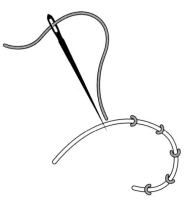

Couching Stitch

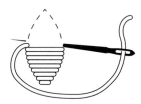

Satin Stitch

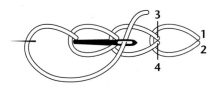

Chain Stitch

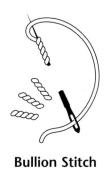

Bullion Stitch

Outline/Stem Stitch

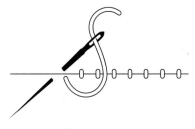

Slip Stitch